Though

His Nature, Productions and Discoveries

Interspersed with Some Particulars

Respecting the Author

William Godwin

Alpha Editions

This edition published in 2023

ISBN : 9789357949552

Design and Setting By
Alpha Editions
www.alphaedis.com
Email - info@alphaedis.com

PREFACE

In the ensuing volume I have attempted to give a defined and permanent form to a variety of thoughts, which have occurred to my mind in the course of thirty-four years, it being so long since I published a volume, entitled, the Enquirer,—thoughts, which, if they have presented themselves to other men, have, at least so far as I am aware, never been given to the public through the medium of the press. During a part of this period I had remained to a considerable degree unoccupied in my character of an author, and had delivered little to the press that bore my name.—And I beg the reader to believe, that, since I entered in 1791 upon that which may be considered as my vocation in life, I have scarcely in any instance contributed a page to any periodical miscellany.

My mind has been constitutionally meditative, and I should not have felt satisfied, if I had not set in order for publication these special fruits of my meditations. I had entered upon a certain career; and I held it for my duty not to abandon it.

One thing further I feel prompted to say. I have always regarded it as my office to address myself to plain men, and in clear and unambiguous terms. It has been my lot to have occasional intercourse with some of those who consider themselves as profound, who deliver their oracles in obscure phraseology, and who make it their boast that few men can understand them, and those few only through a process of abstract reflection, and by means of unwearied application.

To this class of the oracular I certainly did not belong. I felt that I had nothing to say, that it should be very difficult to understand. I resolved, if I could help it, not to "darken counsel by words without knowledge." This was my principle in the Enquiry concerning Political Justice. And I had my reward. I had a numerous audience of all classes, of every age, and of either sex. The young and the fair did not feel deterred from consulting my pages.

It may be that that book was published in a propitious season. I am told that nothing coming from the press will now be welcomed, unless it presents itself in the express form of amusement. He who shall propose to himself for his principal end, to draw aside in one particular or another the veil from the majesty of intellectual or moral truth, must lay his account in being received with little attention.

I have not been willing to believe this: and I publish my speculations accordingly. I have aimed at a popular, and (if I could reach it) an interesting style; and, if I am thrust aside and disregarded, I shall console myself with believing that I have not neglected what it was in my power to achieve.

One characteristic of the present publication will not fail to offer itself to the most superficial reader. I know many men who are misanthropes, and profess to look down with disdain on their species. My creed is of an opposite character. All that we observe that is best and most excellent in the intellectual world, is man: and it is easy to perceive in many cases, that the believer in mysteries does little more, than dress up his deity in the choicest of human attributes and qualifications. I have lived among, and I feel an ardent interest in and love for, my brethren of mankind. This sentiment, which I regard with complacency in my own breast, I would gladly cherish in others. In such a cause I am well pleased to enrol myself a missionary.

February 15, 1831.

The particulars respecting the author, referred to in the title-page, will be found principally in Essays VII, IX, XIV, and XVIII.

ESSAY I. OF BODY AND MIND.

THE PROLOGUE.

There is no subject that more frequently occupies the attention of the contemplative than man: yet there are many circumstances concerning him that we shall hardly admit to have been sufficiently considered.

Familiarity breeds contempt. That which we see every day and every hour, it is difficult for us to regard with admiration. To almost every one of our stronger emotions novelty is a necessary ingredient. The simple appetites of our nature may perhaps form an exception. The appetite for food is perpetually renewed in a healthy subject with scarcely any diminution and love, even the most refined, being combined with one of our original impulses, will sometimes for that reason withstand a thousand trials, and perpetuate itself for years. In all other cases it is required, that a fresh impulse should be given, that attention should anew be excited, or we cannot admire. Things often seen pass feebly before our senses, and scarcely awake the languid soul.

"Man is the most excellent and noble creature of the world, the principal and mighty work of God, the wonder of nature, the marvel of marvels(1)."

(1) Anatomy of Melancholy, p. 1.

Let us have regard to his corporeal structure. There is a simplicity in it, that at first perhaps we slightly consider. But how exactly is it fashioned for strength and agility! It is in no way incumbered. It is like the marble when it comes out of the hand of the consummate sculptor; every thing unnecessary is carefully chiseled away; and the joints, the muscles, the articulations, and the veins come out, clean and finished. It has long ago been observed, that beauty, as well as virtue, is the middle between all extremes: that nose which is neither specially long, nor short, nor thick, nor thin, is the perfect nose; and so of the rest. In like manner, when I speak of man generally, I do not regard any aberrations of form, obesity, a thick calf, a thin calf; I take the middle between all extremes; and this is emphatically man.

Man cannot keep pace with a starting horse: but he can persevere, and beats him in the end.

What an infinite variety of works is man by his corporeal form enabled to accomplish! In this respect he casts the whole creation behind him.

What a machine is the human hand! When we analyse its parts and its uses, it appears to be the most consummate of our members. And yet there are other parts, that may maintain no mean rivalship against it.

What a sublimity is to be attributed to his upright form! He is not fashioned, veluti pecora, quae natura prona atque ventri obedientia finxit. He is made coeli convexa tueri. The looks that are given him in his original structure, are "looks commercing with the skies."

How surpassingly beautiful are the features of his countenance; the eyes, the nose, the mouth! How noble do they appear in a state of repose! With what never-ending variety and emphasis do they express the emotions of his mind! In the visage of man, uncorrupted and undebased, we read the frankness and ingenuousness of his soul, the clearness of his reflections, the penetration of his spirit. What a volume of understanding is unrolled in his broad, expanded, lofty brow! In his countenance we see expressed at one time sedate confidence and awful intrepidity, and at another godlike condescension and the most melting tenderness. Who can behold the human eye, suddenly suffused with moisture, or gushing with tears unbid, and the quivering lip, without unspeakable emotion? Shakespear talks of an eye, "whose bend could awe the world."

What a miraculous thing is the human complexion! We are sent into the world naked, that all the variations of the blood might be made visible. However trite, I cannot avoid quoting here the lines of the most deep-thinking and philosophical of our poets:

We understood

Her by her sight: her pure and eloquent blood

Spoke in her cheeks, and so distinctly wrought,

That one might almost say her body thought.

What a curious phenomenon is that of blushing! It is impossible to witness this phenomenon without interest and sympathy. It comes at once, unanticipated by the person in whom we behold it. It comes from the soul, and expresses with equal certainty shame, modesty, and vivid, uncontrollable affection. It spreads, as it were in so many stages, over the cheeks, the brow, and the neck, of him or her in whom the sentiment that gives birth to it is working.

Thus far I have not mentioned speech, not perhaps the most inestimable of human gifts, but, if it is not that, it is at least the endowment, which makes man social, by which principally we impart our sentiments to each other, and which changes us from solitary individuals, and bestows on us a duplicate and multipliable existence. Beside which it incalculably increases the perfection of one. The man who does not speak, is an unfledged thinker; and the man that does not write, is but half an investigator.

Not to enter into all the mysteries of articulate speech and the irresistible power of eloquence, whether addressed to a single hearer, or instilled into the ears of many,—a topic that belongs perhaps less to the chapter of body than mind,—let us for a moment fix our thoughts steadily upon that little implement, the human voice. Of what unnumbered modulations is it susceptible! What terror may it inspire! How may it electrify the soul, and suspend all its functions! How infinite is its melody! How instantly it subdues the hearer to pity or to love! How does the listener hang upon every note praying that it may last for ever,

> ——that even silence
>
> *Was took ere she was ware, and wished she might*
>
> *Deny her nature, and be never more,*
>
> *Still to be so displaced.*

It is here especially that we are presented with the triumphs of civilisation. How immeasurable is the distance between the voice of the clown, who never thought of the power that dwells in this faculty, who delivers himself in a rude, discordant and unmodulated accent, and is accustomed to confer with his fellow at the distance of two fields, and the man who understands his instrument as Handel understood the organ, and who, whether he thinks of it or no, sways those that hear him as implicitly as Orpheus is said to have subdued the brute creation!

From the countenance of man let us proceed to his figure. Every limb is capable of speaking, and telling its own tale. What can equal the magnificence of the neck, the column upon which the head reposes! The ample chest may denote an almost infinite strength and power. Let us call to mind the Apollo Belvidere, and the Venus de Medicis, whose very "bends are adornings." What loftiness and awe have I seen expressed in the step of an actress, not yet deceased, when first she advanced, and came down towards the audience! I was ravished, and with difficulty kept my seat! Pass we to the mazes of the dance, the inimitable charms and picturesque beauty that may be given to the figure while still unmoved, and the ravishing grace that dwells in it during its endless changes and evolutions.

The upright figure of man produces, incidentally as it were, and by the bye, another memorable effect. Hence we derive the power of meeting in halls, and congregations, and crowded assemblies. We are found "at large, though without number," at solemn commemorations and on festive occasions. We touch each other, as the members of a gay party are accustomed to do, when they wait the stroke of an electrical machine, and the spark spreads along from man to man. It is thus that we have our feelings in common at a theatrical representation and at a public dinner, that indignation is communicated, and patriotism become irrepressible.

One man can convey his sentiments in articulate speech to a thousand; and this is the nursing mother of oratory, of public morality, of public religion, and the drama. The privilege we thus possess, we are indeed too apt to abuse; but man is scarcely ever so magnificent and so awful, as when hundreds of human heads are assembled together, hundreds of faces lifted up to contemplate one object, and hundreds of voices uttered in the expression of one common sentiment.

But, notwithstanding the infinite beauty, the magazine of excellencies and perfections, that appertains to the human body, the mind claims, and justly claims, an undoubted superiority. I am not going into an enumeration of the various faculties and endowments of the mind of man, as I have done of his body. The latter was necessary for my purpose. Before I proceeded to consider the ascendancy of mind, the dominion and loftiness it is accustomed to assert, it appeared but just to recollect what was the nature and value of its subject and its slave.

By the mind we understand that within us which feels and thinks, the seat of sensation and reason. Where it resides we cannot tell, nor can authoritatively pronounce, as the apostle says, relatively to a particular phenomenon, "whether it is in the body, or out of the body." Be it however where or what it may, it is this which constitutes the great essence of, and gives value to, our existence; and all the wonders of our microcosm would without it be a form only, destined immediately to perish, and of no greater account than as a clod of the valley.

It was an important remark, suggested to me many years ago by an eminent physiologer and anatomist, that, when I find my attention called to any particular part or member of my body, I may be morally sure that there is something amiss in the processes of that part or member. As long as the whole economy of the frame goes on well and without interruption, our attention is not called to it. The intellectual man is like a disembodied spirit.

He is almost in the state of the dervise in the Arabian Nights, who had the power of darting his soul into the unanimated body of another, human or brute, while he left his own body in the condition of an insensible carcase, till it should be revivified by the same or some other spirit. When I am, as it is vulgarly understood, in a state of motion, I use my limbs as the implements of my will. When, in a quiescent state of the body, I continue to think, to reflect and to reason, I use, it may be, the substance of the brain as the implement of my thinking, reflecting and reasoning; though of this in fact we know nothing.

We have every reason to believe that the mind cannot subsist without the body; at least we must be very different creatures from what we are at present, when that shall take place. For a man to think, agreeably and with serenity, he must be in some degree of health. The corpus sanum is no less indispensible than the mens sana. We must eat, and drink, and sleep. We must have a reasonably good appetite and digestion, and a fitting temperature, neither too hot nor cold. It is desirable that we should have air and exercise. But this is instrumental merely. All these things are negatives, conditions without which we cannot think to the best purpose, but which lend no active assistance to our thinking.

Man is a godlike being. We launch ourselves in conceit into illimitable space, and take up our rest beyond the fixed stars. We proceed without impediment from country to country, and from century to century, through all the ages of the past, and through the vast creation of the imaginable future. We spurn at the bounds of time and space; nor would the thought be less futile that imagines to imprison the mind within the limits of the body, than the attempt of the booby clown who is said within a thick hedge to have plotted to shut in the flight of an eagle.

We never find our attention called to any particular part or member of the body, except when there is somewhat amiss in that part or member. And, in like manner as we do not think of any one part or member in particular, so neither do we consider our entire microcosm and frame. The body is apprehended as no more important and of intimate connection to a man engaged in a train of reflections, than the house or apartment in which he dwells. The mind may aptly be described under the denomination of the "stranger at home." On set occasions and at appropriate times we examine our stores, and ascertain the various commodities we have, laid up in our presses and our coffers. Like the governor of a fort in time of peace, which was erected to keep out a foreign assailant, we occasionally visit our armoury, and take account of the muskets, the swords, and other implements of war it contains, but for the most part are engaged in the occupations of peace, and do not call the means of warfare in any sort to our recollection.

The mind may aptly be described under the denomination of the "stranger at home." With their bodies most men are little acquainted. We are "like unto a man beholding his natural face in a glass, who beholdeth himself, and goeth his way, and straightway forgetteth what manner of man he is." In the ruminations of the inner man, and the dissecting our thoughts and desires, we employ our intellectual arithmetic, we add, and subtract, and multiply, and divide, without asking the aid, without adverting to the existence, of our joints and members. Even as to the more corporeal part of our avocations, we behold the external world, and proceed straight to the object of our desires, without almost ever thinking of this medium, our own material frame, unaided by which none of these things could be accomplished. In this sense we may properly be said to be spiritual existences, however imperfect may be the idea we are enabled to affix to the term spirit.

Hence arises the notion, which has been entertained ever since the birth of reflection and logical discourse in the world, and which in some faint and confused degree exists probably even among savages, that the body is the prison of the mind. It is in this sense that Waller, after completing fourscore years of age, expresses himself in these affecting and interesting couplets.

When we for age could neither read nor write,

The subject made us able to indite.

The soul's dark cottage, battered and decayed,

Lets in new light by chinks that time hath made:

Stronger by weakness, wiser, men become,

As they draw near to their eternal home.

Thus it is common with persons of elevated soul to talk of neglecting, overlooking, and taking small account of the body. It is in this spirit that the story is recorded of Anaxarchus, who, we are told, was ordered by Nicocreon, tyrant of Salamis, to be pounded in a mortar, and who, in contempt of his mortal sufferings, exclaimed, "Beat on, tyrant! thou dost but strike upon the case of Anaxarchus; thou canst not touch the man himself." And it is in something of the same light that we must regard what is related of the North American savages. Beings, who scoff at their tortures, must have an idea of something that lies beyond the reach of their assailants.

It is just however to observe, that some of the particulars here related, belong not less to the brute creation than to man. If men are imperfectly acquainted with their external figure and appearance, this may well be conceived to be still more predicable of the inferior animals. It is true that all of them seem to be aware of the part in their structure, where lie their main strength and means of hostility. Thus the bull attacks with his horns, and the horse with his heels, the beast of prey with his claws, the bird with his beak, and insects and other venomous creatures with their sting. We know not by what impulse they are prompted to the use of the various means which are so intimately connected with their preservation and welfare; and we call it instinct. We may be certain it does not arise from a careful survey of their parts and members, and a methodised selection of the means which shall be found most effectual for the accomplishment of their ends. There is no premeditation; and, without anatomical knowledge, or any distinct acquaintance with their image and likeness, they proceed straight to their purpose.

Hence, even as men, they are more familiar with the figures and appearance of their fellows, their allies, or their enemies, than with their own.

Man is a creature of mingled substance. I am many times a day compelled to acknowledge what a low, mean and contemptible being I am. Philip of Macedon had no need to give it in charge to a page, to repair to him every morning, and repeat, "Remember, sir, you are a man." A variety of circumstances occur to us, while we eat, and drink, and submit to the humiliating necessities of nature, that may well inculcate into us this salutary lesson. The wonder rather is, that man, who has so many things to put him in mind to be humble and despise himself, should ever have been susceptible of pride and disdain. Nebuchadnezzar must indeed have been the most besotted of mortals, if it were necessary that he should be driven from among men, and made to eat grass like an ox, to convince him that he was not the equal of the power that made him.

But fortunately, as I have said, man is a "stranger at home." Were it not for this, how incomprehensible would be

> *The ceremony that to great ones 'longs,*
>
> *The monarch's crown, and the deputed sword,*
>
> *The marshal's truncheon, and the judge's robe!*

How ludicrous would be the long procession and the caparisoned horse, the gilded chariot and the flowing train, the colours flying, the drums beating, and the sound of trumpets rending the air, which after all only introduce to us an ordinary man, no otherwise perhaps distinguished from the vilest of the ragged spectators, than by the accident of his birth!

But what is of more importance in the temporary oblivion we are enabled to throw over the refuse of the body, it is thus we arrive at the majesty of man. That sublimity of conception which renders the poet, and the man of great literary and original endowments "in apprehension like a God," we could not have, if we were not privileged occasionally to cast away the slough and exuviae of the body from incumbering and dishonouring us, even as Ulysses passed over his threshold, stripped of the rags that had obscured him, while Minerva enlarged his frame, and gave loftiness to his stature, added a youthful beauty and grace to his motions, and caused his eyes to flash with more than mortal fire. With what disdain, when I have been rapt in the loftiest moods of mind, do I look down upon my limbs, the house of clay that contains me, the gross flesh and blood of which my frame is composed, and wonder at a lodging, poorly fitted to entertain so divine a guest!

A still more important chapter in the history of the human mind has its origin in these considerations. Hence it is that unenlightened man, in almost all ages and countries, has been induced, independently of divine revelation, to regard death, the most awful event to which we are subject, as not being the termination of his existence. We see the body of our friend become insensible, and remain without motion, or any external indication of what we call life. We can shut it up in an apartment, and visit it from day to day. If we had perseverance enough, and could so far conquer the repugnance and humiliating feeling with which the experiment would be attended, we might follow step by step the process of decomposition and putrefaction, and observe by what degrees the "dust returned unto earth as it was." But, in spite of this demonstration of the senses, man still believes that there is something in him that lives after death. The mind is so infinitely superior in character to this case of flesh that incloses it, that he cannot persuade himself that it and the body perish together.

There are two considerations, the force of which made man a religious animal. The first is, his proneness to ascribe hostility or benevolent intention to every thing of a memorable sort that occurs to him in the order of nature. The second is that of which I have just treated, the superior dignity of mind over body. This, we persuade ourselves, shall subsist uninjured by the mutations of our corporeal frame, and undestroyed by the wreck of the material universe.

ESSAY II. OF THE DISTRIBUTION OF TALENTS.

{Greek—omitted} Thucydides, Lib.I, cap. 84.

SECTION I.

PRESUMED DEARTH OF INTELLECTUAL POWER.—SCHOOLS FOR THE EDUCATION OF YOUTH CONSIDERED.—THE BOY AND THE MAN COMPARED.

One of the earliest judgments that is usually made by those whose attention is turned to the characters of men in the social state, is of the great inequality with which the gifts of the understanding are distributed among us.

Go into a miscellaneous society; sit down at table with ten or twelve men; repair to a club where as many are assembled in an evening to relax from the toils of the day—it is almost proverbial, that one or two of these persons will perhaps be brilliant, and the rest "weary, stale, flat and unprofitable."

Go into a numerous school—the case will be still more striking. I have been present where two men of superior endowments endeavoured to enter into a calculation on the subject; and they agreed that there was not above one boy in a hundred, who would be found to possess a penetrating understanding, and to be able to strike into a path of intellect that was truly his own. How common is it to hear the master of such a school say, "Aye, I am proud of that lad; I have been a schoolmaster these thirty years, and have never had such another!"

The society above referred to, the dinner-party, or the club, was to a considerable degree select, brought together by a certain supposed congeniality between the individuals thus assembled. Were they taken indiscriminately, as boys are when consigned to the care of a schoolmaster, the proportion of the brilliant would not be a whit greater than in the latter case.

A main criterion of the superiority of the schoolboy will be found in his mode of answering a casual question proposed by the master. The majority will be wholly at fault, will shew that they do not understand the question, and will return an answer altogether from the purpose. One in a hundred perhaps, perhaps in a still less proportion, will reply in a laudable manner, and convey his ideas in perspicuous and spirited language.

It does not certainly go altogether so ill, with men grown up to years of maturity. They do not for the most part answer a plain question in a manner to make you wonder at their fatuity.

A main cause of the disadvantageous appearance exhibited by the ordinary schoolboy, lies in what we denominate sheepishness. He is at a loss, and in the first place stares at you, instead of giving an answer. He does not make by many degrees so poor a figure among his equals, as when he is addressed by his seniors.

One of the reasons of the latter phenomenon consists in the torpedo effect of what we may call, under the circumstances, the difference of ranks. The schoolmaster is a despot to his scholar; for every man is a despot, who delivers his judgment from the single impulse of his own will. The boy answers his questioner, as Dolon answers Ulysses in the Iliad, at the point of the sword. It is to a certain degree the same thing, when the boy is questioned merely by his senior. He fears he knows not what,—a reprimand, a look of lofty contempt, a gesture of summary disdain. He does not think it worth his while under these circumstances, to "gird up the loins of his mind." He cannot return a free and intrepid answer but to the person whom he regards as his equal. There is nothing that has so disqualifying an effect upon him who is to answer, as the consideration that he who questions is universally acknowledged to be a being of a higher sphere, or, as between the boy and the man, that he is the superior in conventional and corporal strength.

Nor is it simple terror that restrains the boy from answering his senior with the same freedom and spirit, as he would answer his equal. He does not think it worth his while to enter the lists. He despairs of doing the thing in the way that shall gain approbation, and therefore will not try. He is like a boxer, who, though skilful, will not fight with one hand tied behind him. He would return you the answer, if it occurred without his giving himself trouble; but he will not rouse his soul, and task his strength to give it. He is careless; and prefers trusting to whatever construction you may put upon him, and whatever treatment you may think proper to bestow upon him. It is the most difficult thing in the world, for the schoolmaster to inspire into his pupil the desire to do his best.

Among full-grown men the case is different. The schoolboy, whether under his domestic roof, or in the gymnasium, is in a situation similar to that of the Christian slaves in Algiers, as described by Cervantes in his History of the Captive. "They were shut up together in a species of bagnio, from whence they were brought out from time to time to perform certain tasks in common: they might also engage in pranks, and get into scrapes, as they pleased; but the master would hang up one, impale another, and cut off the ears of a third, for little occasion, or even wholly without it." Such indeed is the condition of the child almost from the hour of birth. The severities practised upon him are not so great as those resorted to by the proprietor of slaves in Algiers; but they are equally arbitrary and without appeal. He is free to a certain extent, even as the captives described by Cervantes; but his freedom is upon sufferance, and is brought to an end at any time at the pleasure of his seniors. The child therefore feels his way, and ascertains by repeated experiments how far he may proceed with impunity. He is like the slaves of the Romans on the days of the Saturnalia. He may do what he pleases, and command tasks to his masters, but with this difference—the Roman slave knew when the days of his licence would be over, and comported himself accordingly; but the child cannot foresee at any moment when the bell will be struck, and the scene reversed. It is commonly enough incident to this situation, that the being who is at the mercy of another, will practise, what Tacitus calls, a "vernacular urbanity," make his bold jests, and give utterance to his saucy innuendoes, with as much freedom as the best; but he will do it with a wary eye, not knowing how soon he may feel his chain plucked! and himself compulsorily reduced into the established order. His more usual refuge therefore is, to do nothing, and to wrap himself up in that neutrality towards his seniors, that may best protect him from their reprimand and their despotism.

The condition of the full-grown man is different from that of the child, and he conducts himself accordingly. He is always to a certain degree under the control of the political society of which he is a member. He is also exposed to the chance of personal insult and injury from those who are stronger than he, or who may render their strength more considerable by combination and numbers. The political institutions which control him in certain respects, protect him also to a given degree from the robber and assassin, or from the man who, were it not for penalties and statutes, would perpetrate against him all the mischiefs which malignity might suggest. Civil policy however subjects him to a variety of evils, which wealth or corruption are accustomed to inflict under the forms of justice; at the same time that it can never wholly defend him from those violences to which he would be every moment exposed in what is called the state of nature.

The full-grown man in the mean time is well pleased when he escapes from the ergastulum where he had previously dwelt, and in which he had experienced corporal infliction and corporal restraint. At first, in the newness of his freedom, he breaks out into idle sallies and escapes, and is like the full-fed steed that manifests his wantonness in a thousand antics and ruades. But this is a temporary extravagance. He presently becomes as wise and calculating, as the schoolboy was before him.

The human being then, that has attained a certain stature, watches and poises his situation, and considers what he may do with impunity. He ventures at first with no small diffidence, and pretends to be twice as assured as he really is. He accumulates experiment after experiment, till they amount to a considerable volume. It is not till he has passed successive lustres, that he attains that firm step, and temperate and settled accent, which characterise the man complete. He then no longer doubts, but is ranged on the full level of the ripened members of the community.

There is therefore little room for wonder, if we find the same individual, whom we once knew a sheepish and irresolute schoolboy, that hung his head, that replied with inarticulated monotony, and stammered out his meaning, metamorphosed into a thoroughly manly character, who may take his place on the bench with senators, and deliver a grave and matured opinion as well as the best. It appears then that the trial and review of full-grown men is not altogether so disadvantageous to the reckoning of our common nature, as that of boys at school.

It is not however, that the full-grown man is not liable to be checked, reprimanded and rebuked, even as the schoolboy is. He has his wife to read him lectures, and rap his knuckles; he has his master, his landlord, or the mayor of his village, to tell him of his duty in an imperious style, and in measured sentences; if he is a member of a legislature, even there he receives his lessons, and is told, either in phrases of well-conceived irony, or by the exhibition of facts and reasonings which take him by surprise, that he is not altogether the person he deemed himself to be. But he does not mind it. Like Iago in the play, he "knows his price, and, by the faith of man, that he is worth no worse a place" than that which he occupies. He finds out the value of the check he receives, and lets it "pass by him like the idle wind"—a mastery, which the schoolboy, however he may affect it, never thoroughly attains to.

But it unfortunately happens, that, before he has arrived at that degree of independence, the fate of the individual is too often decided for ever. How are the majority of men trampled in the mire, made "hewers of wood, and drawers of water," long, very long, before there was an opportunity of ascertaining what it was of which they were capable! Thus almost every one is put in the place which by nature he was least fit for: and, while perhaps a sufficient quantity of talent is extant in each successive generation, yet, for want of each man's being duly estimated, and assigned his appropriate duty, the very reverse may appear to be the case. By the time that they have attained to that sober self-confidence that might enable them to assert themselves, they are already chained to a fate, or thrust down to a condition, from which no internal energies they possess can ever empower them to escape.

SECTION II.

EQUALITY OF MAN WITH MAN.—TALENTS EXTENSIVELY DISTRIBUTED.—WAY IN WHICH THIS DISTRIBUTION IS COUNTERACTED.—THE APTITUDE OF CHILDREN FOR DIFFERENT PURSUITS SHOULD BE EARLY SOUGHT OUT.— HINTS FOR A BETTER SYSTEM OF EDUCATION.—AMBITION AN UNIVERSAL PRINCIPLE.

The reflections thus put down, may assist us in answering the question as to the way in which talents are distributed among men by the hand of nature.

All things upon the earth and under the earth, and especially all organised bodies of the animal or vegetable kingdom, fall into classes. It is by this means, that the child no sooner learns the terms, man, horse, tree, flower, than, if an object of any of these kinds which he has never seen before, is exhibited to him, he pronounces without hesitation, This is a man, a horse, a tree, a flower.

All organised bodies of the animal or vegetable kingdom are cast in a mould of given dimension and feature belonging to a certain number of individuals, though distinguished by inexhaustible varieties. It is by means of those features that the class of each individual is determined.

To confine ourselves to man.

All men, the monster and the lusus naturae excepted, have a certain form, a certain complement of limbs, a certain internal structure, and organs of sense—may we not add further, certain powers of intellect?

Hence it seems to follow, that man is more like and more equal to man, deformities of body and abortions of intellect excepted, than the disdainful and fastidious censors of our common nature are willing to admit.

I am inclined to believe, that, putting idiots and extraordinary cases out of the question, every human creature is endowed with talents, which, if rightly directed, would shew him to be apt, adroit, intelligent and acute, in the walk for which his organisation especially fitted him.

But the practices and modes of civilised life prompt us to take the inexhaustible varieties of man, as he is given into our guardianship by the bountiful hand of nature, and train him in one uniform exercise, as the raw recruit is treated when he is brought under the direction of his drill-serjeant.

The son of the nobleman, of the country-gentleman, and of those parents who from vanity or whatever other motive are desirous that their offspring should be devoted to some liberal profession, is in nearly all instances sent to the grammar-school. It is in this scene principally, that the judgment is formed that not above one boy in a hundred possesses an acute understanding, or will be able to strike into a path of intellect that shall be truly his own.

I do not object to this destination, if temperately pursued. It is fit that as many children as possible should have their chance of figuring in future life in what are called the higher departments of intellect. A certain familiar acquaintance with language and the shades of language as a lesson, will be beneficial to all. The youth who has expended only six months in acquiring the rudiments of the Latin tongue, will probably be more or less the better for it in all his future life.

But seven years are usually spent at the grammar-school by those who are sent to it. I do not in many cases object to this. The learned languages are assuredly of slow acquisition. In the education of those who are destined to what are called the higher departments of intellect, a long period may advantageously be spent in the study of words, while the progress they make in theory and dogmatical knowledge is too generally a store of learning laid up, to be unlearned again when they reach the period of real investigation and independent judgment. There is small danger of this in the acquisition of words.

But this method, indiscriminately pursued as it is now, is productive of the worst consequences. Very soon a judgment may be formed by the impartial observer, whether the pupil is at home in the study of the learned languages, and is likely to make an adequate progress. But parents are not impartial. There are also two reasons why the schoolmaster is not the proper person to pronounce: first, because, if he pronounces in the negative, he will have reason to fear that the parent will be offended; and secondly, because he does not like to lose his scholar. But the very moment that it can be ascertained, that the pupil is not at home in the study of the learned languages, and is unlikely to make an adequate progress, at that moment he should be taken from it.

The most palpable deficiency that is to be found in relation to the education of children, is a sound judgment to be formed as to the vocation or employment in which each is most fitted to excel.

As, according to the institutions of Lycurgus, as soon as a boy was born, he was visited by the elders of the ward, who were to decide whether he was to be reared, and would be made an efficient member of the commonwealth, so it were to be desired that, as early as a clear discrimination on the subject might be practicable, a competent decision should be given as to the future occupation and destiny of a child.

But this is a question attended with no common degree of difficulty. To the resolving such a question with sufficient evidence, a very considerable series of observations would become necessary. The child should be introduced into a variety of scenes, and a magazine, so to speak, of those things about which human industry and skill may be employed, should be successively set before him. The censor who is to decide on the result of the whole, should be a person of great sagacity, and capable of pronouncing upon a given amount of the most imperfect and incidental indications. He should be clear-sighted, and vigilant to observe the involuntary turns of an eye, expressions of a lip, and demonstrations of a limb.

The declarations of the child himself are often of very small use in the case. He may be directed by an impulse, which occurs in the morning, and vanishes in the evening. His preferences change as rapidly as the shapes we sometimes observe in the evening clouds, and are governed by whim or fantasy, and not by any of those indications which are parcel of his individual constitution. He desires in many instances to be devoted to a particular occupation, because his playfellow has been assigned to it before him.

The parent is not qualified to judge in this fundamental question, because he is under the dominion of partiality, and wishes that his child may become a lord chancellor, an archbishop, or any thing else, the possessor of which condition shall be enabled to make a splendid figure in the world. He is not qualified, because he is an interested party, and, either from an exaggerated estimate of his child's merits, or from a selfish shrinking from the cost it might require to mature them, is anxious to arrive at a conclusion not founded upon the intrinsic claims of the case to be considered.

Even supposing it to be sufficiently ascertained in what calling it is that the child will be most beneficially engaged, a thousand extrinsical circumstances will often prevent that from being the calling chosen. Nature distributes her gifts without any reference to the distinctions of artificial society. The genius that demanded the most careful and assiduous cultivation, that it might hereafter form the boast and ornament of the world, will be reared amidst the chill blasts of poverty; while he who was best adapted to make an exemplary carpenter or artisan, by being the son of a nobleman is thrown a thousand fathoms wide of his true destination.

Human creatures are born into the world with various dispositions. According to the memorable saying of Themistocles, One man can play upon a psaltery or harp, and another can by political skill and ingenuity convert a town of small account, weak and insignificant, into a city noble, magnificent and great.

It is comparatively a very little way that we can penetrate into the mysteries of nature.

Music seems to be one of the faculties most clearly defined in early youth. The child who has received that destination from the hands of nature, will even in infancy manifest a singular delight in musical sounds, and will in no long time imitate snatches of a tune. The present professor of music in the university of Oxford contrived for himself, I believe at three years old, a way for playing on an instrument, the piano forte, unprompted by any of the persons about him. This is called having an ear.

Instances nearly as precocious are related of persons, who afterwards distinguished themselves in the art of painting.

These two kinds of original destination appear to be placed beyond the reach of controversy.

Horace says, The poet is born a poet, and cannot be made so by the ingenuity of art: and this seems to be true. He sees the objects about him with an eye peculiarly his own; the sounds that reach his ear, produce an effect upon him, and leave a memory behind, different from that which is experienced by his fellows. His perceptions have a singular vividness.

The poet's eye, in a fine frenzy rolling,

Doth glance from heaven to earth, from earth to heaven;

And his imagination bodies forth

The forms of things unknown,

It is not probable that any trainings of art can give these endowments to him who has not received them from the gift of nature.

The subtle network of the brain, or whatever else it is, that makes a man more fit for, and more qualified to succeed in, one occupation than another, can scarcely be followed up and detected either in the living subject or the dead one. But, as in the infinite variety of human beings no two faces are so alike that they cannot be distinguished, nor even two leaves plucked from the same tree(2), so it may reasonably be presumed, that there are varieties in the senses, the organs, and the internal structure of the human species, however delicate, and to the touch of the bystander evanescent, which may give to each individual a predisposition to rise to a supreme degree of excellence in some certain art or attainment, over a million of competitors.

(2) Papers between Clarke and Leibnitz, p. 95.

It has been said that all these distinctions and anticipations are idle, because man is born without innate ideas. Whatever is the incomprehensible and inexplicable power, which we call nature, to which he is indebted for his formation, it is groundless to suppose, that that power is cognisant of, and guides itself in its operations by, the infinite divisibleness of human pursuits in civilised society. A child is not designed by his original formation to be a manufacturer of shoes, for he may be born among a people by whom shoes are not worn, and still less is he destined by his structure to be a metaphysician, an astronomer, or a lawyer, a rope-dancer, a fortune-teller, or a juggler.

It is true that we cannot suppose nature to be guided in her operations by the infinite divisibleness of human pursuits in civilised society. But it is not the less true that one man is by his structure best fitted to excel in some one in particular of these multifarious pursuits, however fortuitously his individual structure and that pursuit may be brought into contact. Thus a certain calmness and steadiness of purpose, much flexibility, and a very accurate proportion of the various limbs of the body, are of great advantage in rope-dancing; while lightness of the fingers, and a readiness to direct our thoughts to the rapid execution of a purpose, joined with a steadiness of countenance adapted to what is figuratively called throwing dust in the eyes of the bystander, are of the utmost importance to the juggler: and so of the rest.

It is as much the temper of the individual, as any particular subtlety of organ or capacity, that prepares him to excel in one pursuit rather than a thousand others. And he must have been a very inattentive observer of the indications of temper in an infant in the first months of his existence, who does not confess that there are various peculiarities in that respect which the child brings into the world with him.

There is excellent sense in the fable of Achilles in the island of Scyros. He was placed there by his mother in female attire among the daughters of Lycomedes, that he might not be seduced to engage in the Trojan war. Ulysses was commissioned to discover him, and, while he exhibited jewels and various woman's ornaments to the princesses, contrived to mix with his stores a suit of armour, the sight of which immediately awakened the spirit of the hero.

Every one has probably within him a string more susceptible than the rest, that demands only a kindred impression to be made, to call forth its latent character. Like the war-horse described in the Book of Job: "He paweth in the valley, and rejoiceth in his strength; he goeth on to meet the armed men; he smelleth the battle afar off, the thunder of the captains, and the shouting."

Nothing can be more unlike than the same man to himself, when he is touched, and not touched, upon

> *the master-string*
>
> *That makes most harmony or discord to him.*

It is like the case of Manlius Torquatus in Livy, who by his father was banished among his hinds for his clownish demeanour and untractableness to every species of instruction that was offered him, but who, understanding that his parent was criminally arraigned for barbarous treatment of him, first resolutely resorted to the accuser, compelling him upon pain of death to withdraw his accusation, and subsequently, having surmounted this first step towards an energetic carriage and demeanour, proved one of the most illustrious characters that the Roman republic had to boast.

Those children whose parents have no intention of training them to the highest departments of intellect, and have therefore no thought of bestowing on them a classical education, nevertheless for the most part send them to a school where they are to be taught arithmetic, and the principles of English grammar. I should say in this case, as I said before on the subject of classical education, that a certain initiation in these departments of knowledge, even if they are pursued a very little way, will probably be beneficial to all.

But it will often be found, in these schools for more ordinary education, as in the school for classical instruction, that the majority of the pupils will be seen to be unpromising, and, what is usually called, dull. The mistake is, that the persons by whom this is perceived, are disposed to set aside these pupils as blockheads, and unsusceptible of any species of ingenuity.

It is unreasonable that we should draw such a conclusion.

In the first place, as has been already observed, it is the most difficult thing in the world for the schoolmaster to inspire into his pupil the desire to do his best. An overwhelming majority of lads at school are in their secret hearts rebels to the discipline under which they are placed. The instructor draws, one way, and the pupil another. The object of the latter is to find out how he may escape censure and punishment with the smallest expence of scholastic application. He looks at the task that is set him, without the most distant desire of improvement, but with alienated and averted eye. And, where this is the case, the wonder is not that he does not make a brilliant figure. It is rather an evidence of the slavish and subservient spirit incident to the majority of human beings, that he learns any thing. Certainly the schoolmaster, who judges of the powers of his pupil's mind by the progress he makes in what he would most gladly be excused from learning, must be expected perpetually to fall into the most egregious mistakes.

The true test of the capacity of the individual, is where the desire to succeed, and accomplish something effective, is already awakened in the youthful mind. Whoever has found out what it is in which he is qualified to excel, from that moment becomes a new creature. The general torpor and sleep of the soul, which is incident to the vast multitude of the human species, is departed from him. We begin, from the hour in which our limbs are enabled to exert themselves freely, with a puerile love of sport. Amusement is the order of the day. But no one was ever so fond of play, that he had not also his serious moments. Every human creature perhaps is sensible to the stimulus of ambition. He is delighted with the thought that he also shall be somebody, and not a mere undistinguished pawn, destined to fill up a square in the chess-board of human society. He wishes to be thought something of, and to be gazed upon. Nor is it merely the wish to be admired that excites him: he acts, that he may be satisfied with himself. Self-respect is a sentiment dear to every heart. The emotion can with difficulty be done justice to, that a man feels, who is conscious that he is breathing his true element, that every stroke that he strikes will have the effect he designs, that he has an object before him, and every moment approaches nearer to that object. Before, he was wrapped in an opake cloud, saw nothing distinctly, and struck this way and that at hazard like a blind man. But now the sun of understanding has risen upon him; and every step that he takes, he advances with an assured and undoubting confidence.

It is an admirable remark, that the book which we read at the very time that we feel a desire to read it, affords us ten times the improvement, that we should have derived from it when it was taken up by us as a task. It is just so with the man who chooses his occupation, and feels assured that that about which he is occupied is his true and native field. Compare this person with the boy that studies the classics, or arithmetic, or any thing else, with a secret disinclination, and, as Shakespear expresses it, "creeps like snail, unwillingly, to school." They do not seem as if they belonged to the same species.

The result of these observations certainly strongly tends to support the proposition laid down early in the present Essay, that, putting idiots and extraordinary cases out of the question, every human creature is endowed with talents, which, if rightly directed, would shew him to be apt, adroit, intelligent and acute, in the walk for which his organisation especially fitted him.

SECTION III.

ENCOURAGING VIEW OF OUR COMMON NATURE.—POWER OF SOUND EXPOSITION AFFORDED TO ALL.—DOCTRINE OF THIS ESSAY AND THE HYPOTHESIS OF HELVETIUS COMPARED.—THE WILLING AND UNWILLING PUPIL CONTRASTED.—MISCHIEVOUS TENDENCY OF THE USUAL MODES OF EDUCATION.

What a beautiful and encouraging view is thus afforded us of our common nature! It is not true, as certain disdainful and fastidious censurers of their fellow-men would persuade us to believe, that a thousand seeds are sown in the wide field of humanity, for no other purpose than that half-a-dozen may grow up into something magnificent and splendid, and that the rest, though not absolutely extinguished in the outset, are merely suffered to live that they may furnish manure and nourishment to their betters. On the contrary, each man, according to this hypothesis, has a sphere in which he may shine, and may contemplate the exercise of his own powers with a well-grounded satisfaction. He produces something as perfect in its kind, as that which is effected under another form by the more brilliant and illustrious of his species. He stands forward with a serene confidence in the ranks of his fellow-creatures, and says, "I also have my place in society, that I fill in a manner with which I have a right to be satisfied." He vests a certain portion of ingenuity in the work he turns out. He incorporates his mind with the labour of his hands; and a competent observer will find character and individuality in it.

He has therefore nothing of the sheepishness of the ordinary schoolboy, the tasks imposed upon whom by his instructor are foreign to the true bent of his mind, and who stands cowed before his seniors, shrinking under the judgment they may pass upon him, and the oppression they may exercise towards him. He is probably competent to talk in a manner that may afford instruction to men in other respects wise and accomplished, and is no less clear and well-digested in his discourse respecting the subjects to which his study and labour have been applied, than they are on the questions that have exercised the powers of analysis with which they are endowed. Like Elihu in the Book of Job, he says, "I am young, and you are old; I said therefore, Days shall speak, and multitude of years shall teach wisdom. But there is a spirit in man; and the inspiration of the Almighty giveth him understanding. Great men are not always wise; neither do the aged understand judgment. Hearken therefore to me; and I also will shew my opinion."

What however in the last instance is affirmed, is not always realised in the experiment. The humblest mechanic, who works con amore, and feels that he discharges his office creditably, has a sober satisfaction in the retrospect, and is able to express himself perspicuously and well on the subject that has occupied his industry. He has a just confidence in himself. If the occasion arises, on which he should speak on the subject of what he does, and the methods he adopts for effecting it, he will undoubtedly acquit himself to the satisfaction of those who hear him. He knows that the explanations he can afford will be sound and masculine, and will stand the test of a rigid examination.

But, in proportion as he feels the ground on which he stands, and his own power to make it good, he will not fail to retire from an audience that is not willing to be informed by him. He will often appear in the presence of those, whom the established arrangements of society call his superiors, who are more copiously endowed with the treasures of language, and who, confident perhaps in the advantage of opulence, and what is called, however they may have received it, a liberal education, regard with disdain his artless and unornamented explanations. He did not, it may be, expect this. And, having experienced several times such unmerited treatment, he is not willing again to encounter it. He knew the worth of what he had to offer. And, finding others indisposed to listen to his suggestions, he contentedly confines them within the circle of his own thoughts.

To this it must be added that, though he is able to explain himself perspicuously, yet he is not master of the graces of speech, nor even perhaps of the niceties of grammar. His voice is not tuned to those winning inflections by which men, accustomed to the higher ranks of society, are enabled so to express themselves,

That aged ears play truant at their tales,

And younger hearings are quite ravished,

So sweet and voluble is their discourse.

On the contrary there is a ruggedness in his manner that jars upon the sense. It is easy for the light and supercilious to turn him into ridicule. And those who will not be satisfied with the soundness of his matter, expounded, as he is able to expound it, in clear and appropriate terms, will yield him small credit, and listen to him with little delight.

These considerations therefore bring us back again to the reasons of the prevalent opinion, that the majority of mankind are dull, and of apprehension narrow and confused. The mass of boys in the process of their education appear so, because little of what is addressed to them by their instructors, awakens their curiosity, and inspires them with the desire to excel. The concealed spark of ambition is not yet cleared from the crust that enveloped it as it first came from the hand of nature. And in like manner the elder persons, who have not experienced the advantages of a liberal education, or by whom small profit was made by those advantages, being defective in exterior graces, are generally listened to with impatience, and therefore want the confidence and the inclination to tell what they know.

But these latter, if they are not attended to upon the subjects to which their attention and ingenuity have been applied, do not the less possess a knowledge and skill which are intrinsically worthy of applause. They therefore contentedly shut up the sum of their acquisitions in their own bosoms, and are satisfied with the consciousness that they have not been deficient in performing an adequate part in the generation of men among whom they live.

Those persons who favour the opinion of the incessant improveableness of the human species, have felt strongly prompted to embrace the creed of Helvetius, who affirms that the minds of men, as they are born into the world, are in a state of equality, alike prepared for any kind of discipline and instruction that may be afforded them, and that it depends upon education only, in the largest sense of that word, including every impression that may be made upon the mind, intentional or accidental, from the hour of our birth, whether we shall be poets or philosophers, dancers or singers, chemists or mathematicians, astronomers or dissectors of the faculties of our common nature.

But this is not true. It has already appeared in the course of this Essay, that the talent, or, more accurately speaking, the original suitableness of the individual for the cultivation, of music or painting, depends upon certain peculiarities that we bring into the world with us. The same thing may be affirmed of the poet. As, in the infinite variety of human beings, there are no two faces so alike that they cannot be distinguished, nor even two leaves plucked from the same tree, so there are varieties in the senses, the organs, and the internal structure of the human species, however delicate, and to the touch of the bystander evanescent, which give to each individual a predisposition to rise to excellence in one particular art or attainment, rather than in any other.

And this view of things, if well considered, is as favourable, nay, more so, to the hypothesis of the successive improveableness of the human species, as the creed of Helvetius. According to that philosopher, every human creature that is born into the world, is capable of becoming, or being made, the equal of Homer, Bacon or Newton, and as easily and surely of the one as the other. This creed, if sincerely embraced, no doubt affords a strong stimulus to both preceptor and pupil, since, if true, it teaches us that any thing can be made of any thing, and that, wherever there is mind, it is within the compass of possibility, not only that that mind can be raised to a high pitch of excellence, but even to a high pitch of that excellence, whatever it is, that we shall prefer to all others, and most earnestly desire.

Still this creed will, after all, leave both preceptor and pupil in a state of feeling considerably unsatisfactory. What it sets before us, is too vast and indefinite. We shall be left long perhaps in a state of balance as to what species of excellence we shall choose; and, in the immense field of accessible improvement it offers to us, without land-mark or compass for the direction of our course, it is scarcely possible that we should feel that assured confidence and anticipation of success, which are perhaps indispensibly required to the completion of a truly arduous undertaking.

But, upon the principles laid down in this Essay, the case is widely different. We are here presented in every individual human creature with a subject better fitted for one sort of cultivation than another. We are excited to an earnest study of the individual, that we may the more unerringly discover what pursuit it is for which his nature and qualifications especially prepare him. We may be long in choosing. We may be even on the brink of committing a considerable mistake. Our subsequent observations may enable us to correct the inference we were disposed to make from those which went before. Our sagacity is flattered by the result of the laborious scrutiny which this view of our common nature imposes upon us.

In addition to this we reap two important advantages.

In the first place, we feel assured that every child that is born has his suitable sphere, to which if he is devoted, he will not fail to make an honourable figure, or, in other words, will be seen to be endowed with faculties, apt, adroit, intelligent and acute. This consideration may reasonably stimulate us to call up all our penetration for the purpose of ascertaining the proper destination of the child for whom we are interested.

And, secondly, having arrived at this point, we shall find ourselves placed in a very different predicament from the guardian or instructor, who, having selected at random the pursuit which his fancy dictates, and in the choice of which he is encouraged by the presumptuous assertions of a wild metaphysical philosophy, must often, in spite of himself, feel a secret misgiving as to the final event. He may succeed, and present to a wondering world a consummate musician, painter, poet, or philosopher; for even blind chance may sometimes hit the mark, as truly as the most perfect skill. But he will probably fail. Sudet multum, frustraque laboret. And, if he is disappointed, he will not only feel that disappointment in the ultimate result, but also in every step of his progress. When he has done his best, exerted his utmost industry, and consecrated every power of his soul to the energies he puts forth, he may close every day, sometimes with a faint shadow of success, and sometimes with entire and blank miscarriage. And the latter will happen ten thousand times, for once that the undertaking shall be blessed with a prosperous event.

But, when the destination that is given to a child has been founded upon a careful investigation of the faculties, tokens, and accidental aspirations which characterise his early years, it is then that every step that is made with him, becomes a new and surer source of satisfaction. The moment the pursuit for which his powers are adapted is seriously proposed to him, his eyes sparkle, and a second existence, in addition to that which he received at his birth, descends upon him. He feels that he has now obtained something worth living for. He feels that he is at home, and in a sphere that is appropriately his own. Every effort that he makes is successful. At every resting-place in his race of improvement he pauses, and looks back on what he has done with complacency. The master cannot teach him so fast, as he is prompted to acquire.

What a contrast does this species of instruction exhibit, to the ordinary course of scholastic education! There, every lesson that is prescribed, is a source of indirect warfare between the instructor and the pupil, the one professing to aim at the advancement of him that is taught, in the career of knowledge, and the other contemplating the effect that is intended to be produced upon him with aversion, and longing to be engaged in any thing else, rather than in that which is pressed upon his foremost attention. In this sense a numerous school is, to a degree that can scarcely be adequately described, the slaughter-house of mind. It is like the undertaking, related by Livy, of Accius Navius, the augur, to cut a whetstone with a razor—with this difference, that our modern schoolmasters are not endowed with the gift of working miracles, and, when the experiment falls into their hands, the result of their efforts is a pitiful miscarriage. Knowledge is scarcely in any degree imparted. But, as they are inured to a dogged assiduity, and persist in their unavailing attempts, though the shell of science, so to speak, is scarcely in the smallest measure penetrated, yet that inestimable gift of the author of our being, the sharpness of human faculties, is so blunted and destroyed, that it can scarcely ever be usefully employed even for those purposes which it was originally best qualified to effect.

A numerous school is that mint from which the worst and most flagrant libels on our nature are incessantly issued. Hence it is that we are taught, by a judgment everlastingly repeated, that the majority of our kind are predestinated blockheads.

Not that it is by any means to be recommended, that a little writing and arithmetic, and even the first rudiments of classical knowledge, so far as they can be practicably imparted, should be withheld from any. The mischief is, that we persist, month after month, and year after year, in sowing our seed, when it has already been fully ascertained, that no suitable and wholsome crop will ever be produced.

But what is perhaps worse is, that we are accustomed to pronounce, that that soil, which will not produce the crop of which we have attempted to make it fertile, is fit for nothing. The majority of boys, at the very period when the buds of intellect begin to unfold themselves, are so accustomed to be told that they are dull and fit for nothing, that the most pernicious effects are necessarily produced. They become half convinced by the ill-boding song of the raven, perpetually croaking in their ears; and, for the other half, though by no means assured that the sentence of impotence awarded against them is just, yet, folding up their powers in inactivity, they are contented partly to waste their energies in pure idleness and sport, and partly to wait, with minds scarcely half awake, for the moment when their true destination shall be opened before them.

Not that it is by any means to be desired that the child in his earlier years should meet with no ruggednesses in his way, and that he should perpetually tread "the primrose path of dalliance." Clouds and tempests occasionally clear the atmosphere of intellect, not less than that of the visible world. The road to the hill of science, and to the promontory of heroic virtue, is harsh and steep, and from time to time puts to the proof the energies of him who would ascend their topmost round.

There are many things which every human creature should learn, so far as, agreeably to the constitution of civilised society, they can be brought within his reach. He should be induced to learn them, willingly if possible, but, if that cannot be thoroughly effected, yet with half a will. Such are reading, writing, arithmetic, and the first principles of grammar; to which shall be added, as far as may be, the rudiments of all the sciences that are in ordinary use. The latter however should not be brought forward too soon; and, if wisely delayed, the tyro himself will to a certain degree enter into the views of his instructor, and be disposed to essay Quid valeant humeri, quid ferre recusent. But, above all, the beginnings of those studies should be encouraged, which unfold the imagination, familiarise us with the feelings, the joys and sufferings of our fellow-beings, and teach us to put ourselves in their place and eagerly fly to their assistance.

SECTION IV.

HOW FAR OUR GENUINE PROPENSITIES AND VOCATION SHOULD BE FAVOURED.—SELF-REVERENCE RECOMMENDED.—CONCLUSION.

I knew a man of eminent intellectual faculties(3), one of whose favourite topics of moral prudence was, that it is the greatest mistake in the world to suppose, that, when we have discovered the special aspiration of the youthful mind, we are bound to do every thing in our power to assist its progress. He maintained on the contrary, that it is our true wisdom to place obstacles in its way, and to thwart it: as we may be well assured that, unless it is a mere caprice, it will shew its strength in conquering difficulties, and that all the obstacles that we can conjure up will but inspire it with the greater earnestness to attain final success.

(3) Henry Fuseli.

The maxim here stated, taken to an unlimited extent, is doubtless a very dangerous one. There are obstacles that scarcely any strength of man would be sufficient to conquer. "Chill penury" will sometimes "repress the noblest rage," that almost ever animated a human spirit: and our wisest course will probably be, secretly to favour, even when we seem most to oppose, the genuine bent of the youthful aspirer.

But the thing of greatest importance is, that we should not teach him to estimate his powers at too low a rate. One of the wisest of all the precepts comprised in what are called the Golden Verses of Pythagoras, is that, in which he enjoins his pupil to "reverence himself." Ambition is the noblest root that can be planted in the garden of the human soul: not the ambition to be applauded and admired, to be famous and looked up to, to be the darling theme of "stupid starers and of loud huzzas;" but the ambition to fill a respectable place in the theatre of society, to be useful and to be esteemed, to feel that we have not lived in vain, and that we are entitled to the most honourable of all dismissions, an enlightened self-approbation. And nothing can more powerfully tend to place this beyond our acquisition, even our contemplation, than the perpetual and hourly rebuffs which ingenuous youth is so often doomed to sustain from the supercilious pedant, and the rigid decision of his unfeeling elders.

Self-respect to be nourished in the mind of the pupil, is one of the most valuable results of a well conducted education. To accomplish this, it is most necessary that it should never be inculcated into him, that he is dull. Upon the principles of this Essay, any unfavourable appearances that may present themselves, do not arise from the dulness of the pupil, but from the error of those upon whose superintendence he is cast, who require of him the things for which he is not adapted, and neglect those in which he is qualified to excel.

It is further necessary, if self-respect is one of the most desirable results of a well-conducted education, that, as we should not humble the pupil in his own eyes by disgraceful and humiliating language, so we should abstain, as much as possible, from personal ill-treatment, and the employing towards him the measures of an owner towards his purchased or indentured slave. Indignity is of all things the most hostile to the best purposes of a liberal education. It may be necessary occasionally to employ, towards a human creature in his years of nonage, the stimulants of exhortation and remonstrance even in the pursuits to which he is best adapted, for the purpose of overcoming the instability and fits of idleness to which all men, and most of all in their early years, are subject: though in such pursuits a necessity of this sort can scarcely be supposed. The bow must not always be bent; and it is good for us that we should occasionally relax and play the fool. It may more readily be imagined, that some incitement may be called for in those things which, as has been mentioned above, it may be fit he should learn though with but half a will. All freaks must not be indulged; admonition is salutary, and that the pupil should be awakened by his instructor to sober reflection and to masculine exertion. Every Telemachus should have his Mentor.—But through the whole it is necessary that the spirit of the pupil should not be broken, and that he should not be treated with contumely. Stripes should in all instances be regarded as the last resort, and as a sort of problem set up for the wisdom of the wise to solve, whether the urgent case can arise in which it shall be requisite to have recourse to them.

The principles here laid down have the strongest tendency to prove to us how little progress has yet been made in the art of turning human creatures to the best account. Every man has his place, in which if he can be fixed, the most fastidious judge cannot look upon him with disdain. But, to effect this arrangement, an exact attention is required to ascertain the pursuit in which he will best succeed. In India the whole mass of the members of the community is divided into castes; and, instead of a scrupulous attention being paid to the early intimations of individual character, it is already decided upon each, before he comes into the world, which child shall be a priest, and which a soldier, a physician, a lawyer, a merchant, and an artisan. In Europe we do not carry this so far, and are not so elaborately wrong. But the rudiments of the same folly flourish among us; and the accident of birth for the most part decides the method of life to which each individual with whatever violence shall be dedicated. A very few only, by means of energies that no tyranny can subdue, escape from the operation of this murderous decree.

Nature never made a dunce. Imbecility of mind is as rare, as deformity of the animal frame. If this position be true, we have only to bear it in mind, feelingly to convince ourselves, how wholesale the error is into which society has hitherto fallen in the destination of its members, and how much yet remains to be done, before our common nature can be vindicated from the basest of all libels, the most murderous of all proscriptions.

There is a passage in Voltaire, in which he expresses himself to this effect: "It is after all but a slight line of separation that divides the man of genius from the man of ordinary mould." I remember the place where, and the time when, I read this passage. But I have been unable to find the expression. It is however but reasonable that I should refer to it on this occasion, that I may hereby shew so eminent a modern concurring with the venerable ancient in an early era of letters, whose dictum I have prefixed to this Essay, to vouch to a certain extent for the truth of the doctrine I have delivered.

ESSAY III. OF INTELLECTUAL ABORTION.

In the preceding Essay I have endeavoured to establish the proposition, that every human creature, idiots and extraordinary cases excepted, is endowed with talents, which, if rightly directed, would shew him to be apt, adroit, intelligent and acute, in the walk for which his organisation especially fitted him.

There is however a sort of phenomenon, by no means of rare occurrence, which tends to place the human species under a less favourable point of view. Many men, as has already appeared, are forced into situations and pursuits ill assorted to their talents, and by that means are exhibited to their contemporaries in a light both despicable and ludicrous.

But this is not all. Men are not only placed, by the absurd choice of their parents, or an imperious concurrence of circumstances, in destinations and employments in which they can never appear to advantage: they frequently, without any external compulsion, select for themselves objects of their industry, glaringly unadapted to their powers, and in which all their efforts must necessarily terminate in miscarriage.

I remember a young man, who had been bred a hair-dresser, but who experienced, as he believed, the secret visitations of the Muse, and became inspired. "With sad civility, and aching head," I perused no fewer than six comedies from the pen of this aspiring genius, in no page of which I could discern any glimmering of poetry or wit, or in reality could form a guess what it was that the writer intended in his elaborate effusions. Such are the persons enumerated by Pope in the Prologue to his Satires,

> a parson, much bemused in beer,
>
> A maudlin poetess, a rhyming peer,
>
> A clerk, foredoomed his father's sou to cross,
>
> Who pens a stanza, when he should engross.

Every manager of a theatre, and every publishing bookseller of eminence, can produce you in each revolving season whole reams, almost cartloads, of blurred paper, testifying the frequent recurrence of this phenomenon.

The cause however of this painful mistake does not lie in the circumstance, that each man has not from the hand of nature an appropriate destination, a sphere assigned him, in which, if life should be prolonged to him, he might be secure of the respect of his neighbours, and might write upon his tomb, "I have filled an honourable career; I have finished my course."

One of the most glaring infirmities of our nature is discontent. One of the most unquestionable characteristics of the human mind is the love of novelty. Omne ignotum pro magnifico est. We are satiated with those objects which make a part of our business in every day, and are desirous of trying something that is a stranger to us. Whatever we see through a mist, or in the twilight, is apt to be apprehended by us as something admirable, for the single reason that it is seen imperfectly. What we are sure that we can easily and adequately effect, we despise. He that goes into battle with an adversary of more powerful muscle or of greater practice than himself, feels a tingling sensation, not unallied to delight, very different from that which would occur to him, when his victory was easy and secure.

Each man is conscious what it is that he can certainly effect. This does not therefore present itself to him as an object of ambition. We have many of us internally something of the spirit expressed by the apostle: "Forgetting the things that are behind, we press forward to those that remain." And, so long as this precept is soberly applied, no conduct can be more worthy of praise. Improvement is the appropriate race of man. We cannot stand still. If we do not go forward, we shall inevitably recede. Shakespear, when he wrote his Hamlet, did not know that he could produce Macbeth and Othello.

But the progress of a man of reflection will be, to a considerable degree, in the path he has already entered. If he strikes into a new career, it will not be without deep premeditation. He will attempt nothing wantonly. He will carefully examine his powers, and see for what they are adapted. Sudet multum. He will be like the man, who first in a frail bark committed himself to the treachery of the waves. He will keep near to the shore; he will tremble for the audaciousness of his enterprise; he will feel that it calls for all his alertness and vigilance. The man of reflection will not begin, till he feels his mind swelling with his purposed theme, till his blood flows fitfully and with full pulses through his veins, till his eyes sparkle with the intenseness of his conceptions, and his "bosom labours with the God."

But the fool dashes in at once. He does not calculate the dangers of his enterprise. He does not study the map of the country he has to traverse. He does not measure the bias of the ground, the rising knolls and the descending slopes that are before him. He obeys a blind and unreflecting impulse.

His case bears a striking resemblance to what is related of Oliver Goldsmith. Goldsmith was a man of the most felicitous endowments. His prose flows with such ease, copiousness and grace, that it resembles the song of the sirens. His verses are among the most spirited, natural and unaffected in the English language. Yet he was not contented. If he saw a consummate dancer, he knew no reason why he should not do as well, and immediately felt disposed to essay his powers. If he heard an accomplished musician, he undertook to enter the lists with him. His conduct was of a piece with that of the countryman, who, cheapening spectacles, and making experiment of them for ever in vain upon the book before him, was at length asked, "Could you ever read without spectacles?" to which he was obliged to answer, "I do not know; I never tried." The vanity of Goldsmith was infinite; and his failure in such attempts must necessarily have been ludicrous.

The splendour of the thing presented to our observation, awakens the spirit within us. The applause and admiration excited by certain achievements and accomplishments infects us with desire. We are like the youthful Themistocles, who complained that the trophies of Miltiades would not let him sleep. We are like the novice Guido, who, while looking on the paintings of Michael Angelo, exclaimed, "I also am a painter." Themistocles and Guido were right, for they were of kindred spirit to the great men they admired. But the applause bestowed on others will often generate uneasiness and a sigh, in men least of all qualified by nature to acquire similar applause. We are not contented to proceed in the path of obscure usefulness and worth. We are eager to be admired, and thus often engage in pursuits for which perhaps we are of all men least adapted Each one would be the man above him.

And this is the cause why we see so many individuals, who might have passed their lives with honour, devote themselves to incredible efforts, only that they may be made supremely ridiculous.

To this let it be added, that the wisest man that ever existed, never yet knew himself, especially in the morning of life. The person, who ultimately stamped his history with the most heroic achievements, was far perhaps even from suspecting, in the dawn of his existence, that he should realise the miracles that mark its maturity. He might be ready to exclaim, with Hazael in the Scriptures, "Is thy servant more than man, that he should do this great thing?" The sublimest poet that ever sung, was peradventure, while a stripling, unconscious of the treasures which formed a part of the fabric of his mind, and unsuspicious of the high destiny that in the sequel awaited him. What wonder then, that, awaking from the insensibility and torpor which precede the activity of the soul, some men should believe in a fortune that shall never be theirs, and anticipate a glory they are fated never to sustain! And for the same reason, when unanticipated failure becomes their lot, they are unwilling at first to be discouraged, and find a certain gallantry in persevering, and "against hope believing in hope."

This is the explanation of a countless multitude of failures that occur in the career of literature. Nor is this phenomenon confined to literature. In all the various paths of human existence, that appear to have something in them splendid and alluring, there are perpetual instances of daring adventures, unattended with the smallest rational hope of success. *Optat ephippia bos piger.*

All quit their sphere, and rush into the skies.

But, beside these instances of perfect and glaring miscarriage, there are examples worthy of a deeper regret, where the juvenile candidate sets out in the morning of life with the highest promise, with colours flying, and the spirit-stirring note of gallant preparation, when yet his voyage of life is destined to terminate in total discomfiture. I have seen such an one, whose early instructors regarded him with the most sanguine expectation, and his elders admired him, while his youthful competitors unreluctantly confessed his superiority, and gave way on either side to his triumphant career; and all this has terminated in nothing.

In reality the splendid march of genius is beset with a thousand difficulties. "The race is not always to the swift, nor the battle to the strong." A multitude of unthought-of qualifications are required; and it depends at least as much upon the nicely maintained balance of these, as upon the copiousness and brilliancy of each, whether the result shall be auspicious. The progress of genius is like the flight of an arrow; a breath may turn it out of its course, and cause that course to terminate many a degree wide of its purposed mark. It is therefore scarcely possible that any sharpness of foresight can pronounce of the noblest beginnings whether they shall reach to an adequate conclusion.

I have seen such a man, with the most fervent imagination, with the most diligent study, with the happiest powers of memory, and with an understanding that apparently took in every thing, and arranged every thing, at the same time that by its acuteness it seemed able to add to the accumulated stores of foregone wisdom and learning new treasures of its own; and yet this man shall pass through the successive stages of human life, in appearance for ever active, for ever at work, and leave nothing behind that shall embalm his name to posterity, certainly nothing in any degree adequately representing those excellencies, which a chosen few, admitted to his retired and his serenest hours, knew to reside in him.

There are conceptions of the mind, that come forth like the coruscations of lightning. If you could fix that flash, it would seem as if it would give new brightness to the sons of men, and almost extinguish the luminary of day. But, ere you can say it is here, it is gone. It appears to reveal to us the secrets of the world unknown; but the clouds congregate again, and shut in upon us, before we had time to apprehend its full radiance and splendour.

To give solidity and permanence to the inspirations of genius two things are especially necessary. First, that the idea to be communicated should be powerfully apprehended by the speaker or writer; and next, that he should employ words and phrases which might convey it in all its truth to the mind of another. The man who entertains such conceptions, will not unfrequently want the steadiness of nerve which is required for their adequate transmission. Suitable words will not always wait upon his thoughts. Language is in reality a vast labyrinth, a scene like the Hercinian Forest of old, which, we are told, could not be traversed in less than sixty days. If we do not possess the clue, we shall infallibly perish in the attempt, and our thoughts and our memory will expire with us.

The sentences of this man, when he speaks, or when he writes, will be full of perplexity and confusion. They will be endless, and never arrive at their proper termination. They will include parenthesis on parenthesis. We perceive the person who delivers them, to be perpetually labouring after a meaning, but never reaching it. He is like one flung over into the sea, unprovided with the skill that should enable him to contend with the tumultuous element. He flounders about in pitiable helplessness, without the chance of extricating himself by all his efforts. He is lost in unintelligible embarrassment. It is a delightful and a ravishing sight, to observe another man come after him, and tell, without complexity, and in the simplicity of self-possession, unconscious that there was any difficulty, all that his predecessor had fruitlessly exerted himself to unfold.

There are a multitude of causes that will produce a miscarriage of this sort, where the richest soil, impregnated with the choicest seeds of learning and observation, shall entirely fail to present us with such a crop as might rationally have been anticipated. Many such men waste their lives in indolence and irresolution. They attempt many things, sketch out plans, which, if properly filled up, might illustrate the literature of a nation, and extend the empire of the human mind, but which yet they desert as soon as begun, affording us the promise of a beautiful day, that, ere it is noon, is enveloped in darkest tempests and the clouds of midnight. They skim away from one flower in the parterre of literature to another, like the bee, without, like the bee, gathering sweetness from each, to increase the public stock, and enrich the magazine of thought. The cause of this phenomenon is an unsteadiness, ever seduced by the newness of appearances, and never settling with firmness and determination upon what had been chosen.

Others there are that are turned aside from the career they might have accomplished, by a visionary and impracticable fastidiousness. They can find nothing that possesses all the requisites that should fix their choice, nothing so good that should authorise them to present it to public observation, and enable them to offer it to their contemporaries as something that we should "not willingly let die." They begin often; but nothing they produce appears to them such as that they should say of it, "Let this stand." Or they never begin, none of their thoughts being judged by them to be altogether such as to merit the being preserved. They have a microscopic eye, and discern faults unworthy to be tolerated, in that in which the critic himself might perceive nothing but beauty.

These phenomena have introduced a maxim which is current with many, that the men who write nothing, and bequeath no record of themselves to posterity, are not unfrequently of larger calibre, and more gigantic standard of soul, than such as have inscribed their names upon the columns of the temple of Fame. And certain it is, that there are extraordinary instances which appear in some degree to countenance this assertion. Many men are remembered as authors, who seem to have owed the permanence of their reputation rather to fortune than merit. They were daring, and stepped into a niche that was left in the gallery of art or of science, where others of higher qualifications, but of unconquerable modesty, held back. At the same time persons, whose destiny caused them to live among the elite of an age, have seen reason to confess that they have heard such talk, such glorious and unpremeditated discourse, from men whose thoughts melted away with the breath that uttered them, as the wisest of their vaunted contemporary authors would in vain have sought to rival.

The maxim however, notwithstanding these appearances, may safely be pronounced to be a fallacious one. It has been received in various quarters with the greater indulgence, inasmuch as the human mind is prone in many cases to give a more welcome reception to seeming truths, that present us at the first blush the appearance of falshood.

It must however be recollected that the human mind consists in the first instance merely of faculties prepared to be applied to certain purposes, and susceptible of improvement. It cannot therefore happen, that the man, who has chosen a subject towards which to direct the energy of his faculties, who has sought on all sides for the materials that should enable him to do that subject justice, who has employed upon it his contemplations by day, and his meditations during the watches of the night, should not by such exercise greatly invigorate his powers. In this sense there was much truth in the observation of the author who said, "I did not write upon the subject you mention because I understood it; but I understood it afterward, because I had written upon it."

The man who merely wanders through the fields of knowledge in search of its gayest flowers and of whatever will afford him the most enviable amusement, will necessarily return home at night with a very slender collection. He that shall apply himself with self-denial and an unshrinking resolution to the improvement of his mind, will unquestionably be found more fortunate in the end.

He is not deterred by the gulphs that yawn beneath his feet, or the mountains that may oppose themselves to his progress. He knows that the adventurer of timid mind, and that is infirm of purpose, will never make himself master of those points which it would be most honourable to him to subdue. But he who undertakes to commit to writing the result of his researches, and to communicate his discoveries to mankind, is the genuine hero. Till he enters on this task, every thing is laid up in his memory in a certain confusion. He thinks he possesses a thing whole; but, when he brings it to the test, he is surprised to find how much he was deceived. He that would digest his thoughts and his principles into a regular system, is compelled in the first place to regard them in all their clearness and perspicuity, and in the next place to select the fittest words by which they may be communicated to others. It is through the instrumentality of words that we are taught to think accurately and severely for ourselves; they are part and parcel of all our propositions and theories. It is therefore in this way that a preceptor, by undertaking to enlighten the mind of his pupil, enlightens his own. He becomes twice the man in the sequel, that he was when he entered on his task. We admire the amateur student in his public essays, as we admire a jackdaw or a parrot: he does considerably more than could have been expected from him.

In attending to the subject of this Essay we have been led to observe the different ways, in which the mind of man may be brought into a position tending to exhibit its powers in a less creditable and prepossessing point of view, than that in which all men, idiots and extraordinary cases excepted, are by nature qualified to appear. Many, not contented with those occupations, modest and humble in certain cases, to which their endowments and original bent had designed them, shew themselves immoderately set upon more alluring and splendid pursuits in which they are least qualified to excel. Other instances there are, still more entitled to our regret, where the individual is seen to be gifted with no ordinary qualities, where his morning of life has proved auspicious, and the highest expectations were formed of a triumphant career, while yet in the final experiment he has been found wanting, and the "voyage of his life" has passed "in shallows and in miseries."

But our survey of the subject of which I treat will not be complete, unless we add to what has been said, another striking truth respecting the imperfection of man collectively taken. The examples of which the history of our species consists, not only abound in cases, where, from mistakes in the choice of life, or radical and irremediable imperfection in the adventurer, the most glaring miscarriages are found to result,—but it is also true, that all men, even the most illustrious, have some fatal weakness, obliging both them and their rational admirers to confess, that they partake of human frailty, and belong to a race of beings which has small occasion to be proud. Each man has his assailable part. He is vulnerable, though it be only like the fabled Achilles in his heel. We are like the image that Nebuchadnezzar saw in his dream, of which though the head was of fine gold, and the breast and the arms were silver, yet the feet were partly only of iron, and partly of clay. No man is whole and entire, armed at all points, and qualified for every undertaking, or even for any one undertaking, so as to carry it through, and to make the achievement he would perform, or the work he would produce, in all its parts equal and complete.

It is a gross misapprehension in such men as, smitten with admiration of a certain cluster of excellencies, or series of heroic acts, are willing to predicate of the individual to whom they belong, "This man is consummate, and without alloy." Take the person in his retirement, in his hours of relaxation, when he has no longer a part to play, and one or more spectators before whom he is desirous to appear to advantage, and you shall find him a very ordinary man. He has "passions, dimensions, senses, affections, like the rest of his fellow-creatures, is fed with the same food, hurt with the same weapons, warmed and cooled by the same summer and winter." He will therefore, when narrowly observed, be unquestionably found betraying human weaknesses, and falling into fits of ill humour, spleen, peevishness and folly. No man is always a sage; no bosom at all times beats with sentiments lofty, self-denying and heroic. It is enough if he does so, "when the matter fits his mighty mind."

The literary genius, who undertakes to produce some consummate work, will find himself pitiably in error, if he expects to turn it out of his hands, entire in all its parts, and without a flaw.

There are some of the essentials of which it is constituted, that he has mastered, and is sufficiently familiar with them; but there are others, especially if his work is miscellaneous and comprehensive, to which he is glaringly incompetent. He must deny his nature, and become another man, if he would execute these parts, in a manner equal to that which their intrinsic value demands, or to the perfection he is able to give to his work in those places which are best suited to his powers. There are points in which the wisest man that ever existed is no stronger than a child. In this sense the sublimest genius will be found infelix operas summa, nam ponere totum nescit. And, if he properly knows himself, and is aware where lies his strength, and where his weakness, he will look for nothing more in the particulars which fall under the last of these heads, than to escape as he can, and to pass speedily to things in which he finds himself at home and at his ease.

Shakespear we are accustomed to call the most universal genius that ever existed. He has a truly wonderful variety. It is almost impossible to pronounce in which he has done best, his Hamlet, Macbeth, Lear, or Othello. He is equally excellent in his comic vein as his tragic. Falstaff is in his degree to the full as admirable and astonishing, as what he achieved that is noblest under the auspices of the graver muse. His poetry and the fruits of his imagination are unrivalled. His language, in all that comes from him when his genius is most alive, has a richness, an unction, and all those signs of a character which admits not of mortality and decay, for ever fresh as when it was first uttered, which we recognise, while we can hardly persuade ourselves that we are not in a delusion. As Anthony Wood says(4), "By the writings of Shakespear and others of his time, the English tongue was exceedingly enriched, and made quite another thing than what it was before." His versification on these occasions has a melody, a ripeness and variety that no other pen has reached.

(4) Athenae Oxonienses, vol. i. p. 592.

Yet there were things that Shakespear could not do. He could not make a hero. Familiar as he was with the evanescent touches of mind en dishabille, and in its innermost feelings, he could not sustain the tone of a character, penetrated with a divine enthusiasm, or fervently devoted to a generous cause, though this is truly within the compass of our nature, and is more than any other worthy to be delineated. He could conceive such sentiments, for there are such in his personage of Brutus; but he could not fill out and perfect what he has thus sketched. He seems even to have had a propensity to bring the mountain and the hill to a level with the plain. Caesar is spiritless, and Cicero is ridiculous, in his hands. He appears to have written his Troilus and Cressida partly with a view to degrade, and hold up to contempt, the heroes of Homer; and he has even disfigured the pure, heroic affection which the Greek poet has painted as existing between Achilles and Patroclus with the most odious imputations.

And, as he could not sustain an heroic character throughout, so neither could he construct a perfect plot, in which the interest should be perpetually increasing, and the curiosity of the spectator kept alive and in suspense to the last moment. Several of his plays have an unity of subject to which nothing is wanting; but he has not left us any production that should rival that boast of Ancient Greece in the conduct of a plot, the OEdipus Tyrannus, a piece in which each act rises upon the act before, like a tower that lifts its head story above story to the skies. He has scarcely ever given to any of his plays a fifth act, worthy of those that preceded; the interest generally decreases after the third.

Shakespear is also liable to the charge of obscurity. The most sagacious critics dispute to this very hour, whether Hamlet is or is not mad, and whether Falstaff is a brave man or a coward. This defect is perhaps partly to be imputed to the nature of dramatic writing. It is next to impossible to make words, put into the mouth of a character, develop all those things passing in his mind, which it may be desirable should be known.

I spoke, a short time back, of the language of Shakespear in his finest passages, as of unrivalled excellence and beauty; I might almost have called it miraculous. O, si sic omnia! It is to be lamented that this felicity often deserts him. He is not seldom cramp, rigid and pedantic. What is best in him is eternal, of all ages and times; but what is worst, is crusted with an integument, almost more cumbrous than that of any other writer, his contemporary, the merits of whose works continue to invite us to their perusal.

After Shakespear, it is scarcely worth while to bring forward any other example, of a writer who, notwithstanding his undoubted claims to excellencies of the highest order, yet in his productions fully displays the inequality and non-universality of his genius. One of the most remarkable instances may be alleged in Richardson, the author of Clarissa. In his delineation of female delicacy, of high-souled and generous sentiments, of the subtlest feelings and even mental aberrations of virtuous distress strained beyond the power of human endurance, nothing ever equalled this author. But he could not shape out the image of a perfect gentleman, or of that winning gaiety of soul, which may indeed be exemplified, but can never be defined, and never be resisted. His profligate is a man without taste; and his coquettes are insolent and profoundly revolting. He has no resemblance of the art, so conspicuous in Fletcher and Farquhar, of presenting to the reader or spectator an hilarity, bubbling and spreading forth from a perennial spring, which we love as surely as we feel, which communicates its own tone to the bystander, and makes our very hearts dance within us with a responsive sportiveness. We are astonished however that the formal pedant has acquitted himself of his uncongenial task with so great a display of intellectual wealth; and, though he has not presented to us the genuine picture of an intellectual profligate, or of that lovely gaiety of the female spirit which we have all of us seen, but which it is scarcely possible to fix and to copy, we almost admire the more the astonishing talent, that, having undertaken a task for which it was so eminently unfit, yet has been able to substitute for the substance so amazing a mockery, and has treated with so much copiousness and power what it was unfit ever to have attempted.

ESSAY IV. OF THE DURABILITY OF HUMAN ACHIEVEMENTS AND PRODUCTIONS.

There is a view of the character of man, calculated more perhaps than any other to impress us with reverence and awe.

Man is the only creature we know, that, when the term of his natural life is ended, leaves the memory of himself behind him.

All other animals have but one object in view in their more considerable actions, the supply of the humbler accommodations of their nature. Man has a power sufficient for the accomplishment of this object, and a residue of power beyond, which he is able, and which he not unfrequently feels himself prompted, to employ in consecutive efforts, and thus, first by the application and arrangement of material substances, and afterward by the faculty he is found to possess of giving a permanent record to his thoughts, to realise the archetypes and conceptions which previously existed only in his mind.

One method, calculated to place this fact strongly before us, is, to suppose ourselves elevated, in a balloon or otherwise, so as to enable us to take an extensive prospect of the earth on which we dwell. We shall then see the plains and the everlasting hills, the forests and the rivers, and all the exuberance of production which nature brings forth for the supply of her living progeny. We shall see multitudes of animals, herds of cattle and of beasts of prey, and all the varieties of the winged tenants of the air. But we shall also behold, in a manner almost equally calculated to arrest our attention, the traces and the monuments of human industry. We shall see castles and churches, and hamlets and mighty cities. We shall see this strange creature, man, subjecting all nature to his will. He builds bridges, and he constructs aqueducts. He "goes down to the sea in ships," and variegates the ocean with his squadrons and his fleets. To the person thus mounted in the air to take a wide and magnificent prospect, there seems to be a sort of contest between the face of the earth, as it may be supposed to have been at first, and the ingenuity of man, which shall occupy and possess itself of the greatest number of acres. We cover immense regions of the globe with the tokens of human cultivation.

Thus the matter stands as to the exertions of the power of man in the application and arrangement of material substances.

But there is something to a profound and contemplative mind much more extraordinary, in the effects produced by the faculty we possess of giving a permanent record to our thoughts.

From the development of this faculty all human science and literature take their commencement. Here it is that we most distinctly, and with the greatest astonishment, perceive that man is a miracle. Declaimers are perpetually expatiating to us upon the shortness of human life. And yet all this is performed by us, when the wants of our nature have already by our industry been supplied. We manufacture these sublimities and everlasting monuments out of the bare remnants and shreds of our time.

The labour of the intellect of man is endless. How copious is the volume, and how extraordinary the variety, of our sciences and our arts! The number of men is exceedingly great in every civilised state of society, that make these the sole object of their occupation. And this has been more or less the condition of our species in all ages, ever since we left the savage and the pastoral modes of existence.

From this view of the history of man we are led by an easy transition to the consideration of the nature and influence of the love of fame in modifying the actions of the human mind. We have already stated it to be one of the characteristic distinctions of our species to erect monuments which outlast the existence of the persons that produced them. This at first was accidental, and did not enter the design of the operator. The man who built himself a shed to protect him from the inclemency of the seasons, and afterwards exchanged that shed for a somewhat more commodious dwelling, did not at first advert to the circumstance that the accommodation might last, when he was no longer capable to partake of it.

In this way perhaps the wish to extend the memory of ourselves beyond the term of our mortal existence, and the idea of its being practicable to gratify that wish, descended upon us together. In contemplating the brief duration and the uncertainty of human life, the idea must necessarily have occurred, that we might survive those we loved, or that they might survive us. In the first case we inevitably wish more or less to cherish the memory of the being who once was an object of affection to us, but of whose society death has deprived us. In the second case it can scarcely happen but that we desire ourselves to be kindly recollected by those we leave behind us. So simple is the first germ of that longing after posthumous honour, which presents us with so memorable effects in the page of history.

But, previously to the further consideration of posthumous fame, let us turn our attention for a moment to the fame, or, as in that sense it is more usually styled, popularity, which is the lot of a few favoured individuals while they live. The attending to the subject in this point of view, will be found to throw light upon the more extensive prospect of the question to which we will immediately afterwards proceed.

Popularity is an acquisition more level to the most ordinary capacities, and therefore is a subject of more general ambition, than posthumous fame. It addresses itself to the senses. Applause is a species of good fortune to which perhaps no mortal ear is indifferent. The persons who constitute the circle in which we are applauded, receive us with smiles of approbation and sympathy. They pay their court to us, seem to be made happy by our bare presence among them, and welcome us to their houses with congratulation and joy. The vulgar portion of mankind scarcely understand the question of posthumous fame, they cannot comprehend how panegyric and honour can "soothe the dull, cold ear of death:" but they can all conceive the gratification to be derived from applauding multitudes and loud huzzas.

One of the most obvious features however that attends upon popularity, is its fugitive nature. No man has once been popular, and has lived long, without experiencing neglect at least, if he were not also at some time subjected to the very intelligible disapprobation and censure of his fellows. The good will and kindness of the multitude has a devouring appetite, and is like a wild beast that you should stable under your roof, which, if you do not feed with a continual supply, will turn about and attack its protector.

One touch of nature makes the whole world kin,—

That all, with one consent, praise new-born gauds,

And give to dust, that is a little gilt,

More laud than they will give to gold o'erdusted.

Cromwel well understood the nature of this topic, when he said, as we are told, to one of his military companions, who called his attention to the rapturous approbation with which they were received by the crowd on their return from a successful expedition, "Ah, my friend, they would accompany us with equal demonstrations of delight, if, upon no distant occasion, they were to see us going to be hanged!"

The same thing which happens to the popularity attendant on the real or imaginary hero of the multitude, happens also in the race after posthumous fame.

As has already been said, the number of men is exceedingly great in every civilised state of society, who make the sciences and arts engendered by the human mind, the sole or the principal objects of their occupation.

This will perhaps be most strikingly illustrated by a retrospect of the state of European society in the middle, or, as they are frequently styled, the dark ages.

It has been a vulgar error to imagine, that the mind of man, so far as relates to its active and inventive powers, was sunk into a profound sleep, from which it gradually recovered itself at the period when Constantinople was taken by the Turks, and the books and the teachers of the ancient Greek language were dispersed through Europe. The epoch from which modern invention took its rise, commenced much earlier. The feudal system, one of the most interesting contrivances of man in society, was introduced in the ninth century; and chivalry, the offspring of that system, an institution to which we are mainly indebted for refinement of sentiment, and humane and generous demeanour, in the eleventh. Out of these grew the originality and the poetry of romance.

These were no mean advancements. But perhaps the greatest debt which after ages have contracted to this remote period, arose out of the system of monasteries and ecclesiastical celibacy. Owing to these a numerous race of men succeeded to each other perpetually, who were separated from the world, cut off from the endearments of conjugal and parental affection, and who had a plenitude of leisure for solitary application. To these men we are indebted for the preservation of the literature of Rome, and the multiplied copies of the works of the ancients. Nor were they contented only with the praise of never-ending industry. They forged many works, that afterwards passed for classical, and which have demanded all the perspicacity of comparative criticism to refute. And in these pursuits the indefatigable men who were dedicated to them, were not even goaded by the love of fame. They were satisfied with the consciousness of their own perseverance and ingenuity.

But the most memorable body of men that adorned these ages, were the Schoolmen. They may be considered as the discoverers of the art of logic. The ancients possessed in an eminent degree the gift of genius; but they have little to boast on the score of arrangement, and discover little skill in the strictness of an accurate deduction. They rather arrive at truth by means of a felicity of impulse, than in consequence of having regularly gone through the process which leads to it. The schools of the middle ages gave birth to the Irrefragable and the Seraphic doctors, the subtlety of whose distinctions, and the perseverance of whose investigations, are among the most wonderful monuments of the intellectual power of man. The thirteenth century produced Thomas Aquinas, and Johannes Duns Scotus, and William Occam, and Roger Bacon. In the century before, Thomas a Becket drew around him a circle of literary men, whose correspondence has been handed down to us, and who deemed it their proudest distinction that they called each other philosophers. The Schoolmen often bewildered themselves in their subtleties, and often delivered dogmas and systems that may astonish the common sense of unsophisticated understandings. But such is man. So great is his persevering labour, his invincible industry, and the resolution with which he sets himself, year after year, and lustre after lustre, to accomplish the task which his judgment and his zeal have commanded him to pursue.

But I return to the question of literary fame. All these men, and men of a hundred other classes, who laboured most commendably and gallantly in their day, may be considered as swept away into the gulph of oblivion. As Swift humorously says in his Dedication to Prince Posterity, "I had prepared a copious list of Titles to present to your highness, as an undisputed argument of the prolificness of human genius in my own time: the originals were posted upon all gates and corner's of streets: but, returning in a very few hours to take a review, they were all torn down, and fresh ones put in their places. I enquired after them among readers and booksellers, but in vain: the memorial of them was lost among men; their place was no more to be found."

It is a just remark that had been made by Hume(5): "Theories of abstract philosophy, systems of profound theology, have prevailed during one age. In a successive period these have been universally exploded; their absurdity has been detected; other theories and systems have supplied their place, which again gave way to their successors; and nothing has been experienced more liable to the revolutions of chance and fashion than these pretended decisions of science. The case is not the same with the beauties of eloquence and poetry. Just expressions of passion and nature are sure, after a little time, to gain public applause, which they maintain for ever. Aristotle and Plato and Epicurus and Descartes may successively yield to each other: but Terence and Virgil maintain an universal, undisputed empire over the minds of men. The abstract philosophy of Cicero has lost its credit: the vehemence of his oratory is still the object of our admiration."

(5) Essays, Part 1, Essay xxiii.

A few examples of the instability of fame will place this question in the clearest light.

Nicholas Peiresk was born in the year 1580. His progress in knowledge was so various and unprecedented, that, from the time that he was twenty-one years of age, he was universally considered as holding the helm of learning in his hand, and guiding the commonwealth of letters. He died at the age of fifty-seven. The academy of the Humoristi at Rome paid the most extraordinary honours to his memory; many of the cardinals assisted at his funeral oration; and a collection of verses in his praise was published in more than forty languages.

Salmasius was regarded as a prodigy of learning; and various princes and powers entered into a competition who should be so fortunate as to secure his residence in their states. Christina, queen of Sweden, having obtained the preference, received him with singular reverence and attention; and, Salmasius being taken ill at Stockholm, and confined to his bed, the queen persisted with her own hand to prepare his caudles, and mend his fire. Yet, but for the accident of his having had Milton for his adversary, his name would now be as little remembered, even by the generality of the learned, as that of Peiresk.

Du Bartas, in the reign of Henry the Fourth of France, was one of the most successful poets that ever existed. His poem on the Creation of the World went through upwards of thirty editions in the course of five or six years, was translated into most European languages, and its commentators promised to equal in copiousness and number the commentators on Homer.

One of the most admired of our English poets about the close of the sixteenth century, was Donne. Unlike many of those trivial writers of verse who succeeded him after an interval of forty or fifty years, and who won for themselves a brilliant reputation by the smoothness of their numbers, the elegance of their conceptions, and the politeness of their style, Donne was full of originality, energy and vigour. No man can read him without feeling himself called upon for earnest exercise of his thinking powers, and, even with the most fixed attention and application, the student is often obliged to confess his inability to take in the whole of the meaning with which the poet's mind was perceptibly fraught. Every sentence that Donne writes, whether in verse or prose, is exclusively his own. In addition to this, his thoughts are often in the noblest sense of the word poetical; and passages may be quoted from him that no English poet may attempt to rival, unless it be Milton and Shakespear. Ben Jonson observed of him with great truth and a prophetic spirit: "Donne for not being understood will perish." But this is not all. If Waller and Suckling and Carew sacrificed every thing to the Graces, Donne went into the other extreme. With a few splendid and admirable exceptions, his phraseology and versification are crabbed and repulsive. And, as poetry is read in the first place for pleasure, Donne is left undisturbed on the shelf, or rather in the sepulchre; and not one in an hundred even among persons of cultivation, can give any account of him, if in reality they ever heard of his productions.

The name of Shakespear is that before which every knee must bow. But it was not always so. When the first novelty of his pieces was gone, they were seldom called into requisition. Only three or four of his plays were upon the acting list of the principal company of players during the reign of Charles the Second; and the productions of Beaumont and Fletcher, and of Shirley, were acted three times for once of his. At length Betterton revived, and by his admirable representation gave popularity to, Macbeth, Hamlet and Lear, a popularity they have ever since retained. But Macbeth was not revived (with music, and alterations by sir William Davenant) till 1674; and Lear a few years later, with love scenes and a happy catastrophe by Nahum Tate.

In the latter part of the reign of Charles the Second, Dryden and Otway and Lee held the undisputed supremacy in the serious drama.

Such was the insensibility of the English public to nature, and her high priest, Shakespear. The only one of their productions that has survived upon the theatre, is Venice Preserved: and why it has done so it is difficult to say; or rather it would be impossible to assign a just and honourable reason for it. All the personages in this piece are of an abandoned and profligate character. Pierre is a man resolved to destroy and root up the republic by which he was employed, because his mistress, a courtesan, is mercenary, and endures the amorous visits of an impotent old lecher. Jaffier, without even the profession of any public principle, joins in the conspiracy, because he has been accustomed to luxury and prodigal expence and is poor. He has however no sooner entered into the plot, than he betrays it, and turns informer to the government against his associates. Belvidera instigates him to this treachery, because she cannot bear the thought of having her father murdered, and is absurd enough to imagine that she and her husband shall be tender and happy lovers ever after. Their love in the latter acts of the play is a continued tirade of bombast and sounding nonsense, without one real sentiment, one just reflection, or one strong emotion working from the heart, and analysing the nature of man. The folly of this love can only be exceeded, by the abject and despicable crouching and fawning of Jaffier to the man he had so basely betrayed, and their subsequent reconciliation. There is not a production in the whole realms of fiction, that has less pretension to manly, or even endurable feeling, or to common propriety. The total defect of a moral sense in this piece is strongly characteristic of the reign in which it was written. It has in the mean while a richness of melody, and a picturesqueness of action, that enables it to delude, and that even draws tears from the eyes of, persons who can be won over by the eye and the ear, with almost no participation of the understanding. And this unmeaning rant and senseless declamation sufficed for the time to throw into shade those exquisite delineations of character, those transcendent bursts of passion, and that perfect anatomy of the human heart, which render the master-pieces of Shakespear a property for all nations and all times.

While Shakespear was partly forgotten, it continued to be totally unknown that he had contemporaries as inexpressibly superior to the dramatic writers that have appeared since, as these contemporaries were themselves below the almighty master of scenic composition. It was the fashion to say, that Shakespear existed alone in a barbarous age, and that all his imputed crudities, and intermixture of what was noblest with unparalleled absurdity and buffoonery, were to be allowed for to him on that consideration.

Cowley stands forward as a memorable instance of the inconstancy of fame. He was a most amiable man; and the loveliness of his mind shines out in his productions. He had a truly poetic frame of soul; and he pours out the beautiful feelings that possessed him unreservedly and at large. He was a great sufferer in the Stuart cause, he had been a principal member of the court of the exiled queen; and, when the king was restored, it was a deep sentiment among his followers and friends to admire the verses of Cowley. He was "the Poet." The royalist rhymers were set lightly by in comparison with him. Milton, the republican, who, by his collection published during the civil war, had shewn that he was entitled to the highest eminence, was unanimously consigned to oblivion. Cowley died in 1667; and the duke of Buckingham, the author of the Rehearsal, eight years after, set up his tomb in the cemetery of the nation, with an inscription, declaring him to be at once "the Pindar, the Horace and Virgil of his country, the delight and the glory of his age, which by his death was left a perpetual mourner."—Yet—so capricious is fame—a century has nearly elapsed, since Pope said,

Who now reads Cowley? If he pleases yet,

His moral pleases, not his pointed wit;

Forgot his epic, nay, Pindaric art,

But still I love the language of his heart.

As Cowley was the great royalist poet after the Restoration, Cleveland stood in the same rank during the civil war. In the publication of his works one edition succeeded to another, yearly or oftener, for more than twenty years. His satire is eminently poignant; he is of a strength and energy of thinking uncommonly masculine; and he compresses his meaning so as to give it every advantage. His imagination is full of coruscation and brilliancy. His petition to Cromwel, lord protector of England, when the poet was under confinement for his loyal principles, is a singular example of manly firmness, great independence of mind, and a happy choice of topics to awaken feelings of forbearance and clemency. It is unnecessary to say that Cleveland is now unknown, except to such as feel themselves impelled to search into things forgotten.

It would be endless to adduce all the examples that might be found of the caprices of fame. It has been one of the arts of the envious to set up a contemptible rival to eclipse the splendour of sterling merit. Thus Crowne and Settle for a time disturbed the serenity of Dryden. Voltaire says, the Phaedra of Pradon has not less passion than that of Racine, but expressed in rugged verse and barbarous language. Pradon is now forgotten: and the whole French poetry of the Augustan age of Louis the Fourteenth is threatened with the same fate. Hayley for a few years was applauded as the genuine successor of Pope; and the poem of Sympathy by Pratt went through twelve editions. For a brief period almost each successive age appears fraught with resplendent genius; but they go out one after another; they set, "like stars that fall, to rise no more." Few indeed are endowed with that strength of construction, that should enable them to ride triumphant on the tide of ages.

It is the same with conquerors. What tremendous battles have been fought, what oceans of blood have been spilled, by men who were resolved that their achievements should be remembered for ever! And now even their names are scarcely preserved; and the very effects of the disasters they inflicted on mankind seem to be swept away, as of no more validity than things that never existed. Warriors and poets, the authors of systems and the lights of philosophy, men that astonished the earth, and were looked up to as Gods, even like an actor on the stage, have strutted their hour, and then been heard of no more.

Books have the advantage of all other productions of the human head or hand. Copies of them may be multiplied for ever, the last as good as the first, except so far as some slight inadvertent errors may have insinuated themselves. The Iliad flourishes as green now, as on the day that Pisistratus is said first to have stamped upon it its present order. The songs of the Rhapsodists, the Scalds, and the Minstrels, which once seemed as fugitive as the breath of him who chaunted them, repose in libraries, and are embalmed in collections. The sportive sallies of eminent wits, and the Table Talk of Luther and Selden, may live as long as there shall be men to read, and judges to appreciate them.

But other human productions have their date. Pictures, however admirable, will only last as long as the colours of which they are composed, and the substance on which they are painted. Three or four hundred years ordinarily limit the existence of the most favoured. We have scarcely any paintings of the ancients, and but a small portion of their statues, while of these a great part are mutilated, and various members supplied by later and inferior artists. The library of Bufo is by Pope described,

where busts of poets dead,

And a true Pindar stood without a head.

Monumental records, alike the slightest and the most solid, are subjected to the destructive operation of time, or to the being removed at the caprice or convenience of successive generations. The pyramids of Egypt remain, but the names of him who founded them, and of him whose memory they seemed destined to perpetuate, have perished together. Buildings for the use or habitation of man do not last for ever. Mighty cities, as well as detached edifices, are destined to disappear. Thebes, and Troy, and Persepolis, and Palmyra have vanished from the face of the earth.

"Thorns and brambles have grown up in their palaces: they are habitations for serpents, and a court for the owl."

There are productions of man however that seem more durable than any of the edifices he has raised. Such are, in the first place, modes of government. The constitution of Sparta lasted for seven hundred years. That of Rome for about the same period. Institutions, once deeply rooted in the habits of a people, will operate in their effects through successive revolutions. Modes of faith will sometimes be still more permanent. Not to mention the systems of Moses and Christ, which we consider as delivered to us by divine inspiration, that of Mahomet has continued for twelve hundred years, and may last, for aught that appears, twelve hundred more. The practices of the empire of China are celebrated all over the earth for their immutability.

This brings us naturally to reflect upon the durability of the sciences. According to Bailly, the observation of the heavens, and a calculation of the revolutions of the heavenly bodies, in other words, astronomy, subsisted in maturity in China and the East, for at least three thousand years before the birth of Christ: and, such as it was then, it bids fair to last as long as civilisation shall continue. The additions it has acquired of late years may fall away and perish, but the substance shall remain. The circulation of the blood in man and other animals, is a discovery that shall never be antiquated. And the same may be averred of the fundamental elements of geometry and of some other sciences. Knowledge, in its most considerable branches shall endure, as long as books shall exist to hand it down to successive generations.

It is just therefore, that we should regard with admiration and awe the nature of man, by whom these mighty things have been accomplished, at the same time that the perishable quality of its individual monuments, and the temporary character and inconstancy of that fame which in many instances has filled the whole earth with its renown, may reasonably quell the fumes of an inordinate vanity, and keep alive in us the sentiment of a wholesome diffidence and humility.

ESSAY V. OF THE REBELLIOUSNESS OF MAN.

There is a particular characteristic in the nature of the human mind, which is somewhat difficult to be explained.

Man is a being of a rational and an irrational nature.

It has often been said that we have two souls. Araspes, in the Cyropedia, adopts this language to explain his inconsistency, and desertion of principle and honour. The two souls of man, according to this hypothesis, are, first, animal, and, secondly, intellectual.

But I am not going into any thing of this slight and every-day character.

Man is a rational being. It is by this particular that he is eminently distinguished from the brute creation. He collects premises and deduces conclusions. He enters into systems of thinking, and combines systems of action, which he pursues from day to day, and from year to year. It is by this feature in his constitution that he becomes emphatically the subject of history, of poetry and fiction. It is by this that he is raised above the other inhabitants of the globe of earth, and that the individuals of our race are made the partners of "gods, and men like gods."

But our nature, beside this, has another section. We start occasionally ten thousand miles awry. We resign the sceptre of reason, and the high dignity that belongs to us as beings of a superior species; and, without authority derived to us from any system of thinking, even without the scheme of gratifying any vehement and uncontrolable passion, we are impelled to do, or at least feel ourselves excited to do, something disordinate and strange. It seems as if we had a spring within us, that found the perpetual restraint of being wise and sober insupportable. We long to be something, or to do something, sudden and unexpected, to throw the furniture of our apartment out at window, or, when we are leaving a place of worship, in which perhaps the most solemn feelings of our nature have been excited, to push the grave person that is just before us, from the top of the stairs to the bottom. A thousand absurdities, wild and extravagant vagaries, come into our heads, and we are only restrained from perpetrating them by the fear, that we may be subjected to the treatment appropriated to the insane, or may perhaps be made amenable to the criminal laws of our country.

A story occurs to me, which I learned from the late Dr. Parr at Hatton, that may not unhappily illustrate the point I am endeavouring to explain.

Dr. Samuel Clarke, rector of St. James's, Westminster, the especial friend of Sir Isaac Newton, the distinguished editor of the poems of Homer, and author of the Demonstration of the Being and Attributes of God, was one day summoned from his study, to receive two visitors in the parlour. When he came downstairs, and entered the room, he saw a foreigner, who by his air seemed to be a person of distinction, a professor perhaps of some university on the continent; and an alderman of London, a relation of the doctor, who had come to introduce the foreigner. The alderman, a man of uncultivated mind and manners, and whom the doctor had been accustomed to see in sordid attire, surrounded with the incumbrances of his trade, was decked out for the occasion in a full-dress suit, with a wig of majestic and voluminous structure. Clarke was, as it appears, so much struck with the whimsical nature of this unexpected metamorphosis, and the extraordinary solemnity of his kinsman's demeanour, as to have felt impelled, almost immediately upon entering the room, to snatch the wig from the alderman's head, and throw it against the ceiling: after which this eminent person immediately escaped, and retired to his own apartment. I was informed from the same authority, that Clarke, after exhausting his intellectual faculties by long and intense study, would not unfrequently quit his seat, leap upon the table, and place himself cross-legged like a tailor, being prompted, by these antagonist sallies, to relieve himself from the effect of the too severe strain he had previously put upon his intellectual powers.

But the deviousness and aberration of our human faculties frequently amount to something considerably more serious than this.

I will put a case.

I will suppose myself and another human being together, in some spot secure from the intrusion of spectators. A musket is conveniently at hand. It is already loaded. I say to my companion, "I will place myself before you; I will stand motionless: take up that musket, and shoot me through the heart." I want to know what passes in the mind of the man to whom these words are addressed.

I say, that one of the thoughts that will occur to many of the persons who should be so invited, will be, "Shall I take him at his word?"

There are two things that restrain us from acts of violence and crime. The first is, the laws of morality. The second is, the construction that will be put upon our actions by our fellow-creatures, and the treatment we shall receive from them.—I put out of the question here any particular value I may entertain for my challenger, or any degree of friendship and attachment I may feel for him.

The laws of morality (setting aside the consideration of any documents of religion or otherwise I may have imbibed from my parents and instructors) are matured within us by experience. In proportion as I am rendered familiar with my fellow-creatures, or with society at large, I come to feel the ties which bind men to each other, and the wisdom and necessity of governing my conduct by inexorable rules. We are thus further and further removed from unexpected sallies of the mind, and the danger of suddenly starting away into acts not previously reflected on and considered.

With respect to the censure and retaliation of other men on my proceeding, these, by the terms of my supposition, are left out of the question.

It may be taken for granted, that no man but a madman, would in the case I have stated take the challenger at his word. But what I want to ascertain is, why the bare thought of doing so takes a momentary hold of the mind of the person addressed?

There are three principles in the nature of man which contribute to account for this.

First, the love of novelty.

Secondly, the love of enterprise and adventure. I become insupportably wearied with the repetition of rotatory acts and every-day occurrences. I want to be alive, to be something more than I commonly am, to change the scene, to cut the cable that binds my bark to the shore, to launch into the wide sea of possibilities, and to nourish my thoughts with observing a train of unforeseen consequences as they arise.

A third principle, which discovers itself in early childhood, and which never entirely quits us, is the love of power. We wish to be assured that we are something, and that we can produce notable effects upon other beings out of ourselves. It is this principle, which instigates a child to destroy his playthings, and to torment and kill the animals around him.

But, even independently of the laws of morality, and the fear of censure and retaliation from our fellow-creatures, there are other things which would obviously restrain us from taking the challenger in the above supposition at his word.

If man were an omnipotent being, and at the same time retained all his present mental infirmities, it would be difficult to say of what extravagances he would be guilty. It is proverbially affirmed that power has a tendency to corrupt the best dispositions. Then what would not omnipotence effect?

If, when I put an end to the life of a fellow-creature, all vestiges of what I had done were to disappear, this would take off a great part of the control upon my actions which at present subsists. But, as it is, there are many consequences that "give us pause." I do not like to see his blood streaming on the ground. I do not like to witness the spasms and convulsions of a dying man. Though wounded to the heart, he may speak. Then what may be chance to say? What looks of reproach may he cast upon me? The musket may miss fire. If I wound him, the wound may be less mortal than I contemplated.

Then what may I not have to fear? His dead body will be an incumbrance to me. It must be moved from the place where it lies. It must be buried. How is all this to be done by me? By one precipitate act, I have involved myself in a long train of loathsome and heart-sickening consequences.

If it should be said, that no one but a person of an abandoned character would fail, when the scene was actually before him, to feel an instant repugnance to the proposition, yet it will perhaps be admitted, that almost every reader, when he regards it as a supposition merely, says to himself for a moment, "Would I? Could I?"

But, to bring the irrationality of man more completely to the test, let us change the supposition. Let us imagine him to be gifted with the powers of the fabled basilisk, "to monarchise, be feared, and kill with looks." His present impulses, his passions, his modes of reasoning and choosing shall continue; but his "will is neighboured to his act;" whatever he has formed a conception of with preference, is immediately realised; his thought is succeeded by the effect; and no traces are left behind, by means of which a shadow of censure or suspicion can be reflected on him.

Man is in truth a miracle. The human mind is a creature of celestial origin, shut up and confined in a wall of flesh. We feel a kind of proud impatience of the degradation to which we are condemned. We beat ourselves to pieces against the wires of our cage, and long to escape, to shoot through the elements, and be as free to change at any instant the place where we dwell, as to change the subject to which our thoughts are applied.

This, or something like this, seems to be the source of our most portentous follies and absurdities. This is the original sin upon which St. Austin and Calvin descanted. Certain Arabic writers seem to have had this in their minds, when they tell us, that there is a black drop of blood in the heart of every man, in which is contained the fomes peccati, and add that, when Mahomet was in the fourth year of his age, the angel Gabriel caught him up from among his playfellows, and taking his heart from his bosom, squeezed out of it this first principle of frailty, in consequence of which he for ever after remained inaccessible to the weaknesses of other men(6).

(6) Life of Mahomet, by Prideaux.

It is the observation of sir Thomas Browne: "Man is a noble animal, splendid in ashes, and pompous in the grave." One of the most remarkable examples of this is to be found in the pyramids of Egypt. They are generally considered as having been erected to be the tombs of the kings of that country. They have no opening by which for the light of heaven to enter, and afford no means for the accommodation of living man. An hundred thousand men are said to have been constantly employed in the building; ten years to have been consumed in hewing and conveying the stones, and twenty more in completing the edifice. Of the largest the base is a square, and the sides are triangles, gradually diminishing as they mount in the air. The sides of the base are two hundred and twenty feet in length, and the perpendicular height is above one hundred and fifty-five feet. The figure of the pyramid is precisely that which is most calculated for duration: it cannot perish by accident; and it would require almost as much labour to demolish it, as it did to raise it at first.

What a light does this fact convey into the inmost recesses of the human heart! Man reflects deeply, and with feelings of a mortified nature, upon the perishableness of his frame, and the approaching close, so far as depends upon the evidence of our senses, of his existence. He has indeed an irrepressible "longing after immortality;" and this is one of the various and striking modes in which he has sought to give effect to his desire.

Various obvious causes might be selected, which should be calculated to give birth to the feeling of discontent.

One is, the not being at home.

I will here put together some of the particulars which make up the idea of home in the most emphatical sense of the word.

Home is the place where a man is principally at his ease. It is the place where he most breathes his native air: his lungs play without impediment; and every respiration brings a pure element, and a cheerful and gay frame of mind. Home is the place where he most easily accomplishes all his designs; he has his furniture and materials and the elements of his occupations entirely within his reach. Home is the place where he can be uninterrupted. He is in a castle which is his in full propriety. No unwelcome guests can intrude; no harsh sounds can disturb his contemplations; he is the master, and can command a silence equal to that of the tomb, whenever he pleases.

In this sense every man feels, while cribbed in a cabin of flesh, and shut up by the capricious and arbitrary injunctions of human communities, that he is not at home.

Another cause of our discontent is to be traced to the disparity of the two parts of which we are composed, the thinking principle, and the body in which it acts. The machine which constitutes the visible man, bears no proportion to our thoughts, our wishes and desires. Hence we are never satisfied; we always feel the want of something we have not; and this uneasiness is continually pushing us on to precipitate and abortive resolves.

I find in a book, entitled, Illustrations of Phrenology, by Sir George Mackenzie, Baronet, the following remark. 'If this portrait be correctly drawn, the right side does not quite agree with the left in the region of ideality. This dissimilarity may have produced something contradictory in the feelings of the person it represents, which he may have felt extremely annoying(7).' An observation of this sort may be urged with striking propriety as to the dissimilar attributes of the body and the thinking principle in man.

(7) The remark thus delivered is applied to the portrait of the author

of the present volume.

It is perhaps thus that we are to account for a phenomenon, in itself sufficiently obvious, that our nature has within it a principle of boundless ambition, a desire to be something that we are not, a feeling that we are out of our place, and ought to be where we are not. This feeling produces in us quick and earnest sallies and goings forth of the mind, a restlessness of soul, and an aspiration after some object that we do not find ourselves able to chalk out and define.

Hence comes the practice of castle-building, and of engaging the soul in endless reveries and imaginations of something mysterious and unlike to what we behold in the scenes of sublunary life. Many writers, having remarked this, have endeavoured to explain it from the doctrine of a preexistent state, and have said that, though we have no clear and distinct recollection of what happened to us previously to our being launched in our present condition, yet we have certain broken and imperfect conceptions, as if, when the tablet of the memory was cleared for the most part of the traces of what we had passed through in some other mode of being, there were a few characters that had escaped the diligence of the hand by which the rest had been obliterated.

It is this that, in less enlightened ages of the world, led men to engage so much of their thoughts upon supposed existences, which, though they might never become subject to our organs of vision, were yet conceived to be perpetually near us, fairies, ghosts, witches, demons and angels. Our ancestors often derived suggestions from these, were informed of things beyond the ken of ordinary faculties, were tempted to the commission of forbidden acts, or encouraged to proceed in the paths of virtue.

The most remarkable of these phenomena was that of necromancy, sorcery and magic. There were men who devoted themselves to "curious arts," and had books fraught with hidden knowledge. They could "bedim"

The noon-tide sun, call forth the mutinous winds,

And 'twixt the green sea and the azured vault

Set roaring war: to the dread, rattling thunder

They could give fire, and rift even Jove's stout oak

With his own bolt—graves at their command

Have waked their sleepers, oped and let them forth.

And of these things the actors in them were so certain, that many witches were led to the stake, their guilt being principally established on their own confessions. But the most memorable matters in the history of the black art, were the contracts which those who practised it not unfrequently entered into with the devil, that he should assist them by his supernatural power for ten or twenty years, and, in consideration of this aid, they consented to resign their souls into his possession, when the period of the contract was expired.

In the animal creation there are some species that may be tamed, and others whose wildness is irreclaimable. Horace says, that all men are mad: and no doubt mankind in general has one of the features of madness. In the ordinary current of our existence we are to a considerable degree rational and tractable. But we are not altogether safe. I may converse with a maniac for hours; he shall talk as soberly, and conduct himself with as much propriety, as any other of the species who has never been afflicted with his disease; but touch upon a particular string, and, before you are aware of it, he shall fly out into the wildest and most terrifying extravagances. Such, though in a greatly inferior degree, are the majority of human beings.

The original impulse of man is uncontrollableness. When the spirit of life first descends upon us, we desire and attempt to be as free as air. We are impatient of restraint. This is the period of the empire of will. There is a power within us that wars against the restraint of another. We are eager to follow our own impulses and caprices, and are with difficulty subjected to those who believe they best know how to control inexperienced youth in a way that shall tend to his ultimate advantage.

The most moderate and auspicious method in which the old may endeavour to guide and control the pursuits of the young, undoubtedly is by the conviction of the understanding. But this is not always easy. It is not at all times practicable fully to explain to the apprehension of a very young person the advantage, which at a period a little more advanced he would be able clearly to recognise.

There is a further evil appertaining to this view of the subject.

A young man even, in the early season of life, is not always disposed to obey the convictions of his understanding. He has prescribed to himself a task which returns with the returning day; but he is often not disposed to apply. The very sense that it is what he conceives to be an incumbent duty, inspires him with reluctance.

An obvious source of this reluctance is, that the convictions of our understanding are not always equally present to us. I have entered into a deduction of premises, and arrived at a conclusion; but some of the steps of the chain are scarcely obvious to me, at the time that I am called upon to act upon the conclusion I have drawn. Beside which, there was a freshness in the first conception of the reasons on which my conduct was to be framed, which, by successive rehearsals, and by process of time, is no longer in any degree spirit-stirring and pregnant.

This restiveness and impracticability are principally incident to us in the period of youth. By degrees the novelties of life wear out, and we become sober. We are like soldiers at drill, and in a review. At first we perform our exercise from necessity, and with an ill grace. We had rather be doing almost any thing else.

By degrees we are reconciled to our occupation. We are like horses in a manege, or oxen or dogs taught to draw the plough, or be harnessed to a carriage. Our stubbornness is subdued; we no longer exhaust our strength in vain efforts to free ourselves from the yoke.

Conviction at first is strong. Having arrived at years of discretion, I revolve with a sobered mind the different occupations to which my efforts and my time may be devoted, and determine at length upon that which under all the circumstances displays the most cogent recommendations. Having done so, I rouse my faculties and direct my energies to the performance of my task. By degrees however my resolution grows less vigorous, and my exertions relax. I accept any pretence to be let off, and fly into a thousand episodes and eccentricities.

But, as the newness of life subsides, the power of temptation becomes less. That conviction, which was at first strong, and gradually became fainter and less impressive, is made by incessant repetitions a part of my nature. I no more think of doubting its truth, than of my own existence. Practice has rendered the pursuits that engage me more easy, till at length I grow disturbed and uncomfortable if I am withheld from them. They are like my daily bread. If they are not afforded me, I grow sick and attenuated, and my life verges to a close. The sun is not surer to rise, than I am to feel the want of my stated employment.

It is the business of education to tame the wild ass, the restive and rebellious principle, in our nature. The judicious parent or instructor essays a thousand methods to accomplish his end. The considerate elder tempts the child with inticements and caresses, that he may win his attention to the first rudiments of learning.

He sets before him, as he grows older, all the considerations and reasons he can devise, to make him apprehend the advantage of improvement and literature. He does his utmost to make his progress easy, and to remove all impediments. He smooths the path by which he is to proceed, and endeavours to root out all its thorns. He exerts his eloquence to inspire his pupil with a love for the studies in which he is engaged. He opens to him the beauties and genius of the authors he reads, and endeavours to proceed with him hand in hand, and step by step. He persuades, he exhorts, and occasionally he reproves. He awakens in him the love of excellence, the fear of disgrace, and an ambition to accomplish that which "the excellent of the earth" accomplished before him.

At a certain period the young man is delivered into his own hands, and becomes an instructor to himself. And, if he is blessed with an ingenuous disposition, he will enter on his task with an earnest desire and a devoted spirit. No person of a sober and enlarged mind can for a moment delude himself into the opinion that, when he is delivered into his own hands, his education is ended. In a sense to which no one is a stranger, the education of man and his life terminate together. We should at no period of our existence be backward to receive information, and should at all times preserve our minds open to conviction. We should through every day of our lives seek to add to the stores of our knowledge and refinement. But, independently of this more extended sense of the word, a great portion of the education of the young man is left to the direction of the man himself. The epoch of entire liberty is a dangerous period, and calls upon him for all his discretion, that he may not make an ill use of that, which is in itself perhaps the first of sublunary blessings. The season of puberty also, and all the excitements from this source, "that flesh is heir to," demand the utmost vigilance and the strictest restraint. In a word, if we would counteract the innate rebelliousness of man, that indocility of mind which is at all times at hand to plunge us into folly, we must never slumber at our post, but govern ourselves with steady severity, and by the dictates of an enlightened understanding. We must be like a skilful pilot in a perilous sea, and be thoroughly aware of all the rocks and quicksands, and the multiplied and hourly dangers that beset our navigation.

In this Essay I have treated of nothing more than the inherent restiveness and indocility of man, which accompany him at least through all the earlier sections and divisions of his life. I have not treated of those temptations calculated to lead him into a thousand excesses and miseries, which originate in our lower nature, and are connected with what we call the passion of love. Nor have I entered upon the still more copious chapter, of the incentives and provocations which are administered to us by those wants which at all times beset us as living creatures, and by the unequal distribution of property generally in civil society. I have not considered those attributes of man which may serve indifferently for good or for ill, as he may happen to be or not to be the subject of those fiercer excitements, that will oft times corrupt the most ingenuous nature, and have a tendency to inspire into us subtle schemes and a deep contrivance. I have confined myself to the consideration of man, as yet untamed to the modes of civilised community, and unbroken to the steps which are not only prescribed by the interests of our social existence, but which are even in some degree indispensible to the improvement and welfare of the individual. I have considered him, not as he is often acted upon by causes and motives which seem almost to compel him to vice, but merely as he is restless, and impatient, and disdainful both of the control of others, and the shackles of system.

For the same reason I have not taken notice of another species of irrationality, and which seems to answer more exactly to the Arabic notion of the fomes peccati, the black drop of blood at the bottom of the heart. We act from motives apprehended by the judgment; but we do not stop at them. Once set in motion, it will not seldom happen that we proceed beyond our original mark. We are like Othello in the play:

Our blood begins our safer guides to rule;

And passion, having our best judgment quelled,

Assays to lead the way.

This is the explanation of the greatest enormities that have been perpetrated by man, and the inhuman deeds of Nero and Caligula. We proceed from bad to worse. The reins of our discretion drop from our hands. It fortunately happens however, that we do not in the majority of cases, like Phaeton in the fable, set the world on fire; but that, with ordinary men, the fiercest excesses of passion extend to no greater distance than can be reached by the sound of their voice.

ESSAY VI. OF HUMAN INNOCENCE.

One of the most obvious views which are presented to us by man in society is the inoffensiveness and innocence that ordinarily characterise him.

Society for the greater part carries on its own organization. Each man pursues his proper occupation, and there are few individuals that feel the propensity to interrupt the pursuits of their neighbours by personal violence. When we observe the quiet manner in which the inhabitants of a great city, and, in the country, the frequenters of the fields, the high roads, and the heaths, pass along, each engrossed by his private contemplations, feeling no disposition to molest the strangers he encounters, but on the contrary prepared to afford them every courteous assistance, we cannot in equity do less than admire the innocence of our species, and fancy that, like the patriarchs of old, we have fallen in with "angels unawares."

There are a few men in every community, that are sons of riot and plunder, and for the sake of these the satirical and censorious throw a general slur and aspersion upon the whole species.

When we look at human society with kind and complacent survey, we are more than half tempted to imagine that men might subsist very well in clusters and congregated bodies without the coercion of law; and in truth criminal laws were only made to prevent the ill-disposed few from interrupting the regular and inoffensive proceedings of the vast majority.

From what disposition in human nature is it that all this accommodation and concurrence proceed?

It is not primarily love. We feel in a very slight degree excited to good will towards the stranger whom we accidentally light upon in our path.

Neither is it fear.

It is principally forecast and prudence. We have a sensitiveness, that forbids us for a slight cause to expose ourselves to we know not what. We are unwilling to be disturbed.

We have a mental vis inertiae, analogous to that quality in material substances, by means of which, being at rest, they resist being put into a state of motion. We love our security; we love our respectability; and both of these may be put to hazard by our rashly and unadvisedly thrusting ourselves upon the course of another. We like to act for ourselves. We like to act with others, when we think we can foresee the way in which the proposed transaction will proceed, and that it will proceed to our wish.

Let us put the case, that I am passing along the highway, destitute and pennyless, and without foresight of any means by which I am to procure the next meal that my nature requires.

The vagrant, who revolves in his mind the thought of extorting from another the supply of which he is urgently in need, surveys the person upon whom he meditates this violence with a scrutinising eye. He considers, Will this man submit to my summons without resistance, or in what manner will he repel my trespass? He watches his eye, he measures his limbs, his strength, and his agility. Though they have met in the deserts of Africa, where there is no law to punish the violator, he knows that he exposes himself to a fearful hazard; and he enters upon his purpose with desperate resolve. All this and more must occur to the man of violence, within the pale of a civilised community.

Begging is the mildest form in which a man can obtain from the stranger he meets, the means of supplying his urgent necessities.

But, even here, the beggar knows that he exposes himself not only to refusal, but to the harsh and opprobrious terms in which that refusal may be conveyed. In this city there are laws against begging; and the man that asks alms of me, is an offender against the state. In country-towns it is usual to remark a notice upon entering, to say, Whoever shall be found begging in this place, shall be set in the stocks.

There are modes however in which I may accost a stranger, with small apprehension that I shall be made to repent of it. I may enquire of him my way to the place towards which my business or my pleasure invites me. Ennius of old has observed, that lumen de lumine, to light my candle at my neighbour's lamp, is one of the privileges that the practices of civil society concede.

But it is not merely from forecast and prudence that we refrain from interrupting the stranger in his way. We have all of us a certain degree of kindness for a being of our own species. A multitude of men feel this kindness for every thing that has animal life. We would not willingly molest the stranger who has done us no injury. On the contrary we would all of us to a certain extent assist him, under any unforeseen casualty and tribulation. A part therefore of the innocence that characterises our species is to be attributed to philanthropy.

Childhood is diffident. Children for the most part are averse to the addressing themselves to strangers, unless in cases where, from the mere want of anticipation and reflection, they proceed as if they were wholly without the faculty of making calculations and deducing conclusions. The child neither knows himself nor the stranger he meets in his path. He has not measured either the one or the other. He does not know what the stranger may be able, or may likely be prompted to do to him, nor what are his own means of defence or escape. He takes refuge therefore in a wary, sometimes an obstinate silence. It is for this reason that a boy at school often appears duller and more inept, than would be the amount of a fair proportion to what he is found to be when grown up to a man.

As we improve in judgment and strength, we know better ourselves and others, and in a majority of instances take our due place in the ranks of society. We acquire a modest and cautious firmness, yield what belongs to another, and assert what is due to ourselves. To the last however, we for the most part retain the inoffensiveness described in the beginning of this Essay.

How comes it then that our nature labours under so bitter an aspersion? We have been described as cunning, malicious and treacherous. Other animals herd together for mutual convenience; and their intercourse with their species is for the most part a reciprocation of social feeling and kindness. But community among men, we are told, is that condition of human existence, which brings out all our evil qualities to the face of day. We lie in wait for, and circumvent each other by multiplied artifices. We cannot depend upon each other for the truth of what is stated to us; and promises and the most solemn engagements often seem as if they were made only to mislead. We are violent and deadly in our animosities, easily worked up to ferocity, and satisfied with scarcely any thing short of mutilation and blood. We are revengeful: we lay up an injury, real or imaginary, in the store-house of an undecaying memory, waiting only till we can repay the evil we have sustained tenfold, at a time when our adversary shall be lulled in unsuspecting security. We are rapacious, with no symptom that the appetite for gain within us will ever be appeased; and we practise a thousand deceits, that it may be the sooner, and to the greater degree glutted. The ambition of man is unbounded; and he hesitates at no means in the course it prompts him to pursue. In short, man is to man ever the most fearful and dangerous foe: and it is in this view of his nature that the king of Brobdingnag says to Gulliver, "I cannot but conclude the bulk of your race to be the most pernicious generation of little, odious vermin, that were ever suffered to crawl upon the surface of the earth." The comprehensive faculties of man therefore, and the refinements and subtlety of his intellect, serve only to render him the more formidable companion, and to hold us up as a species to merited condemnation.

It is obvious however that the picture thus drawn is greatly overcharged, that it describes a very small part of our race, and that even as to them it sets before us a few features only, and a partial representation.

History—the successive scenes of the drama in which individuals play their part—is a labyrinth, of which no man has as yet exactly seized the clue.

It has long since been observed, that the history of the four great monarchies, of tyrannies and free states, of chivalry and clanship, of Mahometanism and the Christian church, of the balance of Europe and the revolution of empires, is little else than a tissue of crimes, exhibiting nations as if they were so many herds of ferocious animals, whose genuine occupation was to tear each other to pieces, and to deform their mother-earth with mangled carcases and seas of blood.

But it is not just that we should establish our opinion of human nature purely from the records of history. Man is alternately devoted to tranquillity and to violence. But the latter only affords the proper materials of narration. When he is wrought upon by some powerful impulse, our curiosity is most roused to observe him. We remark his emotions, his energies, his tempest. It is then that he becomes the person of a drama. And, where this disquietude is not the affair of a single individual, but of several persons together, of nations, it is there that history finds her harvest. She goes into the field with all the implements of her industry, and fills her storehouses and magazines with the abundance of her crop. But times of tranquillity and peace furnish her with no materials. They are dismissed in a few slight sentences, and leave no memory behind.

Let us divide this spacious earth into equal compartments, and see in which violence, and in which tranquillity prevails. Let us look through the various ranks and occupations of human society, and endeavour to arrive at a conclusion of a similar sort. The soldier by occupation, and the officer who commands him, would seem, when they are employed in their express functions, to be men of strife. Kings and ministers of state have in a multitude of instances fallen under this description. Conquerors, the firebrands of the earth, have sufficiently displayed their noxious propensities.

But these are but a small part of the tenantry of the many-peopled globe. Man lives by the sweat of his brow. The teeming earth is given him, that by his labour he may raise from it the means of his subsistence. Agriculture is, at least among civilised nations, the first, and certainly the most indispensible of professions. The profession itself is the emblem of peace. All its occupations, from seed-time to harvest, are tranquil; and there is nothing which belongs to it, that can obviously be applied to rouse the angry passions, and place men in a frame of hostility to each other. Next to the cultivator, come the manufacturer, the artificer, the carpenter, the mason, the joiner, the cabinet-maker, all those numerous classes of persons, who are employed in forming garments for us to wear, houses to live in, and moveables and instruments for the accommodation of the species. All these persons are, of necessity, of a peaceable demeanour. So are those who are not employed in producing the conveniencies of life, but in conducting the affairs of barter and exchange. Add to these, such as are engaged in literature, either in the study of what has already been produced, or in adding to the stock, in science or the liberal arts, in the instructing mankind in religion and their duties, or in the education of youth. "Civility," "civil," are indeed terms which express a state of peaceable occupation, in opposition to what is military, and imply a tranquil frame of mind, and the absence of contention, uproar and violence. It is therefore clear, that the majority of mankind are civil, devoted to the arts of peace, and so far as relates to acts of violence innocent, and that the sons of rapine constitute the exception to the general character.

We come into the world under a hard and unpalatable law, "In the sweat of thy brow shalt thou eat bread." It is a bitter decree that is promulgated against us, "He that will not work, neither shall he eat." We all of us love to do our own will, and to be free from the manacles of restraint. What our hearts "find us to do," that we are disposed to execute "with all our might." Some men are lovers of strenuous occupation. They build and they plant; they raise splendid edifices, and lay out pleasure-grounds of mighty extent. Or they devote their minds to the acquisition of knowledge; they

  ——*outwatch the bear,*

With thrice great Hermes, or unsphere

The spirit of Plato, to unfold

What worlds, or what vast regions hold

The immortal mind.

Others again would waste perhaps their whole lives in reverie and idleness. They are constituted of materials so kindly and serene, that their spirits never flag from want of occupation and external excitement. They could lie for ever on a sunny bank, in a condition divided between thinking and no thinking, refreshed by the fanning breeze, viewing the undulations of the soil, and the rippling of the brook, admiring the azure heavens, and the vast, the bold, and the sublime figure of the clouds, yielding themselves occasionally to "thick-coming fancies," and day-dreams, and the endless romances of an undisciplined mind;

And find no end, in wandering mazes lost.

But all men, alike the busy of constitution and the idle, would desire to follow the impulses of their own minds, unbroken in upon by harsh necessity, or the imperious commands of their fellows.

We cannot however, by the resistless law of our existence, live, except the few who by the accident of their birth are privileged to draw their supplies from the labour of others, without exerting ourselves to procure by our efforts or ingenuity the necessaries of food, lodging and attire. He that would obtain them for himself in an uninhabited island, would find that this amounted to a severe tax upon that freedom of motion and thought which would otherwise be his inheritance. And he who has his lot cast in a populous community, exists in a condition somewhat analogous to that of a negro slave, except that he may to a limited extent select the occupation to which he shall addict himself, or may at least starve, in part or in whole, uncontroled, and at his choice. Such is, as it were, the universal lot.

'Tis destiny unshunnable like death:

Even then this dire necessity falls on us,

When we do quicken.

I go forth in the streets, and observe the occupations of other men. I remark the shops that on every side beset my path. It is curious and striking, how vast are the ingenuity and contrivance of human beings, to wring from their fellow-creatures, "from the hard hands of peasants" and artisans, a part of their earnings, that they also may live. We soon become feelingly convinced, that we also must enter into the vast procession of industry, upon pain that otherwise,

Like to an entered tide, they all rush by,

And leave you hindmost: there you lie,

For pavement to the abject rear, o'errun

And trampled on.

It is through the effect of this necessity, that civilised communities become what they are. We all fall into our ranks. Each one is member of a certain company or squadron. We know our respective places, and are marshaled and disciplined with an exactness scarcely less than that of the individuals of a mighty army. We are therefore little disposed to interrupt the occupations of each other. We are intent upon the peculiar employment to which we have become devoted. We "rise up early, and lie down late," and have no leisure to trouble ourselves with the pursuits of others. Hence of necessity it happens in a civilised community, that a vast majority of the species are innocent, and have no inclination to molest or interrupt each other's avocations.

But, as this condition of human society preserves us in comparative innocence, and renders the social arrangement in the midst of which we exist, to a certain degree a soothing and agreeable spectacle, so on the other hand it is not less true that its immediate tendency is, to clip the wings of the thinking principle within us, and plunge the members of the community in which we live into a barren and ungratifying mediocrity. Hence it should be the aim of those persons, who from their situation have more or less the means of looking through the vast assemblage of their countrymen, of penetrating "into the seeds" of character, and determining "which grain will grow, and which will not," to apply themselves to the redeeming such as are worthy of their care from the oblivious gulph into which the mass of the species is of necessity plunged. It is therefore an ill saying, when applied in the most rigorous extent, "Let every man maintain himself, and be his own provider: why should we help him?"

The help however that we should afford to our fellow-men requires of us great discernment in its administration. The deceitfulness of appearances is endless. And nothing can well be at the same time more lamentable and more ludicrous, than the spectacle of those persons, the weaver, the thresher, and the mechanic, who by injudicious patronage are drawn from their proper sphere, only to exhibit upon a larger stage their imbecility and inanity, to shew those moderate powers, which in their proper application would have carried their possessors through life with respect, distorted into absurdity, and used in the attempt to make us look upon a dwarf, as if he were one of the Titans who in the commencement of recorded time astonished the earth.

It is also true to a great degree, that those efforts of the human mind are most healthful and vigorous, in which the possessor of talents "administers to himself," and contends with the different obstacles that arise,

————throwing them aside,

And stemming them with hearts of controversy.

Many illustrious examples however may be found in the annals of literature, of patronage judiciously and generously applied, where men have been raised by the kindness of others from the obscurest situations, and placed on high, like beacons, to illuminate the world. And, independently of all examples, a sound application of the common sense of the human mind would teach us, that the worthies of the earth, though miracles, are not omnipotent, and that a certain aid, from those who by counsel or opulence are enabled to afford it, have oft times produced the noblest effects, have carried on the generous impulse that works within us, and prompted us manfully to proceed, when the weakness of our nature was ready to give in from despair.

But the thing that in this place it was most appropriate to say, is, that we ought not quietly to affirm, of the man whose mind nature or education has enriched with extraordinary powers, "Let him maintain himself, and be his own provider: why should we help him?" It is a thing deeply to be regretted, that such a man will frequently be compelled to devote himself to pursuits comparatively vulgar and inglorious, because he must live. Much of this is certainly inevitable. But what glorious things might a man with extraordinary powers effect, were he not hurried unnumbered miles awry by the unconquerable power of circumstances? The life of such a man is divided between the things which his internal monitor strongly prompts him to do, and those which the external power of nature and circumstances compels him to submit to. The struggle on the part of his better self is noble and admirable. The less he gives way, provided he can accomplish the purpose to which he has vowed himself, the more he is worthy of the admiration of the world. If, in consequence of listening too much to the loftier aspirations of his nature, he fails, it is deeply to be regretted—it is a man to a certain degree lost—but surely, if his miscarriage be not caused by undue presumption, or the clouds and unhealthful atmosphere of self-conceit, he is entitled to the affectionate sympathy and sorrow of every generous mind.

ESSAY VII. OF THE DURATION OF HUMAN LIFE.

The active and industrious portion of the human species in civilised countries, is composed of those who are occupied in the labour of the hand, and in the labour of the head.

The following remarks expressly apply only to the latter of these classes, principally to such as are occupied in productive literature. They may however have their use to all persons a considerable portion of whose time is employed in study and contemplation, as, if well founded, they will form no unimportant chapter in the science of the human mind.

In relation to all the members of the second class then, I should say, that human life is made up of term and vacation, in other words, of hours that may be intellectually employed, and of hours that cannot be so employed.

Human life consists of years, months and days: each day contains twenty-four hours. Of these hours how many belong to the province of intellect?

"There is," as Solomon says, "a time for all things." There must be a time for sleep, a time for recreation, a time for exercise, a time for supplying the machine with nourishment, and a time for digestion. When all these demands have been supplied, how many hours will be left for intellectual occupation?

These remarks, as I have said, are intended principally to apply to the subject of productive literature. Now, of the hours that remain when all the necessary demands of human life have been supplied, it is but a portion, perhaps a small portion, that can be beneficially, judiciously, employed in productive literature, or literary composition.

It is true, that there are many men who will occupy eight, ten, or twelve hours in a day, in the labour of composition. But it may be doubted whether they are wisely so occupied.

It is the duty of an author, inasmuch as he is an author, to consider, that he is to employ his pen in putting down that which shall be fit for other men to read. He is not writing a letter of business, a letter of amusement, or a letter of sentiment, to his private friend. He is writing that which shall be perused by as many men as can be prevailed on to become his readers. If he is an author of spirit and ambition, he wishes his productions to be read, not only by the idle, but by the busy, by those who cannot spare time to peruse them but at the expence of some occupations which ought not to be suspended without an adequate occasion. He wishes to be read not only by the frivolous and the lounger, but by the wise, the elegant, and the fair, by those who are qualified to appreciate the merit of a work, who are endowed with a quick sensibility and a discriminating taste, and are able to pass a sound judgment on its beauties and defects. He advances his claim to permanent honours, and desires that his lucubrations should be considered by generations yet unborn.

A person, so occupied, and with such aims, must not attempt to pass his crudities upon the public. If I may parody a celebrated aphorism of Quintilian, I would say, "Magna debetur hominibus reverentia(8):" in other words, we should carefully examine what it is that we propose to deliver in a permanent form to the taste and understanding of our species. An author ought only to commit to the press the first fruits of his field, his best and choicest thoughts. He ought not to take up the pen, till he has brought his mind into a fitting tone, and ought to lay it down, the instant his intellect becomes in any degree clouded, and his vital spirits abate of their elasticity.

(8) Mankind is to be considered with reverence.

There are extraordinary cases. A man may have so thoroughly prepared himself by long meditation and study, he may have his mind so charged with an abundance of thought, that it may employ him for ten or twelve hours consecutively, merely to put down or to unravel the conceptions already matured in his soul. It was in some such way, that Dryden, we are told, occupied a whole night, and to a late hour in the next morning, in penning his Alexander's Feast. But these are the exceptions. In most instances two or three hours are as much as an author can spend at a time in delivering the first fruits of his field, his choicest thoughts, before his intellect becomes in some degree clouded, and his vital spirits abate of their elasticity.

Nor is this all. He might go on perhaps for some time longer with a reasonable degree of clearness. But the fertility which ought to be his boast, is exhausted. He no longer sports in the meadows of thought, or revels in the exuberance of imagination, but becomes barren and unsatisfactory. Repose is necessary, and that the soil should be refreshed with the dews of another evening, the sleep of a night, and the freshness and revivifying influence of another morning.

These observations lead, by a natural transition, to the question of the true estimate and value of human life, considered as the means of the operations of intellect.

A primary enquiry under this head is as to the duration of life: Is it long, or short?

The instant this question is proposed, I hear myself replied to from all quarters: What is there so well known as the brevity of human life? "Life is but a span." It is "as a tale that is told." "Man cometh forth like a flower, and is cut down: he fleeth also as a shadow, and continueth not." We are "as a sleep; or as grass: in the morning it flourisheth, and groweth up; in the evening it is cut down, and withereth."

The foundation of this sentiment is obvious. Men do not live for ever. The longest duration of human existence has an end: and whatever it is of which that may be affirmed, may in some sense be pronounced to be short. The estimation of our existence depends upon the point of view from which we behold it. Hope is one of our greatest enjoyments. Possession is something. But the past is as nothing. Remorse may give it a certain solidity; the recollection of a life spent in acts of virtue may be refreshing. But fruition, and honours, and fame, and even pain, and privations, and torment, when they ere departed, are but like a feather; we regard them as of no account. Taken in this sense, Dryden's celebrated verses are but a maniac's rant:

To-morrow, do thy worst, for I have lived to-day:

Be fair, or foul, or rain, or shine,

The joys I have possessed, in spite of fate are mine.

Not heaven itself upon the past has power,

But what has been has been, and I have had my hour.

But this way of removing the picture of human life to a certain distance from us, and considering those things which were once in a high degree interesting as frivolous and unworthy of regard, is not the way by which we shall arrive at a true and just estimation of life. Whatever is now past, and is of little value, was once present: and he who would form a sound judgment, must look upon every part of our lives as present in its turn, and not suffer his opinion to be warped by the consideration of the nearness or remoteness of the object he contemplates.

One sentence, which has grown into a maxim for ever repeated, is remarkable for the grossest fallacy: Ars longa, vita brevis(9). I would fain know, what art, compared with the natural duration of human life from puberty to old age, is long.

(9) Art is long; life is short.

If it is intended to say, that no one man can be expected to master all possible arts, or all arts that have at one time or another been the subject of human industry, this indeed is true. But the cause of this does not lie in the limited duration of human life, but in the nature of the faculties of the mind. Human understanding and human industry cannot embrace every thing. When we take hold of one thing, we must let go another. Science and art, if we would pursue them to the furthest extent of which we are capable, must be pursued without interruption. It would therefore be more to the purpose to say, Man cannot be for ever young. In the stream of human existence, different things have their appropriate period. The knowledge of languages can perhaps be most effectually acquired in the season of nonage.

At riper years one man devotes himself to one science or art, and another man to another. This man is a mathematician; a second studies music; a third painting. This man is a logician; and that man an orator. The same person cannot be expected to excel in the abstruseness of metaphysical science, and in the ravishing effusions of poetical genius. When a man, who has arrived at great excellence in one department of art or science, would engage himself in another, he will be apt to find the freshness of his mind gone, and his faculties no longer distinguished by the same degree of tenacity and vigour that they formerly displayed. It is with the organs of the brain, as it is with the organs of speech, in the latter of which we find the tender fibres of the child easily accommodating themselves to the minuter inflections and variations of sound, which the more rigid muscles of the adult will for the most part attempt in vain.

If again, by the maxim, Ars longa, vita brevis, it is intended to signify, that we cannot in any art arrive at perfection; that in reality all the progress we can make is insignificant; and that, as St. Paul says, we must "not count ourselves to have already attained; but that, forgetting the things that are behind, it becomes us to press forward to the prize of our calling,"—this also is true. But this is only ascribable to the limitation of our faculties, and that even the shadow of perfection which man is capable to reach, can only be attained by the labour of successive generations. The cause does not lie in the shortness of human life, unless we would include in its protracted duration the privilege of being for ever young; to which we ought perhaps to add, that our activity should never be exhausted, the freshness of our minds never abate, and our faculties for ever retain the same degree of tenacity and vigour, as they had in the morning of life, when every thing was new, when all that allured or delighted us was seen accompanied with charms inexpressible, and, as Dryden expresses it(10), "the first sprightly running" of the wine of life afforded a zest never after to be hoped for.

(10) Aurengzebe.

I return then to the consideration of the alleged shortness of life. I mentioned in the beginning of this Essay, that "human life consists of years, months and days; each day containing twenty-four hours." But, when I said this, I by no means carried on the division so far as it might be carried. It has been calculated that the human mind is capable of being impressed with three hundred and twenty sensations in a second of time.(11)

(11) See Watson on Time, Chapter II.

"How infinitely rapid is the succession of thought! While I am speaking, perhaps no two ideas are in my mind at the same time, and yet with what facility do I slide from one to another! If my discourse be argumentative, how often do I pass in review the topics of which it consists, before I utter them; and, even while I am speaking, continue the review at intervals, without producing any pause in my discourse! How many other sensations are experienced by me during this period, without so much as interrupting, that is, without materially diverting, the train of my ideas! My eye successively remarks a thousand objects that present themselves. My mind wanders to the different parts of my body, and receives a sensation from the chair on which I sit, or the table on which I lean. It reverts to a variety of things that occurred in the course of the morning, in the course of yesterday, the most remote from, the most unconnected with, the subject that might seem wholly to engross me. I see the window, the opening of a door, the snuffing of a candle. When these most perceptibly occur, my mind passes from one to the other, without feeling the minutest obstacle, or being in any degree distracted by their multiplicity(12)."

(12) Political Justice, Book IV, Chapter ix.

If this statement should appear to some persons too subtle, it may however prepare us to form a due estimate of the following remarks.

"Art is long." No, certainly, no art is long, compared with the natural duration of human life from puberty to old age. There is perhaps no art that may not with reasonable diligence be acquired in three years, that is, as to its essential members and its skilful exercise. We may improve afterwards, but it will be only in minute particulars, and only by fits. Our subsequent advancement less depends upon the continuance of our application, than upon the improvement of the mind generally, the refining of our taste, the strengthening our judgment, and the accumulation of our experience.

The idea which prevails among the vulgar of mankind is, that we must make haste to be wise. The erroneousness of this notion however has from time to time been detected by moralists and philosophers; and it has been felt that he who proceeds in a hurry towards the goal, exposes himself to the imminent risk of never reaching it.

The consciousness of this danger has led to the adoption of the modified maxim, Festina lente, Hasten, but with steps deliberate and cautious.

It would however be a more correct advice to the aspirant, to say, Be earnest in your application, but let your march be vigilant and slow.

There is a doggrel couplet which I have met with in a book on elocution:

Learn to speak slow: all other graces

Will follow in their proper places.

I could wish to recommend a similar process to the student in the course of his reading.

Toplady, a celebrated methodist preacher of the last age, somewhere relates a story of a coxcomb, who told him that he had read over Euclid's Elements of Geometry one afternoon at his tea, only leaving out the A's and B's and crooked lines, which seemed to be intruded merely to retard his progress.

Nothing is more easy than to gabble through a work replete with the profoundest elements of thinking, and to carry away almost nothing, when we have finished.

The book does not deserve even to be read, which does not impose on us the duty of frequent pauses, much reflecting and inward debate, or require that we should often go back, compare one observation and statement with another, and does not call upon us to combine and knit together the disjecta membra.

It is an observation which has often been repeated, that, when we come to read an excellent author a second and a third time, we find in him a multitude of things, that we did not in the slightest degree perceive in a first reading. A careful first reading would have a tendency in a considerable degree to anticipate this following crop.

Nothing is more certain than that a schoolboy gathers much of his most valuable instruction when his lesson is not absolutely before him. In the same sense the more mature student will receive most important benefit, when he shuts his book, and goes forth in the field, and ruminates on what he has read. It is with the intellectual, as with the corporeal eye: we must retire to a certain distance from the object we would examine, before we can truly take in the whole. We must view it in every direction, "survey it," as Sterne says, "transversely, then foreright, then this way, and then that, in all its possible directions and foreshortenings(13);" and thus only can it be expected that we should adequately comprehend it.

(13) Tristram Shandy, Vol. IV, Chap. ii.

But the thing it was principally in my purpose to say is, that it is one of the great desiderata of human life, not to accomplish our purposes in the briefest time, to consider "life as short, and art as long," and therefore to master our ends in the smallest number of days or of years, but rather to consider it as an ample field that is spread before us, and to examine how it is to be filled with pleasure, with advantage, and with usefulness. Life is like a lordly garden, which it calls forth all the skill of the artist to adorn with exhaustless variety and beauty; or like a spacious park or pleasure-ground, all of whose inequalities are to be embellished, and whose various capacities of fertilisation, sublimity or grace, are to be turned to account, so that we may wander in it for ever, and never be wearied.

We shall perhaps understand this best, if we take up the subject on a limited scale, and, before we consider life in its assigned period of seventy years, first confine our attention to the space of a single day. And we will consider that day, not as it relates to the man who earns his subsistence by the labour of his hands, or to him who is immersed in the endless details of commerce. But we will take the case of the man, the whole of whose day is to be disposed of at his own discretion.

The attention of the curious observer has often been called to the tediousness of existence, how our time hangs upon our hands, and in how high estimation the art is held, of giving wings to our hours, and making them pass rapidly and cheerfully away. And moralists of a cynical disposition have poured forth many a sorrowful ditty upon the inconsistency of man, who complains of the shortness of life, at the same time that he is put to the greatest straits how to give an agreeable and pleasant occupation to its separate portions. "Let us hear no more," say these moralists, "of the transitoriness of human existence, from men to whom life is a burthen, and who are willing to assign a reward to him that shall suggest to them an occupation or an amusement untried before."

But this inconsistency, if it merits the name, is not an affair of artificial and supersubtle refinement, but is based in the fundamental principles of our nature. It is unavoidable that, when we have reached the close of any great epoch of our existence, and still more when we have arrived at its final term, we should regret its transitory nature, and lament that we have made no more effectual use of it. And yet the periods and portions of the stream of time, as they pass by us, will often be felt by us as insufferably slow in their progress, and we would give no inconsiderable sum to procure that the present section of our lives might come to an end, and that we might turn over a new leaf in the volume of existence.

I have heard various men profess that they never knew the minutes that hung upon their hands, and were totally unacquainted with what, borrowing a term from the French language, we call ennui. I own I have listened to these persons with a certain degree of incredulity, always excepting such as earn their subsistence by constant labour, or as, being placed in a situation of active engagement, have not the leisure to feel apathy and disgust.

But we are talking here of that numerous class of human beings, who are their own masters, and spend every hour of the day at the choice of their discretion. To these we may add the persons who are partially so, and who, having occupied three or four hours of every day in discharge of some function necessarily imposed on them, at the striking of a given hour go out of school, and employ themselves in a certain industry or sport purely of their own election.

To go back then to the consideration of the single day of a man, all of whose hours are at his disposal to spend them well or ill, at the bidding of his own judgment, or the impulse of his own caprice.

We will suppose that, when he rises from his bed, he has sixteen hours before him, to be employed in whatever mode his will shall decide. I bar the case of travelling, or any of those schemes for passing the day, which by their very nature take the election out of his hands, and fill up his time with a perpetual motion, the nature of which is ascertained from the beginning.

With such a man then it is in the first place indispensibly necessary, that he should have various successive occupations. There is no one study or intellectual enquiry to which a man can apply sixteen hours consecutively, unless in some extraordinary instances which can occur but seldom in the course of a life. And even then the attention will from time to time relax, and the freshness of mental zeal and activity give way, though perhaps, after the lapse of a few minutes they may be revived and brought into action again.

In the ordinary series of human existence it is desirable that, in the course of the same day, a man should have various successive occupations. I myself for the most part read in one language at one part of the day, and in another at another. I am then in the best health and tone of spirits, when I employ two or three hours, and no more, in the act of writing and composition. There must also in the sixteen hours be a time for meals. There should be a time for fresh air and bodily exercise. It is in the nature of man, that we should spend a part of every day in the society of our fellows, either at public spectacles and places of concourse, or in the familiar interchange of conversation with one, two, or more persons with whom we can give ourselves up to unrestrained communication. All human life, as I have said, every day of our existence, consists of term and vacation; and the perfection of practical wisdom is to interpose these one with another, so as to produce a perpetual change, a well-chosen relief, and a freshness and elastic tone which may bid defiance to weariness.

Taken then in this point of view, what an empire does the man of leisure possess in each single day of his life! He disposes of his hours much in the same manner, as the commander of a company of men whom it is his business to train in the discipline of war.

This officer directs one party of his men to climb a mountain, and another to ford or swim a stream which rushes along the valley. He orders this set to rush forward with headlong course, and the other to wheel, and approach by circuitous progress perhaps to the very same point. He marches them to the right and the left. He then dismisses them from the scene of exercise, to furbish their arms, to attend to their accoutrements, or to partake of necessary refection. Not inferior to this is the authority of the man of leisure in disposing of the hours of one single day of his existence. And human life consists of many such days, there being three hundred and sixty-five in each year that we live.

How infinitely various may be the occupations of the life of man from puberty to old age! We may acquire languages; we may devote ourselves to arts; we may give ourselves up to the profoundness of science. Nor is any one of these objects incompatible with the others, nor is there any reason why the same man should not embrace many. We may devote one portion of the year to travelling, and another to all the abstractions of study. I remember when I was a boy, looking forward with terror to the ample field of human life, and saying, When I have read through all the books that have been written, what shall I do afterwards? And there is infinitely more sense in this, than in the ludicrous exclamations of men who complain of the want of time, and say that life affords them no space in which to act their imaginings.

On the contrary, when a man has got to the end of one art or course of study, he is compelled to consider what he shall do next. And, when we have gone through a cycle of as many acquisitions, as, from the limitation of human faculties, are not destructive of each other, we shall find ourselves frequently reduced to the beginning some of them over again. Nor is this the least agreeable occupation of human leisure. The book that I read when I was a boy, presents quite a new face to me as I advance in the vale of years. The same words and phrases suggest to me a new train of ideas. And it is no mean pleasure that I derive from the singular sensation of finding the same author and the same book, old and yet not old, presenting to me cherished and inestimable recollections, and at the same time communicating mines of wealth, the shaft of which was till now unexplored.

The result then of these various observations is to persuade the candid and ingenuous man, to consider life as an important and ample possession, to resolve that it shall be administered with as much judgment and deliberation as a person of true philanthropy and wisdom would administer a splendid income, and upon no occasion so much to think upon the point of in how short a time an interesting pursuit is to be accomplished, as by what means it shall be accomplished in a consummate and masterly style. Let us hear no more, from those who have to a considerable degree the command of their hours, the querulous and pitiful complaint that they have no time to do what they ought to do and would wish to do; but let them feel that they have a gigantic store of minutes and hours and days and months, abundantly sufficient to enable them to effect what it is especially worthy of a noble mind to perform!

ESSAY VIII. OF HUMAN VEGETATION.

There is another point of view from which we may look at the subject of time as it is concerned with the business of human life, that will lead us to conclusions of a very different sort from those which are set down in the preceding Essay.

Man has two states of existence in a striking degree distinguished from each other: the state in which he is found during his waking hours; and the state in which he is during sleep.

The question has been agitated by Locke and other philosophers, "whether the soul always thinks," in other words, whether the mind, during those hours in which our limbs lie for the most part in a state of inactivity, is or is not engaged by a perpetual succession of images and impressions. This is a point that can perhaps never be settled. When the empire of sleep ceases, or when we are roused from sleep, we are often conscious that we have been to that moment busily employed with that sort of conceptions and scenes which we call dreams. And at times when, on waking, we have no such consciousness, we can never perhaps be sure that the shock that waked us, had not the effect of driving away these fugitive and unsubstantial images. There are men who are accustomed to say, they never dream. If in reality the mind of man, from the hour of his birth, must by the law of its nature be constantly occupied with sensations or images (and of the contrary we can never be sure), then these men are all their lives in the state of persons, upon whom the shock that wakes them, has the effect of driving away such fugitive and unsubstantial images.—Add to which, there may be sensations in the human subject, of a species confused and unpronounced, which never arrive at that degree of distinctness as to take the shape of what we call dreaming.

So much for man in the state of sleep.

But during our waking hours, our minds are very differently occupied at different periods of the day. I would particularly distinguish the two dissimilar states of the waking man, when the mind is indolent, and when it is on the alert.

While I am writing this Essay, my mind may be said to be on the alert. It is on the alert, so long as I am attentively reading a book of philosophy, of argumentation, of eloquence, or of poetry.

It is on the alert, so long as I am addressing a smaller or a greater audience, and endeavouring either to amuse or instruct them. It is on the alert, while in silence and solitude I endeavour to follow a train of reasoning, to marshal and arrange a connected set of ideas, or in any other way to improve my mind, to purify my conceptions, and to advance myself in any of the thousand kinds of intellectual process. It is on the alert, when I am engaged in animated conversation, whether my cue be to take a part in the reciprocation of alternate facts and remarks in society, or merely to sit an attentive listener to the facts and remarks of others.

This state of the human mind may emphatically be called the state of activity and attention.

So long as I am engaged in any of the ways here enumerated, or in any other equally stirring mental occupations which are not here set down, my mind is in a frame of activity.

But there is another state in which men pass their minutes and hours, that is strongly contrasted with this. It depends in some men upon constitution, and in others upon accident, how their time shall be divided, how much shall be given to the state of activity, and how much to the state of indolence.

In an Essay I published many years ago there is this passage.

"The chief point of difference between the man of talent and the man without, consists in the different ways in which their minds are employed during the same interval. They are obliged, let us suppose, to walk from Temple-Bar to Hyde-Park-Corner. The dull man goes straight forward; he has so many furlongs to traverse. He observes if he meets any of his acquaintance; he enquires respecting their health and their family. He glances perhaps the shops as he passes; he admires the fashion of a buckle, and the metal of a tea-urn. If he experiences any flights of fancy, they are of a short extent; of the same nature as the flights of a forest-bird, clipped of his wings, and condemned to pass the rest of his life in a farm-yard. On the other hand the man of talent gives full scope to his imagination. He laughs and cries. Unindebted to the suggestions of surrounding objects, his whole soul is employed. He enters into nice calculations; he digests sagacious reasonings. In imagination he declaims or describes, impressed with the deepest sympathy, or elevated to the loftiest rapture. He makes a thousand new and admirable combinations. He passes through a thousand imaginary scenes, tries his courage, tasks his ingenuity, and thus becomes gradually prepared to meet almost any of the many-coloured events of human life. He consults by the aid of memory the books he has read, and projects others for the future instruction and delight of mankind. If he observe the passengers, he reads their countenances, conjectures their past history, and forms a superficial notion of their wisdom or folly, their virtue or vice, their satisfaction or misery. If he observe the scenes that occur, it is with the eye of a connoisseur or an artist. Every object is capable of suggesting to him a volume of reflections. The time of these two persons in one respect resembles; it has brought them both to Hyde-Park-Corner. In almost every other respect it is dissimilar;(14)."

(14) Enquirer, Part 1, Essay V.

This passage undoubtedly contains a true description of what may happen, and has happened.

But there lurks in this statement a considerable error.

It has appeared in the second Essay of this volume, that there is not that broad and strong line of distinction between the wise man and the dull that has often been supposed. We are all of us by turns both the one and the other. Or, at least, the wisest man that ever existed spends a portion of his time in vacancy and dulness; and the man, whose faculties are seemingly the most obtuse, might, under proper management from the hour of his birth, barring those rare exceptions from the ordinary standard of mind which do not deserve to be taken into the account, have proved apt, adroit, intelligent and acute, in the walk for which his organisation especially fitted him(15).

(15) See above, Essay 3.

Many men without question, in a walk of the same duration as that above described between Temple-Bar and Hyde-Park-Corner, have passed their time in as much activity, and amidst as strong and various excitements, as those enumerated in the passage above quoted.

But the lives of all men, the wise, and those whom by way of contrast we are accustomed to call the dull, are divided between animation and comparative vacancy; and many a man, who by the bursts of his genius has astonished the world, and commanded the veneration of successive ages, has spent a period of time equal to that occupied by a walk from Temple-Bar to Hyde-Park-Corner, in a state of mind as idle, and as little affording materials for recollection, as the dullest man that ever breathed the vital air.

The two states of man which are here attempted to be distinguished, are, first, that in which reason is said to fill her throne, in which will prevails, and directs the powers of mind or of bodily action in one channel or another; and, secondly, that in which these faculties, tired of for ever exercising their prerogatives, or, being awakened as it were from sleep, and having not yet assumed them, abandon the helm, even as a mariner might be supposed to do, in a wide sea, and in a time when no disaster could be apprehended, and leave the vessel of the mind to drift, exactly as chance might direct.

To describe this last state of mind I know not a better term that can be chosen, than that of reverie. It is of the nature of what I have seen denominated BROWN STUDY(16) a species of dozing and drowsiness, in which all men spend a portion of the waking part of every day of their lives. Every man must be conscious of passing minutes, perhaps hours of the day, particularly when engaged in exercise in the open air, in this species of neutrality and eviration. It is often not unpleasant at the time, and leaves no sinking of the spirits behind. It is probably of a salutary nature, and may be among the means, in a certain degree beneficial like sleep, by which the machine is restored, and the man comes forth from its discipline reinvigorated, and afresh capable of his active duties.

(16) Norris, and Johnson, Dictionary of the English Language.

This condition of our nature has considerably less vitality in it, than we experience in a complete and perfect dream. In dreaming we are often conscious of lively impressions, of a busy scene, and of objects and feelings succeeding each other with rapidity. We sometimes imagine ourselves earnestly speaking: and the topics we treat, and the words we employ, are supplied to us with extraordinary fluency. But the sort of vacancy and inoccupation of which I here treat, has a greater resemblance to the state of mind, without distinct and clearly unfolded ideas, which we experience before we sink into sleep. The mind is in reality in a condition, more properly accessible to feeling and capable of thought, than actually in the exercise of either the one or the other. We are conscious of existence and of little more. We move our legs, and continue in a peripatetic state; for the man who has gone out of his house with a purpose to walk, exercises the power of volition when he sets out, but proceeds in his motion by a semi-voluntary act, by a sort of vis inertiae, which will not cease to operate without an express reason for doing so, and advances a thousand steps without distinctly willing any but the first. When it is necessary to turn to the right or the left, or to choose between any two directions on which he is called upon to decide, his mind is so far brought into action as the case may expressly require, and no further.

I have here instanced in the case of the peripatetic: but of how many classes and occupations of human life may not the same thing be affirmed? It happens to the equestrian, as well as to him that walks on foot. It occurs to him who cultivates the fruits of the earth, and to him who is occupied in any of the thousand manufactures which are the result of human ingenuity. It happens to the soldier in his march, and to the mariner on board his vessel. It attends the individuals of the female sex through all their diversified modes of industry, the laundress, the housemaid, the sempstress, the netter of purses, the knotter of fringe, and the worker in tambour, tapestry and embroidery. In all, the limbs or the fingers are employed mechanically; the attention of the mind is only required at intervals; and the thoughts remain for the most part in a state of non-excitation and repose.

It is a curious question, but extremely difficult of solution, what portion of the day of every human creature must necessarily be spent in this sort of intellectual indolence. In the lower classes of society its empire is certainly very great; its influence is extensive over a large portion of the opulent and luxurious; it is least among those who are intrusted in the more serious affairs of mankind, and among the literary and the learned, those who waste their lives, and consume the midnight-oil, in the search after knowledge.

It appeared with sufficient clearness in the immediately preceding Essay, that the intellect cannot be always on the stretch, nor the bow of the mind for ever bent. In the act of composition, unless where the province is of a very inferior kind, it is likely that not more than two or three hours at a time can be advantageously occupied. But in literary labour it will often occur, that, in addition to the hours expressly engaged in composition, much time may be required for the collecting materials, the collating of authorities, and the bringing together a variety of particulars, so as to sift from the mass those circumstances which may best conduce to the purpose of the writer. In all these preliminary and inferior enquiries it is less necessary that the mind should be perpetually awake and on the alert, than in the direct office of composition. The situation is considerably similar of the experimental philosopher, the man who by obstinate and unconquerable application resolves to wrest from nature her secrets, and apply them to the improvement of social life, or to the giving to the human mind a wider range or a more elevated sphere. A great portion of this employment consists more in the motion of the hands and the opportune glance of the eye, than in the labour of the head, and allows to the operator from time to time an interval of rest from the momentous efforts of invention and discovery, and the careful deduction of consequences in the points to be elucidated.

There is a distinction, sufficiently familiar to all persons who occupy a portion of their time in reading, that is made between books of instruction, and books of amusement. From the student of mathematics or any of the higher departments of science, from the reader of books of investigation and argument, an active attention is demanded. Even in the perusal of the history of kingdoms and nations, or of certain memorable periods of public affairs, we can scarcely proceed with any satisfaction, unless in so far as we collect our thoughts, compare one part of the narrative with another, and hold the mind in a state of activity.

We are obliged to reason while we read, and in some degree to construct a discourse of our own, at the same time that we follow the statements of the author before us. Unless we do this, the sense and spirit of what we read will be apt to slip from under our observation, and we shall by and by discover that we are putting together words and sounds only, when we purposed to store our minds with facts and reflections. We apprehended not the sense of the writer even when his pages were under our eye, and of consequence have nothing laid up in the memory after the hour of reading is completed.

In works of amusement it is otherwise, and most especially in writings of fiction. These are sought after with avidity by the idle, because for the most part they are found to have the virtue of communicating impressions to the reader, even while his mind remains in a state of passiveness. He finds himself agreeably affected with fits of mirth or of sorrow, and carries away the facts of the tale, at the same time that he is not called upon for the act of attention. This is therefore one of the modes of luxury especially cultivated in a highly civilized state of society.

The same considerations will also explain to us the principal part of the pleasure that is experienced by mankind in all states of society from public shews and exhibitions. The spectator is not called upon to exert himself; the amusement and pleasure come to him, while he remains voluptuously at his ease; and it is certain that the exertion we make when we are compelled to contribute to, and become in part the cause of our own entertainment, is more than the human mind is willing to sustain, except at seasons in which we are specially on the alert and awake.

This is further one of the causes why men in general feel prompted to seek the society of their fellows. We are in part no doubt called upon in select society to bring our own information along with us, and a certain vein of wit, humour or narrative, that we may contribute our proportion to the general stock. We read the newspapers, the newest publications, and repair to places of fashionable amusement and resort; partly that we may at least be upon a par with the majority of the persons we are likely to meet. But many do not thus prepare themselves, nor does perhaps any one upon all occasions.

There is another state of human existence in which we expressly dismiss from our hands the reins of the mind, and suffer our minutes and our hours to glide by us undisciplined and at random.

This is, generally speaking, the case in a period of sickness. We have no longer the courage to be on the alert, and to superintend the march of our thoughts. It is the same with us for the most part when at any time we lie awake in our beds. To speak from my own experience, I am in a restless and uneasy state while I am alone in my sitting-room, unless I have some occupation of my own choice, writing or reading, or any of those employments the pursuit of which was chosen at first, and which is more or less under the direction of the will afterwards. But when awake in my bed, either in health or sickness, I am reasonably content to let my thoughts flow on agreeably to those laws of association by which I find them directed, without giving myself the trouble to direct them into one channel rather than another, or to marshal and actively to prescribe the various turns and mutations they may be impelled to pursue.

It is thus that we are sick; and it is thus that we die. The man that guides the operations of his own mind, is either to a certain degree in bodily health, or in that health of mind which shall for a longer or shorter time stand forward as the substitute of the health of the body. When we die, we give up the game, and are not disposed to contend any further. It is a very usual thing to talk of the struggles of a man in articulo mortis. But this is probably, like so many other things that occur to us in this sublunary stage, a delusion. The bystander mistakes for a spontaneous contention and unwillingness to die, what is in reality nothing more than an involuntary contraction and convulsion of the nerves, to which the mind is no party, and is even very probably unconscious.—But enough of this, the final and most humiliating state through which mortal men may be called on to pass.

I find then in the history of almost every human creature four different states or modes of existence. First, there is sleep. In the strongest degree of contrast to this there is the frame in which we find ourselves, when we write! or invent and steadily pursue a consecutive train of thinking unattended with the implements of writing, or read in some book of science or otherwise which calls upon us for a fixed attention, or address ourselves to a smaller or greater audience, or are engaged in animated conversation. In each of these occupations the mind may emphatically be said to be on the alert.

But there are further two distinct states or kinds of mental indolence. The first is that which we frequently experience during a walk or any other species of bodily exercise, where, when the whole is at an end, we scarcely recollect any thing in which the mind has been employed, but have been in what I may call a healthful torpor, where our limbs have been sufficiently in action to continue our exercise, we have felt the fresh breeze playing on our cheeks, and have been in other respects in a frame of no unpleasing neutrality. This may be supposed greatly to contribute to our bodily health. It is the holiday of the faculties: and, as the bow, when it has been for a considerable time unbent, is said to recover its elasticity, so the mind, after a holiday of this sort, comes fresh, and with an increased alacrity, to those occupations which advance man most highly in the scale of being.

But there is a second state of mental indolence, not so complete as this, but which is still indolence, inasmuch as in it the mind is passive, and does not assume the reins of empire. Such is the state in which we are during our sleepless hours in bed; and in this state our ideas, and the topics that successively occur, appear to go forward without remission, while it seems that it is this busy condition of the mind, and the involuntary activity of our thoughts, that prevent us from sleeping.

The distinction then between these two sorts of indolence is, that in the latter our ideas are perfectly distinct, are attended with consciousness, and can, as we please, be called up to recollection. This therefore is not what we understand by reverie. In these waking hours which are spent by us in bed, the mind is no less busy, than it is in sleep during a dream. The other and more perfect sort of mental indolence, is that which we often experience during our exercise in the open air. This is of the same nature as the condition of thought which seems to be the necessary precursor of sleep, and is attended with no precise consciousness.

By the whole of the above statement we are led to a new and a modified estimate of the duration of human life.

If by life we understand mere susceptibility, a state of existence in which we are accessible at any moment to the onset of sensation, for example, of pain—in this sense our life is commensurate, or nearly commensurate, to the entire period, from the quickening of the child in the womb, to the minute at which sense deserts the dying man, and his body becomes an inanimate mass.

But life, in the emphatical sense, and par excellence, is reduced to much narrower limits. From this species of life it is unavoidable that we should strike off the whole of the interval that is spent in sleep; and thus, as a general rule, the natural day of twenty-four hours is immediately reduced to sixteen.

Of these sixteen hours again, there is a portion that falls under the direction of will and attention, and a portion that is passed by us in a state of mental indolence. By the ordinary and least cultivated class of mankind, the husbandman, the manufacturer, the soldier, the sailor, and the main body of the female sex, much the greater part of every day is resigned to a state of mental indolence. The will does not actively interfere, and the attention is not roused. Even the most intellectual beings of our species pass no inconsiderable portion of every day in a similar condition. Such is our state for the most part during the time that is given to bodily exercise, and during the time in which we read books of amusement merely, or are employed in witnessing public shews and exhibitions.

That portion of every day of our existence which is occupied by us with a mind attentive and on the alert, I would call life in a transcendant sense. The rest is scarcely better than a state of vegetation.

And yet not so either. The happiest and most valuable thoughts of the human mind will sometimes come when they are least sought for, and we least anticipated any such thing. In reading a romance, in witnessing a performance at a theatre, in our idlest and most sportive moods, a vein in the soil of intellect will sometimes unexpectedly be broken up, "richer than all the tribe" of contemporaneous thoughts, that shall raise him to whom it occurs, to a rank among his species altogether different from any thing he had looked for. Newton was led to the doctrine of gravitation by the fall of an apple, as he indolently reclined under the tree on which it grew. "A verse may find him, who a sermon flies." Polemon, when intoxicated, entered the school of Xenocrates, and was so struck with the energy displayed by the master, and the thoughts he delivered, that from that moment he renounced the life of dissipation he had previously led, and applied himself entirely to the study of philosophy. —But these instances are comparatively of rare occurrence, and do not require to be taken into the account.

It is still true therefore for the most part, that not more than eight hours in the day are passed by the wisest and most energetic, with a mind attentive and on the alert. The remainder is a period of vegetation only. In the mean time we have all of us undoubtedly to a certain degree the power of enlarging the extent of the period of transcendant life in each day of our healthful existence, and causing it to encroach upon the period either of mental indolence or of sleep.—With the greater part of the human species the whole of their lives while awake, with the exception of a few brief and insulated intervals, is spent in a passive state of the intellectual powers. Thoughts come and go, as chance, or some undefined power in nature may direct, uninterfered with by the sovereign will, the steersman of the mind. And often the understanding appears to be a blank, upon which if any impressions are then made, they are like figures drawn in the sand which the next tide obliterates, or are even lighter and more evanescent than this.

Let me add, that the existence of the child for two or three years from the period of his birth, is almost entirely a state of vegetation. The impressions that are made upon his sensorium come and go, without either their advent or departure being anticipated, and without the interference of the will. It is only under some express excitement, that the faculty of will mounts its throne, and exercises its empire. When the child smiles, that act is involuntary; but, when he cries, will presently comes to mix itself with the phenomenon. Wilfulness, impatience and rebellion are infallible symptoms of a mind on the alert. And, as the child in the first stages of its existence puts forth the faculty of will only at intervals, so for a similar reason this period is but rarely accompanied with memory, or leaves any traces of recollection for our after-life.

There are other memorable states of the intellectual powers, which if I did not mention, the survey here taken would seem to be glaringly imperfect. The first of these is madness. In this humiliating condition of our nature the sovereignty of reason is deposed:

Chaos umpire sits,

And by decision more embroils the fray.

The mind is in a state of turbulence and tempest in one instant, and in another subsides into the deepest imbecility; and, even when the will is occasionally roused, the link which preserved its union with good sense and sobriety is dissolved, and the views by which it has the appearance of being regulated, are all based in misconstruction and delusion.

Next to madness occur the different stages of spleen, dejection and listlessness. The essence of these lies in the passiveness and neutrality of the intellectual powers. In as far as the unhappy sufferer could be roused to act, the disease would be essentially diminished, and might finally be expelled. But long days and months are spent by the patient in the midst of all harassing imaginations, and an everlasting nightmare seems to sit on the soul, and lock up its powers in interminable inactivity. Almost the only interruption to this, is when the demands of nature require our attention, or we pay a slight and uncertain attention to the decencies of cleanliness and attire.

In all these considerations then we find abundant occasion to humble the pride and vain-glory of man. But they do not overturn the principles delivered in the preceding Essay respecting the duration of human life, though they certainly interpose additional boundaries to limit the prospects of individual improvement.

ESSAY IX. OF LEISURE.

The river of human life is divided into two streams; occupation and leisure—or, to express the thing more accurately, that occupation, which is prescribed, and may be called the business of life, and that occupation, which arises contingently, and not so much of absolute and set purpose, not being prescribed: such being the more exact description of these two divisions of human life, inasmuch as the latter is often not less earnest and intent in its pursuits than the former.

It would be a curious question to ascertain which of these is of the highest value.

To this enquiry I hear myself loudly and vehemently answered from all hands in favour of the first. "This," I am told by unanimous acclamation, "is the business of life."

The decision in favour of what we primarily called occupation, above what we called leisure, may in a mitigated sense be entertained as true. Man can live with little or no leisure, for millions of human beings do so live: but the species to which we belong, and of consequence the individuals of that species, cannot exist as they ought to exist, without occupation.

Granting however the paramount claims that occupation has to our regard, let us endeavour to arrive at a just estimate of the value of leisure.

It has been said by some one, with great appearance of truth, that schoolboys learn as much, perhaps more, of beneficial knowledge in their hours of play, as in their hours of study.

The wisdom of ages has been applied to ascertain what are the most desirable topics for the study of the schoolboy. They are selected for the most part by the parent. There are few parents that do not feel a sincere and disinterested desire for the welfare of their children. It is an unquestionable maxim, that we are the best judges of that of which we have ourselves had experience; and all parents have been children. It is therefore idle and ridiculous to suppose that those studies which have for centuries been chosen by the enlightened mature for the occupation of the young, have not for the most part been well chosen. Of these studies the earliest consist in the arts of reading and writing. Next follows arithmetic, with perhaps some rudiments of algebra and geometry. Afterward comes in due order the acquisition of languages, particularly the dead languages; a most fortunate occupation for those years of man, in which the memory is most retentive, and the reasoning powers have yet acquired neither solidity nor enlargement. Such are the occupations of the schoolboy in his prescribed hours of study.

But the schoolboy is cooped up in an apartment, it may be with a number of his fellows. He is seated at a desk, diligently conning the portion of learning that is doled out to him, or, when he has mastered his lesson, reciting it with anxious brow and unassured lips to the senior, who is to correct his errors, and pronounce upon the sufficiency of his industry. All this may be well: but it is a new and more exhilarating spectacle that presents itself to our observation, when he is dismissed from his temporary labours, and rushes impetuously out to the open air, and gives free scope to his limbs and his voice, and is no longer under the eye of a censor that shall make him feel his subordination and dependence.

Meanwhile the question under consideration was, not in which state he experienced the most happiness, but which was productive of the greatest improvement.

The review of the human subject is conveniently divided under the heads of body and mind.

There can be no doubt that the health of the body is most promoted by those exercises in which the schoolboy is engaged during the hours of play. And it is further to be considered that health is required, not only that we may be serene, contented and happy, but that we may be enabled effectually to exert the faculties of the mind.

But there is another way, in which we are called upon to consider the division of the human subject under the heads of body and mind.

The body is the implement and instrument of the mind, the tool by which most of its purposes are to be effected. We live in the midst of a material world, or of what we call such. The greater part of the pursuits in which we engage, are achieved by the action of the limbs and members of the body upon external matter.

Our communications with our fellow-men are all of them carried on by means of the body.

Now the action of the limbs and members of the body is infinitely improved by those exercises in which the schoolboy becomes engaged during his hours of play. In the first place it is to be considered that we do those things most thoroughly and in the shortest time, which are spontaneous, the result of our own volition; and such are the exercises in which the schoolboy engages during this period. His heart and soul are in what he does. The man or the boy must be a poor creature indeed, who never does any thing but as he is bid by another. It is in his voluntary acts and his sports, that he learns the skilful and effective use of his eye and his limbs. He selects his mark, and he hits it. He tries again and again, effort after effort, and day after day, till he has surmounted the difficulty of the attempt, and the rebellion of his members. Every articulation and muscle of his frame is called into action, till all are obedient to the master-will; and his limbs are lubricated and rendered pliant by exercise, as the limbs of the Grecian athleta were lubricated with oil.

Thus he acquires, first dexterity of motion, and next, which is of no less importance, a confidence in his own powers, a consciousness that he is able to effect what he purposes, a calmness and serenity which resemble the sweeping of the area, and scattering of the saw-dust, upon which the dancer or the athlete is to exhibit with grace, strength and effect.

So much for the advantages reaped by the schoolboy during his hours of play as to the maturing his bodily powers, and the improvement of those faculties of his mind which more immediately apply to the exercise of his bodily powers.

But, beside this, it is indispensible to the well-being and advantage of the individual, that he should employ the faculties of his mind in spontaneous exertions. I do not object, especially during the period of nonage, to a considerable degree of dependence and control. But his greatest advancement, even then, seems to arise from the interior impulses of his mind. The schoolboy exercises his wit, and indulges in sallies of the thinking principle. This is wholsome; this is fresh; it has twice the quickness, clearness and decision in it, that are to be found in those acts of the mind which are employed about the lessons prescribed to him.

In school our youth are employed about the thoughts, the acts and suggestions of other men. This is all mimicry, and a sort of second-hand business. It resembles the proceeding of the fresh-listed soldier at drill; he has ever his eye on his right-hand man, and does not raise his arm, nor advance his foot, nor move his finger, but as he sees another perform the same motion before him. It is when the schoolboy proceeds to the playground, that he engages in real action and real discussion. It is then that he is an absolute human being and a genuine individual.

The debates of schoolboys, their discussions what they shall do, and how it shall be done, are anticipations of the scenes of maturer life. They are the dawnings of committees, and vestries, and hundred-courts, and ward-motes, and folk-motes, and parliaments. When boys consult when and where their next cricket-match shall be played, it may be regarded as the embryo representation of a consult respecting a grave enterprise to be formed, or a colony to be planted. And, when they enquire respecting poetry and prose, and figures and tropes, and the dictates of taste, this happily prepares them for the investigations of prudence, and morals, and religious principles, and what is science, and what is truth.

It is thus that the wit of man, to use the word in the old Saxon sense, begins to be cultivated. One boy gives utterance to an assertion; and another joins issue with him, and retorts. The wheels of the engine of the brain are set in motion, and, without force, perform their healthful revolutions. The stripling feels himself called upon to exert his presence of mind, and becomes conscious of the necessity of an immediate reply. Like the unfledged bird, he spreads his wings, and essays their powers. He does not answer, like a boy in his class, who tasks his understanding or not, as the whim of the moment shall prompt him, where one boy honestly performs to the extent of his ability, and others disdain the empire assumed over them, and get off as cheaply as they can. He is no longer under review, but is engaged in real action. The debate of the schoolboy is the combat of the intellectual gladiator, where he fences and parries and thrusts with all the skill and judgment he possesses.

There is another way in which the schoolboy exercises his powers during his periods of leisure. He is often in society; but he is ever and anon in solitude. At no period of human life are our reveries so free and untrammeled, as at the period here spoken of. He climbs the mountain-cliff; and penetrates into the depths of the woods. His joints are well strung; he is a stranger to fatigue. He rushes down the precipice, and mounts again with ease, as though he had the wings of a bird. He ruminates, and pursues his own trains of reflection and discovery, "exhausting worlds," as it appears to him, "and then imagining new." He hovers on the brink of the deepest philosophy, enquiring how came I here, and to what end. He becomes a castle-builder, constructing imaginary colleges and states, and searching out the businesses in which they are to be employed, and the schemes by which they are to be regulated. He thinks what he would do, if he possessed uncontrolable strength, if he could fly, if he could make himself invisible. In this train of mind he cons his first lessons of liberty and independence. He learns self-reverence, and says to himself, I also am an artist, and a maker. He ruffles himself under the yoke, and feels that he suffers foul tyranny when he is driven, and when brute force is exercised upon him, to compel him to a certain course, or to chastise his faults, imputed or real.

Such are the benefits of leisure to the schoolboy: and they are not less to man when arrived at years of discretion. It is good for us to have some regular and stated occupation. Man may be practically too free; this is frequently the case with those who have been nurtured in the lap of opulence and luxury. We were sent into the world under the condition, "In the sweat of thy brow shalt thou eat bread." And those who, by the artificial institutions of society, are discharged from this necessity, are placed in a critical and perilous situation. They are bound, if they would consult their own well-being, to contrive for themselves a factitious necessity, that may stand them in the place of that necessity which is imposed without appeal on the vast majority of their brethren.

But, if it is desirable that every man should have some regular and stated occupation, so it is certainly not less desirable, that every man should have his seasons of relaxation and leisure.

Unhappy is the wretch, whose condition it is to be perpetually bound to the oar, and who is condemned to labour in one certain mode, during all the hours that are not claimed by sleep, or as long as the muscles of his frame, or the fibres of his fingers will enable him to persevere. "Apollo himself," says the poet, "does not always bend the bow." There should be a season, when the mind is free as air, when not only we should follow without restraint any train of thinking or action, within the bounds of sobriety, and that is not attended with injury to others, that our own minds may suggest to us, but should sacrifice at the shrine of intellectual liberty, and spread our wings, and take our flight into untried regions. It is good for man that he should feel himself at some time unshackled and autocratical, that he should say, This I do, because it is prescribed to me by the conditions without which I cannot exist, or by the election which in past time I deliberately made; and this, because it is dictated by the present frame of my spirit, and is therefore that in which the powers my nature has entailed upon me may be most fully manifested. In addition to which we are to consider, that a certain variety and mutation of employments is best adapted to humanity. When my mind or my body seems to be overwrought by one species of occupation, the substitution of another will often impart to me new life, and make me feel as fresh as if no labour had before engaged me. For all these reasons it is to be desired, that we should possess the inestimable privilege of leisure, that in the revolving hours of every day a period should arrive, at which we should lay down the weapons of our labour, and engage in a sport that may be no less active and strenuous than the occupation which preceded it.

A question, which deserves our attention in this place, is, how much of every day it behoves us to give to regular and stated occupation, and how much is the just and legitimate province of leisure. It has been remarked in a preceding Essay(17), that, if my main and leading pursuit is literary composition, two or three hours in the twenty-four will often be as much as can advantageously and effectually be so employed. But this will unavoidably vary according to the nature of the occupation: the period above named may be taken as the MINIMUM.

(17) See above, Essay 7.

Such, let us say, is the portion of time which the man of letters is called on to devote to literary composition.

It may next be fitting to enquire as to the humbler classes of society, and those persons who are engaged in the labour of the hands, how much time they ought to be expected to consume in their regular and stated occupations, and how much would remain to them for relaxation and leisure. It has been said(18), that half an hour in the day given by every member of the community to manual labour, might be sufficient for supplying the whole with the absolute necessaries of life. But there are various considerations that would inevitably lengthen this period. In a community which has made any considerable advance in the race of civilisation, many individuals must be expected to be excused from any portion of manual labour. It is not desirable that any community should be contented to supply itself with necessaries only. There are many refinements in life, and many advances in literature and the arts, which indispensibly conduce to the rendering man in society a nobler and more exalted creature than he could otherwise be; and these ought not to be consigned to neglect.

(18) Political Justice, Book VIII, Chap. VI.

On the other hand however it is certain, that much of the ostentation and a multitude of the luxuries which subsist in European and Asiatic society are just topics of regret, and that, if ever those improvements in civilisation take place which philosophy has essayed to delineate, there would be a great abridgment of the manual labour that we now see around us, and the humbler classes of the community would enter into the inheritance of a more considerable portion of leisure than at present falls to their lot.

But it has been much the habit, for persons not belonging to the humbler classes of the community, and who profess to speculate upon the genuine interests of human society, to suppose, however certain intervals of leisure may conduce to the benefit of men whose tastes have been cultivated and refined, and who from education have many resources of literature and reflection at all times at their beck, yet that leisure might prove rather pernicious than otherwise to the uneducated and the ignorant. Let us enquire then how these persons would be likely to employ the remainder of their time, if they had a greater portion of leisure than they at present enjoy.—I would add, that the individuals of the humbler classes of the community need not for ever to merit the appellation of the uneducated and ignorant.

In the first place, they would engage, like the schoolboy, in active sports, thereby giving to their limbs, which, in rural occupation and mechanical labour, are somewhat too monotonously employed, and contract the stiffness and experience the waste of a premature old age, the activity and freedom of an athlete, a cricketer, or a hunter. Nor do these occupations only conduce to the health of the body, they also impart a spirit and a juvenile earnestness to the mind.

In the next place, they may be expected to devote a part of the day, more than they do at present, to their wives and families, cultivating the domestic affections, watching the expanding bodies and minds of their children, leading them on in the road of improvement, warning them against the perils with which they are surrounded, and observing with somewhat of a more jealous and parental care, what it is for which by their individual qualities they are best adapted, and in what particular walk of life they may most advantageously be engaged. The father and the son would grow in a much greater degree friends, anticipating each other's wishes, and sympathising in each other's pleasures and pains.

Thirdly, one infallible consequence of a greater degree of leisure in the lower classes would be that reading would become a more common propensity and amusement. It is the aphorism of one of the most enlightened of my contemporaries, "The schoolmaster is abroad:" and many more than at present would desire to store up in their little hoard a certain portion of the general improvement. We should no longer have occasion to say,

> But knowledge to their eyes her ample page,
>
> Rich with the spoils of time, did ne'er unrol.

Nor should we be incited to fear that ever wakeful anticipation of the illiberal, that, by the too great diffusion of the wisdom of the wise, we might cease to have a race of men adapted to the ordinary pursuits of life. Our ploughmen and artificers, who obtained the improvements of intellect through the medium of leisure, would have already received their destination, and formed their habits, and would be disposed to consider the new lights that were opened upon them, as the ornament of existence, not its substance. Add to which, as leisure became more abundant, and the opportunities of intellectual improvement increased, they would have less motive to repine at their lot. It is principally while knowledge and information are new, that they are likely to intoxicate the brain of those to whose share they have fallen; and, when they are made a common stock upon which all men may draw, sound thinking and sobriety may be expected to be the general result.

One of the scenes to which the leisure of the laborious classes is seen to induce them to resort, is the public-house; and it is inferred that, if their leisure were greater, a greater degree of drunkenness, dissipation and riot would inevitably prevail.

In answer to this anticipation, I would in the first place assert, that the merits and demerits of the public-house are very unjustly rated by the fastidious among the more favoured orders of society.

We ought to consider that the opportunities and amusements of the lower orders of society are few. They do not frequent coffee-houses; theatres and places of public exhibition are ordinarily too expensive for them; and they cannot engage in rounds of visiting, thus cultivating a private and familiar intercourse with the few whose conversation might be most congenial to them. We certainly bear hard upon persons in this rank of society, if we expect that they should take all the severer labour, and have no periods of unbending and amusement.

But in reality what occurs in the public-house we are too much in the habit of calumniating. If we would visit this scene, we should find it pretty extensively a theatre of eager and earnest discussion. It is here that the ardent and "unwashed artificer," and the sturdy husbandman, compare notes and measure wits with each other. It is their arena of intellectual combat, the ludus literarius of their unrefined university. It is here they learn to think. Their minds are awakened from the sleep of ignorance; and their attention is turned into a thousand channels of improvement. They study the art of speaking, of question, allegation and rejoinder. They fix their thought steadily on the statement that is made, acknowledge its force, or detect its insufficiency. They examine the most interesting topics, and form opinions the result of that examination. They learn maxims of life, and become politicians. They canvas the civil and criminal laws of their country, and learn the value of political liberty. They talk over measures of state, judge of the intentions, sagacity and sincerity of public men, and are likely in time to become in no contemptible degree capable of estimating what modes of conducting national affairs, whether for the preservation of the rights of all, or for the vindication and assertion of justice between man and man, may be expected to be crowned with the greatest success: in a word, they thus become, in the best sense of the word, citizens.

As to excess in drinking, the same thing may be expected to occur here, as has been remarked of late years in better company in England. In proportion as the understanding is cultivated, men are found to be less the victims of drinking and the grosser provocatives of sense. The king of Persia of old made it his boast that he could drink large quantities of liquor with greater impunity than any of his subjects. Such was not the case with the more polished Greeks. In the dark ages the most glaring enormities of that kind prevailed. Under our Charles the Second coarse dissipation and riot characterised the highest circles. Rochester, the most accomplished man and the greatest wit of our island, related of himself that, for five years together, he could not affirm that for any one day he had been thoroughly sober. In Ireland, a country less refined than our own, the period is not long past, when on convivial occasions the master of the house took the key from his door, that no one of his guests might escape without having had his dose. No small number of the contemporaries of my youth fell premature victims to the intemperance which was then practised. Now wine is merely used to excite a gayer and livelier tone of the spirits; and inebriety is scarcely known in the higher circles. In like manner, it may readily be believed that, as men in the lower classes of society become less ignorant and obtuse, as their thoughts are less gross, as they wear off the vestigia ruris, the remains of a barbarous state, they will find less need to set their spirits afloat by this animal excitement, and will devote themselves to those thoughts and that intercourse which shall inspire them with better and more honourable thoughts of our common nature.

ESSAY X. OF IMITATION AND INVENTION.

Of the sayings of the wise men of former times none has been oftener repeated than that of Solomon, "The thing that hath been, is that which is; and that which is done, is that which shall be done; and there is no new thing under the sun."

The books of the Old Testament are apparently a collection of the whole literary remains of an ancient and memorable people, whose wisdom may furnish instruction to us, and whose poetry abounds in lofty flights and sublime imagery. How this collection came indiscriminately to be considered as written by divine inspiration, it is difficult to pronounce. The history of the Jews, as contained in the Books of Kings and of Chronicles, certainly did not require the interposition of the Almighty for its production; and the pieces we receive as the compositions of Solomon have conspicuously the air of having emanated from a conception entirely human.

In the book of Ecclesiastes, from which the above sentence is taken, are many sentiments not in accordance with the religion of Christ. For example; "That which befalleth the sons of men, befalleth beasts; as the one dieth, so dieth the other; yea, they have all one breath, so that a man hath no preeminence above a beast: all go to one place; all are of the dust, and turn to dust again. Wherefore I perceive that there is nothing better, than that a man should rejoice in his works." And again, "The living know that they shall die; but the dead know not any thing; their love, and their hatred, and their envy are perished; neither have they any more a reward." Add to this, "Wherefore I praise the dead which are already dead, more than the living which are yet alive: yea, better is he than both they, which hath not yet been." There can therefore be no just exception taken against our allowing ourselves freely to canvas the maxim cited at the head of this Essay.

It certainly contains a sufficient quantity of unquestionable truth, to induce us to regard it as springing from profound observation, and comprehensive views of what is acted "under the sun."

A wise man would look at the labours of his own species, in much the same spirit as he would view an ant-hill through a microscope. He would see them tugging a grain of corn up a declivity; he would see the tracks that are made by those who go, and who return; their incessant activity; and would find one day the copy of that which went before; and their labours ending in nothing: I mean, in nothing that shall carry forward the improvement of the head and the heart, either in the individual or society, or that shall add to the conveniences of life, or the better providing for the welfare of communities of men. He would smile at their earnestness and zeal, all spent in supplying the necessaries of the day, or, at most, providing for the revolution of the seasons, or for that ephemeral thing we call the life of man.

Few things can appear more singular, when duly analysed, than that articulated air, which we denominate speech. It is not to be wondered at that we are proud of the prerogative, which so eminently distinguishes us from the rest of the animal creation. The dog, the cat, the horse, the bear, the lion, all of them have voice. But we may almost consider this as their reproach. They can utter for the greater part but one monotonous, eternal sound.

The lips, the teeth, the palate, the throat, which in man are instruments of modifying the voice in such endless variety, are in this respect given to them in vain: while all the thoughts that occur, at least to the bulk of mankind, we are able to express in words, to communicate facts, feelings, passions, sentiments, to discuss, to argue, to agree, to issue commands on the one part, and report the execution on the other, to inspire lofty conceptions, to excite the deepest feeling of commiseration, and to thrill the soul with extacy, almost too mighty to be endured.

Yet what is human speech for the most part but mere imitation? In the most obvious sense this stands out on the surface. We learn the same words, we speak the same language, as our elders. Not only our words, but our phrases are the same. We are like players, who come out as if they were real persons, but only utter what is set down for them. We represent the same drama every day; and, however stale is the eternal repetition, pass it off upon others, and even upon ourselves, as if it were the suggestion of the moment. In reality, in rural or vulgar life, the invention of a new phrase ought to be marked down among the memorable things in the calendar. We afford too much honour to ordinary conversation, when we compare it to the exhibition of the recognised theatres, since men ought for the most part to be considered as no more than puppets. They perform the gesticulations; but the words come from some one else, who is hid from the sight of the general observer. And not only the words, but the cadence: they have not even so much honour as players have, to choose the manner they may deem fittest by which to convey the sense and the passion of what they speak. The pronunciation, the dialect, all, are supplied to them, and are but a servile repetition. Our tempers are merely the work of the transcriber. We are angry, where we saw that others were angry; and we are pleased, because it is the tone to be pleased. We pretend to have each of us a judgment of our own: but in truth we wait with the most patient docility, till he whom we regard as the leader of the chorus gives us the signal, Here you are to applaud, and Here you are to condemn.

What is it that constitutes the manners of nations, by which the people of one country are so eminently distinguished from the people of another, so that you cannot cross the channel from Dover to Calais, twenty-one miles, without finding yourself in a new world? Nay, I need not go among the subjects of another government to find examples of this; if I pass into Ireland, Scotland or Wales, I see myself surrounded with a new people, all of whose characters are in a manner cast in one mould, and all different from the citizens of the principal state and from one another. We may go further than this. Not only nations, but classes of men, are contrasted with each other. What can be more different than the gentry of the west end of this metropolis, and the money-making dwellers in the east? From them I will pass to Billingsgate and Wapping. What more unlike than a soldier and a sailor? the children of fashion that stroll in St. James's and Hyde Park, and the care-worn hirelings, that recreate themselves, with their wives and their brats, with a little fresh air on a Sunday near Islington? The houses of lords and commons have each their characteristic manners. Each profession has its own, the lawyer, the divine, and the man of medicine. We are all apes, fixing our eyes upon a model, and copying him, gesture by gesture. We are sheep, rushing headlong through the gap, when the bell-wether shews us the way. We are choristers, mechanically singing in a certain key, and giving breath to a certain tone.

Our religion, our civil practices, our political creed, are all imitation. How many men are there, that have examined the evidences of their religious belief, and can give a sound "reason of the faith that is in them?" When I was a child, I was taught that there were four religions in the world, the Popish, the Protestant, the Mahometan, the Pagan. It is a phenomenon to find the man, who has held the balance steadily, and rendered full and exact justice to the pretensions of each of these. No: tell me the longitude and latitude in which a man is born, and I will tell you his religion.

> *By education most have been misled;*
>
> *So they believe, because they so were bred:*
>
> *The priest continues what the nurse began,*
>
> *And thus the child imposes on the man.*

And, if this happens, where we are told our everlasting salvation is at issue, we may easily judge of the rest.

The author, with one of whose dicta I began this Essay, has observed, "One generation passeth away, and another generation cometh; but the earth abideth for ever." It is a maxim of the English constitution, that "the king never dies;" and the same may with nearly equal propriety be observed of every private man, especially if he have children. "Death," say the writers of natural history, "is the generator of life:" and what is thus true of animal corruption, may with small variation be affirmed of human mortality. I turn off my footman, and hire another; and he puts on the livery of his predecessor: he thinks himself somebody; but he is only a tenant. The same thing is true, when a country-gentleman, a noble, a bishop, or a king dies. He puts off his garments, and another puts them on. Every one knows the story of the Tartarian dervise, who mistook the royal palace for a caravansera, and who proved to his majesty by genealogical deduction, that he was only a lodger. In this sense the mutability, which so eminently characterises every thing sublunary, is immutability under another name.

The most calamitous, and the most stupendous scenes are nothing but an eternal and wearisome repetition: executions, murders, plagues, famine and battle. Military execution, the demolition of cities, the conquest of nations, have been acted a hundred times before. The mighty conqueror, who "smote the people in wrath with a continual stroke," who "sat in the seat of God, shewing himself that he was God," and assuredly persuaded himself that he was doing something to be had in everlasting remembrance, only did that which a hundred other vulgar conquerors had done in successive ages of the world, whose very names have long since perished from the records of mankind.

Thus it is that the human species is for ever engaged in laborious idleness. We put our shoulder to the wheel, and raise the vehicle out of the mire in which it was swallowed, and we say, I have done something; but the same feat under the same circumstances has been performed a thousand times before. We make what strikes us as a profound observation; and, when fairly analysed, it turns out to be about as sagacious, as if we told what's o'clock, or whether it is rain or sunshine. Nothing can be more delightfully ludicrous, than the important and emphatical air with which the herd of mankind enunciate the most trifling observations. With much labour we are delivered of what is to us a new thought; and, after a time, we find the same in a musty volume, thrown by in a corner, and covered with cobwebs and dust.

This is pleasantly ridiculed in the well known exclamation, "Deuce take the old fellows who gave utterance to our wit, before we ever thought of it!"

The greater part of the life of the mightiest genius that ever existed is spent in doing nothing, and saying nothing. Pope has observed of Shakespear's plays, that, "had all the speeches been printed without the names of the persons, we might have applied them with certainty to every speaker." To which another critic has rejoined, that that was impossible, since the greater part of what every man says is unstamped with peculiarity. We have all more in us of what belongs to the common nature of man, than of what is peculiar to the individual.

It is from this beaten, turnpike road, that the favoured few of mankind are for ever exerting themselves to escape. The multitude grow up, and are carried away, as grass is carried away by the mower. The parish-register tells when they were born, and when they died: "known by the ends of being to have been." We pass away, and leave nothing behind. Kings, at whose very glance thousands have trembled, for the most part serve for nothing when their breath has ceased, but as a sort of distance-posts in the race of chronology. "The dull swain treads on" their relics "with his clouted shoon." Our monuments are as perishable as ourselves; and it is the most hopeless of all problems for the most part, to tell where the mighty ones of the earth repose.

All men are aware of the frailty of life, and how short is the span assigned us. Hence every one, who feels, or thinks he feels the power to do so, is desirous to embalm his memory, and to be thought of by a late posterity, to whom his personal presence shall be unknown. Mighty are the struggles; everlasting the efforts. The greater part of these we well know are in vain. It is Aesop's mountain in labour: "Dire was the tossing, deep the groans:" and the result is a mouse. But is it always so?

This brings us back to the question: "Is there indeed nothing new under the sun?"

Most certainly there is something that is new. If, as the beast dies, so died man, then indeed we should be without hope. But it is his distinguishing faculty, that he can leave something behind, to testify that he has lived. And this is not only true of the pyramids of Egypt, and certain other works of human industry, that time seems to have no force to destroy. It is often true of a single sentence, a single word, which the multitudinous sea is incapable of washing away:

Quod non imber edax, non Aquilo impotens

Possit diruere, aut innumerabilis

Annorum series, et fuga temporum.

It is the characteristic of the mind and the heart of man, that they are progressive. One word, happily interposed, reaching to the inmost soul, may "take away the heart of stone, and introduce a heart of flesh." And, if an individual may be thus changed, then his children, and his connections, to the latest page of unborn history.

This is the true glory of man, that "one generation doth not pass away, and another come, velut unda supervenit undam;" but that we leave our improvements behind us. What infinite ages of refinement on refinement, and ingenuity on ingenuity, seem each to have contributed its quota, to make up the accommodations of every day of civilised man; his table, his chair, the bed he lies on, the food he eats, the garments that cover him! It has often been said, that the four quarters of the world are put under contribution, to provide the most moderate table. To this what mills, what looms, what machinery of a thousand denominations, what ship-building, what navigation, what fleets are required! Man seems to have been sent into the world a naked, forked, helpless animal, on purpose to call forth his ingenuity to supply the accommodations that may conduce to his well-being. The saying, that "there is nothing new under the sun," could never have been struck out, but in one of the two extreme states of man, by the naked savage, or by the highly civilised beings among whom the perfection of refinement has produced an artificial feeling of uniformity.

The thing most obviously calculated to impress us with a sense of the power, and the comparative sublimity of man, is, if we could make a voyage of some duration in a balloon, over a considerable tract of the cultivated and the desert parts of the earth. A brute can scarcely move a stone out of his way, if it has fallen upon the couch where he would repose. But man cultivates fields, and plants gardens; he constructs parks and canals; he turns the course of rivers, and stretches vast artificial moles into the sea; he levels mountains, and builds a bridge, joining in giddy height one segment of the Alps to another; lastly, he founds castles, and churches, and towers, and distributes mighty cities at his pleasure over the face of the globe. "The first earth has passed away, and another earth has come; and all things are made new."

It is true, that the basest treacheries, the most atrocious cruelties, butcheries, massacres, violations of all the restraints of decency, and all the ties of nature, fields covered with dead bodies, and flooded with human gore, are all of them vulgar repetitions of what had been acted countless times already. If Nero or Caligula thought to perpetrate that which should stand unparalleled, they fell into the grossest error. The conqueror, who should lay waste vast portions of the globe, and destroy mighty cities, so that "thorns should come up in the palaces, and nettles in the fortresses thereof, and they should be a habitation of serpents, and a court for owls, and the wild beasts of the desert should meet there," would only do what Tamerlane, and Aurengzebe, and Zingis, and a hundred other conquerors, in every age and quarter of the world, had done before. The splendour of triumphs, and the magnificence of courts, are so essentially vulgar, that history almost disdains to record them.

And yet there is something that is new, and that by the reader of discernment is immediately felt to be so.

We read of Moses, that he was a child of ordinary birth, and, when he was born, was presently marked, as well as all the male children of his race, for destruction. He was unexpectedly preserved; and his first act, when he grew up, was to slay an Egyptian, one of the race to whom all his countrymen were slaves, and to fly into exile. This man, thus friendless and alone, in due time returned, and by the mere energy of his character prevailed upon his whole race to make common cause with him, and to migrate to a region, in which they should become sovereign and independent. He had no soldiers, but what were made so by the ascendancy of his spirit no counsellors but such as he taught to be wise, no friends but those who were moved by the sentiment they caught from him. The Jews he commanded were sordid and low of disposition, perpetually murmuring against his rule, and at every unfavourable accident calling to remembrance "the land of Egypt, where they had sat by the fleshpots, and were full." Yet over this race he retained a constant mastery, and finally made of them a nation whose customs and habits and ways of thinking no time has availed to destroy. This was a man then, that possessed the true secret to make other men his creatures, and lead them with an irresistible power wherever he pleased. This history, taken entire, has probably no parallel in the annals of the world.

The invasion of Greece by the Persians, and its result, seem to constitute an event that stands alone among men. Xerxes led against this little territory an army of 5,280,000 men. They drank up rivers, and cut their way through giant-mountains. They were first stopped at Thermopylae by Leonidas and his three hundred Spartans. They fought for a country too narrow to contain the army by which the question was to be tried. The contest was here to be decided between despotism and liberty, whether there is a principle in man, by which a handful of individuals, pervaded with lofty sentiments, and a conviction of what is of most worth in our nature, can defy the brute force, and put to flight the attack, of bones, joints and sinews, though congregated in multitudes, numberless as the waves of the sea, or the sands on its shore. The flood finally rolled back: and in process of time Alexander, with these Greeks whom the ignorance of the East affected to despise, founded another universal monarchy on the ruins of Persia. This is certainly no vulgar history.

Christianity is another of those memorable chapters in the annals of mankind, to which there is probably no second. The son of a carpenter in a little, rocky country, among a nation despised and enslaved, undertook to reform the manners of the people of whom he was a citizen. The reformation he preached was unpalatable to the leaders of the state; he was persecuted; and finally suffered the death reserved for the lowest malefactors, being nailed to a cross. He was cut off in the very beginning of his career, before he had time to form a sect. His immediate representatives and successors were tax-gatherers and fishermen. What could be more incredible, till proved by the event, than that a religion thus begun, should have embraced in a manner the whole civilised world, and that of its kingdom there should be no visible end? This is a novelty in the history of the world, equally if we consider it as brought about by the immediate interposition of the author of all things, or regard it, as some pretend to do, as happening in the course of mere human events.

Rome, "the eternal city," is likewise a subject that stands out from the vulgar history of the human race. Three times, in three successive forms, has she been the mistress of the world. First, by the purity, the simplicity, the single-heartedness, the fervour and perseverance of her original character she qualified herself to subdue all the nations of mankind. Next, having conquered the earth by her virtue and by the spirit of liberty, she was able to maintain her ascendancy for centuries under the emperors, notwithstanding all her astonishing profligacy and anarchy. And, lastly, after her secular ascendancy had been destroyed by the inroads of the northern barbarians, she rose like the phoenix from her ashes, and, though powerless in material force, held mankind in subjection by the chains of the mind, and the consummateness of her policy. Never was any thing so admirably contrived as the Catholic religion, to subdue the souls of men by the power of its worship over the senses, and, by its contrivances in auricular confession, purgatory, masses for the dead, and its claim magisterially to determine controversies, to hold the subjects it had gained in everlasting submission.

The great principle of originality is in the soul of man. And here again we may recur to Greece, the parent of all that is excellent in art. Painting, statuary, architecture, poetry, in their most exquisite and ravishing forms, originated in this little province. Is not the Iliad a thing new, and that will for ever remain new? Whether it was written by one man, as I believe, or, as the levellers of human glory would have us think, by many, there it stands: all the ages of the world present us nothing that can come in competition with it.

Shakespear is another example of unrivalled originality. His fame is like the giant-rivers of the world: the further it flows, the wider it spreads out its stream, and the more marvellous is the power with which it sweeps along.

But, in reality, all poetry and all art, that have a genuine claim to originality, are new, the smallest, as well as the greatest.

It is the mistake of dull minds only, to suppose that every thing has been said, that human wit is exhausted, and that we, who have unfortunately fallen upon the dregs of time, have no alternative left, but either to be silent, or to say over and over again, what has been well said already.

There remain yet immense tracts of invention, the mines of which have been untouched. We perceive nothing of the strata of earth, and the hidden fountains of water, that we travel over, unconscious of the treasures that are immediately within our reach, till some person, endowed with the gift of a superior sagacity, comes into the country, who appears to see through the opake and solid mass, as we see through the translucent air, and tells us of things yet undiscovered, and enriches us with treasures, of which we had been hitherto entirely ignorant. The nature of the human mind, and the capabilities of our species are in like manner a magazine of undiscovered things, till some mighty genius comes to break the surface, and shew us the wonderful treasures that lay beneath uncalled for and idle.

Human character is like the contents of an ample cabinet, brought together by the untired zeal of some curious collector, who tickets his rarities with numbers, and has a catalogue in many volumes, in which are recorded the description and qualities of the things presented to our view. Among the most splendid examples of character which the genius of man has brought to light, are Don Quixote and his trusty squire, sir Roger de Coverley, Parson Adams, Walter Shandy and his brother Toby. Who shall set bounds to the everlasting variety of nature, as she has recorded her creations in the heart of man? Most of these instances are recent, and sufficiently shew that the enterprising adventurer, who would aspire to emulate the illustrious men from whose writings these examples are drawn, has no cause to despair.

Vulgar observers pass carelessly by a thousand figures in the crowded masquerade of human society, which, when inscribed on the tablet by the pencil of a master, would prove not less wondrous in the power of affording pleasure, nor less rich as themes for inexhaustible reflection, than the most admirable of these. The things are there, and all that is wanting is an eye to perceive, and a pen to record them.

As to a great degree we may subscribe to the saying of the wise man, that "there is nothing new under the sun," so in a certain sense it may also be affirmed that nothing is old. Both of these maxims may be equally true. The prima materia, the atoms of which the universe is composed, is of a date beyond all record; and the figures which have yet been introduced into the most fantastic chronology, may perhaps be incompetent to represent the period of its birth. But the ways in which they may be compounded are exhaustless. It is like what the writers on the Doctrine of Chances tell us of the throwing of dice. How many men now exist on the face of the earth? Yet, if all these were brought together, and if, in addition to this, we could call up all the men that ever lived, it may be doubted, whether any two would be found so much alike, that a clear-sighted and acute observer might not surely distinguish the one from the other. Leibnitz informs us, that no two leaves of a tree exist in the most spacious garden, that, upon examination, could be pronounced perfectly similar(19).

(19) See above, Essay 2.

The true question is not, whether any thing can be found that is new, but whether the particulars in which any thing is new may not be so minute and trifling, as scarcely to enter for any thing, into that grand and comprehensive view of the whole, in which matters of obvious insignificance are of no account.

But, if art and the invention of the human mind are exhaustless, science is even more notoriously so. We stand but on the threshold of the knowledge of nature, and of the various ways in which physical power may be brought to operate for the accommodation of man. This is a business that seems to be perpetually in progress; and, like the fall of bodies by the power of gravitation, appears to gain in momentum, in proportion as it advances to a greater distance from the point at which the impulse was given. The discoveries which at no remote period have been made, would, if prophesied of, have been laughed to scorn by the ignorant sluggishness of former generations; and we are equally ready to regard with incredulity the discoveries yet unmade, which will be familiar to our posterity. Indeed every man of a capacious and liberal mind is willing to admit, that the progress of human understanding in science, which is now going on, is altogether without any limits that by the most penetrating genius can be assigned. It is like a mighty river, that flows on for ever and for ever, as far as the words, "for ever," can have a meaning to the comprehension of mortals. The question that remains is, our practicable improvement in literature and morals, and here those persons who entertain a mean opinion of human nature, are constantly ready to tell us that it will be found to amount to nothing. However we may be continually improving in mechanical knowledge and ingenuity, we are assured by this party, that we shall never surpass what has already been done in poetry and literature, and, which is still worse, that, however marvellous may be our future acquisitions in science and the application of science, we shall be, as much as ever, the creatures of that vanity, ostentation, opulence and the spirit of exclusive accumulation, which has hitherto, in most countries (not in all countries), generated the glaring inequality of property, and the oppression of the many for the sake of pampering the folly of the few.

There is another circumstance that may be mentioned, which, particularly as regards the question of repetition and novelty that is now under consideration, may seem to operate in an eminent degree in favour of science, while it casts a most discouraging veil over poetry and the pure growth of human fancy and invention. Poetry is, after all, nothing more than new combinations of old materials. Nihil est in intellectu, quod non fuit prius in sensu. The poet has perhaps in all languages been called a maker, a creator: but this seems to be a vain-glorious and an empty boast. He is a collector of materials only, which he afterwards uses as best he may be able. He answers to the description I have heard given of a tailor, a man who cuts to pieces whatever is delivered to him from the loom, that he may afterwards sew it together again. The poet therefore, we may be told, adds nothing to the stock of ideas and conceptions already laid up in the storehouse of mind. But the man who is employed upon the secrets of nature, is eternally in progress; day after day he delivers in to the magazine of materials for thinking and acting, what was not there before; he increases the stock, upon which human ingenuity and the arts of life are destined to operate. He does not, as the poet may be affirmed by his censurers to do, travel for ever in a circle, but continues to hasten towards a goal, while at every interval we may mark how much further he has proceeded from the point at which his race began.

Much may be said in answer to this, and in vindication and honour of the poet and the artist. All that is here alleged to their disadvantage, is in reality little better than a sophism. The consideration of the articles he makes use of, does not in sound estimate detract from the glories of which he is the artificer. Materiem superat opus. He changes the nature of what he handles; all that he touches is turned into gold. The manufacture he delivers to us is so new, that the thing it previously was, is no longer recognisable. The impression that he makes upon the imagination and the heart, the impulses that he communicates to the understanding and the moral feeling, are all his own; and, "if there is any thing lovely and of good report, if there is any virtue and any praise," he may well claim our applauses and our thankfulness for what he has effected.

There is a still further advantage that belongs to the poet and the votarist of polite literature, which ought to be mentioned, as strongly calculated to repress the arrogance of the men of science, and the supercilious contempt they are apt to express for those who are engrossed by the pursuits of imagination and taste. They are for ever talking of the reality and progressiveness of their pursuits, and telling us that every step they take is a point gained, and gained for the latest posterity, while the poet merely suits himself to the taste of the men among whom he lives, writes up to the fashion of the day, and, as our manners turn, is sure to be swept away to the gulph of oblivion. But how does the matter really stand? It is to a great degree the very reverse of this.

The natural and experimental philosopher has nothing sacred and indestructible in the language and form in which he delivers truths. New discoveries and experiments come, and his individual terms and phrases and theories perish. One race of natural philosophers does but prepare the way for another race, which is to succeed. They "blow the trumpet, and give out the play." And they must be contented to perish before the brighter knowledge, of which their efforts were but the harbingers. The Ptolemaic system gave way to Tycho Brahe, and his to that of Copernicus. The vortices of Descartes perished before the discoveries of Newton; and the philosophy of Newton already begins to grow old, and is found to have weak and decaying parts mixed with those which are immortal and divine. In the science of mind Aristotle and Plato are set aside; the depth of Malebranche, and the patient investigation of Locke have had their day; more penetrating, and concise, and lynx-eyed reasoners of our own country have succeeded; the German metaphysicians seem to have thrust these aside; and it perhaps needs no great degree of sagacity to foresee, that Kant and Fichte will at last fare no better than those that went before them.

But the poet is immortal. The verses of Homer are of workmanship no less divine, than the armour of his own Achilles. His poems are as fresh and consummate to us now, as they were to the Greeks, when the old man of Chios wandered in person through the different cities, rehearsing his rhapsodies to the accompaniment of his lute. The language and the thoughts of the poet are inextricably woven together; and the first is no more exposed to decay and to perish than the last. Presumptuous innovators have attempted to modernise Chaucer, and Spenser, and other authors, whose style was supposed to have grown obsolete. But true taste cannot endure the impious mockery. The very words that occurred to these men, when the God descended, and a fire from heaven tingled in all their veins, are sacred, are part of themselves; and you may as well attempt to preserve the man when you have deprived him of all his members, as think to preserve the poet when you have taken away the words that he spoke. No part of his glorious effusions must perish; and "the hairs of his head are all numbered."

ESSAY XI. OF SELF-LOVE AND BENEVOLENCE.

NO question has more memorably exercised the ingenuity of men who have speculated upon the structure of the human mind, than that of the motives by which we are actuated in our intercourse with our fellow-creatures. The dictates of a plain and unsophisticated understanding on the subject are manifest; and they have been asserted in the broadest way by the authors of religion, the reformers of mankind, and all persons who have been penetrated with zeal and enthusiasm for the true interests of the race to which they belong.

"The end of the commandment," say the authors of the New Testament, "is love." "This is the great commandment of the law, Thou shalt love thy maker with all thy heart; and the second is like unto it, Thou shalt love thy neighbour as thyself." "Though I bestow all my goods to feed the poor, and give my body to be burned, and have not love, it profiteth me nothing." "For none of us liveth to himself; and no man dieth to himself."

The sentiments of the ancient Greeks and Romans, for so many centuries as their institutions retained their original purity, were cast in a mould of a similar nature. A Spartan was seldom alone; they were always in society with each other. The love of their country and of the public good was their predominant passion, they did not imagine that they belonged to themselves, but to the state. After the battle of Leuctra, in which the Spartans were defeated by the Thebans, the mothers of those who were slain congratulated one another, and went to the temples to thank the Gods, that their children had done their duty; while the relations of those who survived the defeat were inconsolable.

The Romans were not less distinguished by their self-denying patriotism. It was in this spirit that Brutus put his two sons to death for conspiring against their country. It was in this spirit that the Fabii perished at their fort on the Cremera, and the Decii devoted themselves for the public. The rigour of self-denial in a true Roman approached to a temper which moderns are inclined to denominate savage.

In the times of the ancient republics the impulse of the citizens was to merge their own individuality in the interests of the state. They held it their duty to live but for their country. In this spirit they were educated; and the lessons of their early youth regulated the conduct of their riper years.

In a more recent period we have learned to model our characters by a different standard. We seldom recollect the society of which we are politically members, as a whole, but are broken into detached parties, thinking only for the most part of ourselves and our immediate connections and attachments.

This change in the sentiments and manners of modern times has among its other consequences given birth to a new species of philosophy. We have been taught to affirm, that we can have no express and pure regard for our fellow-creatures, but that all our benevolence and affection come to us through the strainers of a gross or a refined self-love. The coarser adherents of this doctrine maintain, that mankind are in all cases guided by views of the narrowest self-interest, and that those who advance the highest claims to philanthropy, patriotism, generosity and self-sacrifice, are all the time deceiving others, or deceiving themselves, and use a plausible and high-sounding language merely, that serves no other purpose than to veil from observation "that hideous sight, a naked human heart."

The more delicate and fastidious supporters of the doctrine of universal self-love, take a different ground. They affirm that "such persons as talk to us of disinterestedness and pure benevolence, have not considered with sufficient accuracy the nature of mind, feeling and will. To understand," they say, "is one thing, and to choose another." The clearest proposition that ever was stated, has, in itself, no tendency to produce voluntary action on the part of the percipient. It can be only something apprehended as agreeable or disagreeable to us, that can operate so as to determine the will. Such is the law of universal nature. We act from the impulse of our own desires and aversions; and we seek to effect or avert a thing, merely because it is viewed by us as an object of gratification or the contrary.

The virtuous man and the vicious are alike governed by the same principle; and it is therefore the proper business of a wise instructor of youth, and of a man who would bring his own sentiments and feelings into the most praise-worthy frame, to teach us to find our interest and gratification in that which shall be most beneficial to others."

When we proceed to examine the truth of these statements, it certainly is not strictly an argument to say, that the advocate of self-love on either of these hypotheses cannot consistently be a believer in Christianity, or even a theist, as theism is ordinarily understood. The commandments of the author of the Christian religion are, as we have seen, purely disinterested: and, especially if we admit the latter of the two explanations of self-love, we shall be obliged to confess, on the hypothesis of this new philosophy, that the almighty author of the universe never acts in any of his designs either of creation or providence, but from a principle of self-love. In the mean time, if this is not strictly an argument, it is however but fair to warn the adherents of the doctrine I oppose, of the consequences to which their theory leads. It is my purpose to subvert that doctrine by means of the severest demonstration; but

I am not unwilling, before I begin, to conciliate, as far as may be, the good-will of my readers to the propositions I proceed to establish.

I will therefore further venture to add, that, upon the hypothesis of self-love, there can be no such thing as virtue. There are two circumstances required, to entitle an action to be denominated virtuous. It must have a tendency to produce good rather than evil to the race of man, and it must have been generated by an intention to produce such good. The most beneficent action that ever was performed, if it did not spring from the intention of good to others, is not of the nature of virtue. Virtue, where it exists in any eminence, is a species of conduct, modelled upon a true estimate of the good intended to be produced. He that makes a false estimate, and prefers a trivial and partial good to an important and comprehensive one, is vicious(20).

(20) *Political Justice, Book 11, Chap. IV.*

It is admitted on all hands, that it is possible for a man to sacrifice his own existence to that of twenty others. But the advocates of the doctrine of self-love must say, that he does this that he may escape from uneasiness, and because he could not bear to encounter the inward upbraiding with which he would be visited, if he acted otherwise. This in reality would change his action from an act of virtue to an act of vice. So far as belongs to the real merits of the case, his own advantage or pleasure is a very insignificant consideration, and the benefit to be produced, suppose to a world, is inestimable. Yet he falsely and unjustly prefers the first, and views the latter as trivial; nay, separately taken, as not entitled to the smallest regard. If the dictates of impartial justice be taken into the account, then, according to the system of self-love, the best action that ever was performed, may, for any thing we know, have been the action, in the whole world, of the most exquisite and deliberate injustice. Nay, it could not have been otherwise, since it produced the greatest good, and therefore was the individual instance, in which the greatest good was most directly postponed to personal gratification(21). Such is the spirit of the doctrine I undertake to refute.

(21) *Political Justice, Book IV, Chap. X.*

But man is not in truth so poor and pusillanimous a creature as this system would represent.

It is time however to proceed to the real merits of the question, to examine what in fact is the motive which induces a good man to elect a generous mode of proceeding.

Locke is the philosopher, who, in writing on Human Understanding, has specially delivered the doctrine, that uneasiness is the cause which determines the will, and urges us to act. He says(22), "The motive we have for continuing in the same state, is only the present satisfaction we feel in it; the motive to change is always some uneasiness: nothing setting us upon the change of state, or upon any new action, but some uneasiness. This is the great motive that works on the mind."

(22) Book II, Chap. XXI, Sect. 29.

It is not my concern to enquire, whether Locke by this statement meant to assert that self-love is the only principle of human action. It has at any rate been taken to express the doctrine which I here propose to refute.

And, in the first place, I say, that, if our business is to discover the consideration entertained by the mind which induces us to act, this tells us nothing. It is like the case of the Indian philosopher(23), who, being asked what it was that kept the earth in its place, answered, that it was supported by an elephant, and that elephant again rested on a tortoise. He must be endowed with a slender portion of curiosity, who, being told that uneasiness is that which spurs on the mind to act, shall rest satisfied with this explanation, and does not proceed to enquire, what makes us uneasy?

(23) Locke on Understanding, Book 11, Chap. XIII, Sect. 19.

An explanation like this is no more instructive, than it would be, if, when we saw a man walking, or grasping a sword or a bludgeon, and we enquired into the cause of this phenomenon, any one should inform us that he walks, because he has feet, and he grasps, because he has hands.

I could not commodiously give to my thoughts their present form, unless I had been previously furnished with pens and paper. But it would be absurd to say, that my being furnished with pens and paper, is the cause of my writing this Essay on Self-love and Benevolence.

The advocates of self-love have, very inartificially and unjustly, substituted the abstract definition of a voluntary agent, and made that stand for the motive by which he is prompted to act. It is true, that we cannot act without the impulse of desire or uneasiness; but we do not think of that desire and uneasiness; and it is the thing upon which the mind is fixed that constitutes our motive. In the boundless variety of the acts, passions and pursuits of human beings, it is absurd on the face of it to say that we are all governed by one motive, and that, however dissimilar are the ends we pursue, all this dissimilarity is the fruit of a single cause.

One man chooses travelling, another ambition, a third study, a fourth voluptuousness and a mistress. Why do these men take so different courses?

Because one is partial to new scenes, new buildings, new manners, and the study of character. Because a second is attracted by the contemplation of wealth and power. Because a third feels a decided preference for the works of Homer, or Shakespear, or Bacon, or Euclid. Because a fourth finds nothing calculated to stir his mind in comparison with female beauty, female allurements, or expensive living.

Each of these finds the qualities he likes, intrinsically in the thing he chooses. One man feels himself strongly moved, and raised to extacy, by the beauties of nature, or the magnificence of architecture. Another is ravished with the divine excellencies of Homer, or of some other of the heroes of literature. A third finds nothing delights him so much as the happiness of others, the beholding that happiness increased, and seeing pain and oppression and sorrow put to flight. The cause of these differences is, that each man has an individual internal structure, directing his partialities, one man to one thing, and another to another.

Few things can exceed the characters of human beings in variety. There must be something abstractedly in the nature of mind, which renders it accessible to these varieties. For the present we will call it taste. One man feels his spirits regaled with the sight of those things which constitute wealth, another in meditating the triumphs of Alexander or Caesar, and a third in viewing the galleries of the Louvre. Not one of these thinks in the outset of appropriating these objects to himself; not one of them begins with aspiring to be the possessor of vast opulence, or emulating the triumphs of Caesar, or obtaining in property the pictures and statues the sight of which affords him so exquisite delight. Even the admirer of female beauty, does not at first think of converting this attractive object into a mistress, but on the contrary desires, like Pygmalion, that the figure he beholds might become his solace and companion, because he had previously admired it for itself.

Just so the benevolent man is an individual who finds a peculiar delight in contemplating the contentment, the peace and heart's ease of other men, and sympathises in no ordinary degree with their sufferings. He rejoices in the existence and diffusion of human happiness, though he should not have had the smallest share in giving birth to the thing he loves. It is because such are his tastes, and what above all things he prefers, that he afterwards becomes distinguished by the benevolence of his conduct.

The reflex act of the mind, which these new philosophers put forward as the solution of all human pursuits, rarely presents itself but to the speculative enquirer in his closet. The savage never dreams of it. The active man, engaged in the busy scenes of life, thinks little, and on rare occasions of himself, but much, and in a manner for ever, of the objects of his pursuit.

Some men are uniform in their character, and from the cradle to the grave prefer the same objects that first awakened their partialities. Other men are inconsistent and given to change, are "every thing by starts, and nothing long." Still it is probable that, in most cases, he who performs an act of benevolence, feels for the time that he has a peculiar delight in contemplating the good of his fellow-man.

The doctrine of the modern philosophers on this point, is in many ways imbecil and unsound. It is inauspicious to their creed, that the reflex act of the mind is purely the affair of experience. Why did the liberal-minded man perform his first act of benevolence? The answer of these persons ought to be, because the recollection of a generous deed is a source of the truest delight. But there is an absurdity on the face of this solution.

We do not experimentally know the delight which attends the recollection of a generous deed, till a generous deed has been performed by us. We do not learn these things from books. And least of all is this solution to the purpose, when the business is to find a solution that suits the human mind universally, the unlearned as well as the learned, the savage as well as the sage.

And surely it is inconsistent with all sound reasoning, to represent that as the sole spring of our benevolent actions, which by the very terms will not fit the first benevolent act in which any man engaged.

The advocates of the doctrine of "self-love the source of all our actions," are still more puzzled, when the case set before them is that of the man, who flies, at an instant's warning, to save the life of the child who has fallen into the river, or the unfortunate whom he beholds in the upper story of a house in flames. This man, as might be illustrated in a thousand instances, treats his own existence as unworthy of notice, and exposes it to multiplied risks to effect the object to which he devotes himself.

They are obliged to say, that this man anticipates the joy he will feel in the recollection of a noble act, and the cutting and intolerable pain he will experience in the consciousness that a human being has perished, whom it was in his power to save. It is in vain that we tell them that, without a moment's consideration, he tore off his clothes, or plunged into the stream with his clothes on, or rushed up a flaming stair-case. Still they tell us, that he recollected what compunctious visitings would be his lot if he remained supine—he felt the sharpest uneasiness at sight of the accident before him, and it was to get rid of that uneasiness, and not for the smallest regard to the unhappy being he has been the means to save, that he entered on the hazardous undertaking.

Uneasiness, the knowledge of what inwardly passes in the mind, is a thing not in the slightest degree adverted to but in an interval of leisure. No; the man here spoken of thinks of nothing but the object immediately before his eyes; he adverts not at all to himself; he acts only with an undeveloped, confused and hurried consciousness that he may be of some use, and may avert the instantly impending calamity. He has scarcely even so much reflection as amounts to this.

The history of man, whether national or individual, and consequently the acts of human creatures which it describes, are cast in another mould than that which the philosophy of self-love sets before us. A topic that from the earliest accounts perpetually presents itself in the records of mankind, is self-sacrifice, parents sacrificing themselves for their children, and children for their parents. Cimon, the Athenian, yet in the flower of his youth, voluntarily became the inmate of a prison, that the body of his father might receive the honours of sepulture. Various and unquestionable are the examples of persons who have exposed themselves to destruction, and even petitioned to die, that so they might save the lives of those, whose lives they held dearer than their own. Life is indeed a thing, that is notoriously set at nothing by generous souls, who have fervently devoted themselves to an overwhelming purpose. There have been instances of persons, exposed to all the horrors of famine, where one has determined to perish by that slowest and most humiliating of all the modes of animal destruction, that another, dearer to him than life itself, might, if possible, be preserved.

What is the true explanation of these determinations of the human will? Is it, that the person, thus consigning himself to death, loved nothing but himself, regarded only the pleasure he might reap, or the uneasiness he was eager to avoid? Or, is it, that he had arrived at the exalted point of self-oblivion, and that his whole soul was penetrated and ingrossed with the love of those for whom he conceived so exalted a partiality?

This sentiment so truly forms a part of our nature, that a multitude of absurd practices, and a multitude of heart-rending fables, have been founded upon the consciousness of man in different ages and nations, that these modes of thinking form a constituent part of our common existence. In India there was found a woman, whose love to the deceased partner of her soul was so overwhelming, that she resolved voluntarily to perish on his funeral pile. And this example became so fascinating and admirable, that, by insensible degrees, it grew into a national custom with the Hindoos, that, by a sort of voluntary constraint, the widows of all men of a certain caste, should consign themselves to the flames with the dead bodies of their husbands. The story of Zopyrus cutting off his nose and ears, and of Curtius leaping into the gulph, may be fictitious: but it was the consciousness of those by whom these narratives were written that they drew their materials from the mighty store-house of the heart of man, that prompted them to record them. The institutions of clientship and clans, so extensively diffused in different ages of the world, rests upon this characteristic of our nature, that multitudes of men may be trained and educated so, as to hold their existence at no price, when the life of the individual they were taught unlimitedly to reverence might be preserved, or might be defended at the risk of their destruction.

The principal circumstance that divides our feelings for others from our feelings for ourselves, and that gives, to satirical observers, and superficial thinkers, an air of exclusive selfishness to the human mind, lies in this, that we can fly from others, but cannot fly from ourselves. While I am sitting by the bed-side of the sufferer, while I am listening to the tale of his woes, there is comparatively but a slight line of demarcation, whether they are his sorrows or my own. My sympathy is vehemently excited towards him, and I feel his twinges and anguish in a most painful degree. But I can quit his apartment and the house in which he dwells, can go out in the fields, and feel the fresh air of heaven fanning my hair, and playing upon my cheeks. This is at first but a very imperfect relief. His image follows me; I cannot forget what I have heard and seen; I even reproach myself for the mitigation I involuntarily experience. But man is the creature of his senses. I am every moment further removed, both in time and place, from the object that distressed me. There he still lies upon the bed of agony: but the sound of his complaint, and the sight of all that expresses his suffering, are no longer before me. A short experience of human life convinces us that we have this remedy always at hand ("I am unhappy, only while I please")(24); and we soon come therefore to anticipate the cure, and so, even while we are in the presence of the sufferer, to feel that he and ourselves are not perfectly one.

(24) Douglas.

But with our own distempers and adversities it is altogether different. It is this that barbs the arrow. We may change the place of our local existence; but we cannot go away from ourselves. With chariots, and embarking ourselves on board of ships, we may seek to escape from the enemy. But grief and apprehension enter the vessel along with us; and, when we mount on horseback, the discontent that specially annoyed us, gets up behind, and clings to our sides with a hold never to be loosened(25).

(25) Horace.

Is it then indeed a proof of selfishness, that we are in a greater or less degree relieved from the anguish we endured for our friend, when other objects occupy us, and we are no longer the witnesses of his sufferings? If this were true, the same argument would irresistibly prove, that we are the most generous of imaginable beings, the most disregardful of whatever relates to ourselves. Is it not the first ejaculation of the miserable, "Oh, that I could fly from myself? Oh, for a thick, substantial sleep!" What the desperate man hates is his own identity. But he knows that, if for a few moments he loses himself in forgetfulness, he will presently awake to all that distracted him. He knows that he must act his part to the end, and drink the bitter cup to the dregs. He can do none of these things by proxy. It is the consciousness of the indubitable future, from which we can never be divorced, that gives to our present calamity its most fearful empire. Were it not for this great line of distinction, there are many that would feel not less for their friend than for themselves. But they are aware, that his ruin will not make them beggars, his mortal disease will not bring them to the tomb, and that, when he is dead, they may yet be reserved for many years of health, of consciousness and vigour.

The language of the hypothesis of self-love was well adapted to the courtiers of the reign of Louis the Fourteenth. The language of disinterestedness was adapted to the ancient republicans in the purest times of Sparta and Rome.

But these ancients were not always disinterested; and the moderns are not always narrow, self-centred and cold. The ancients paid, though with comparative infrequency, the tax imposed upon mortals, and thought of their own gratification and ease; and the moderns are not utterly disqualified for acts of heroic affection.

It is of great consequence that men should come to think correctly on this subject. The most snail-blooded man that exists, is not so selfish as he pretends to be. In spite of all the indifference he professes towards the good of others, he will sometimes be detected in a very heretical state of sensibility towards his wife, his child or his friend; he will shed tears at a tale of distress, and make considerable sacrifices of his own gratification for the relief of others.

But his creed is a pernicious one. He who for ever thinks, that his "charity must begin at home," is in great danger of becoming an indifferent citizen, and of withering those feelings of philanthropy, which in all sound estimation constitute the crowning glory of man. He will perhaps have a reasonable affection towards what he calls his own flesh and blood, and may assist even a stranger in a case of urgent distress.—But it is dangerous to trifle with the first principles and sentiments of morality. And this man will scarcely in any case have his mind prepared to hail the first dawnings of human improvement, and to regard all that belongs to the welfare of his kind as parcel of his own particular estate.

The creed of self-love will always have a tendency to make us Frenchmen in the frivolous part of that character, and Dutchmen in the plodding and shopkeeping spirit of barter and sale. There is no need that we should beat down the impulse of heroism in the human character, and be upon our guard against the effervescences and excess of a generous sentiment. One of the instructors of my youth was accustomed to say to his pupils, "Do not be afraid to commit your thoughts to paper in all the fervour and glow of your first conception: when you come to look at them the next day, you will find this gone off to a surprising degree." As this was no ill precept for literary composition, even so in our actions and moral conduct we shall be in small danger of being too warm-hearted and too generous.

Modern improvements in education are earnest in recommending to us the study of facts, and that we should not waste the time of young persons upon the flights of imagination. But it is to imagination that we are indebted for our highest enjoyments; it tames the ruggedness of uncivilised nature, and is the never-failing associate of all the considerable advances of social man, whether in throwing down the strong fences of intellectual slavery, or in giving firmness and duration to the edifice of political freedom.

And who does not feel that every thing depends upon the creed we embrace, and the discipline we exercise over our own souls?

The disciple of the theory of self-love, if of a liberal disposition, will perpetually whip himself forward "with loose reins," upon a spiritless Pegasus, and say, "I will do generous things; I will not bring into contempt the master I serve—though I am conscious all the while that this is but a delusion, and that, however I brag of generosity, I do not set a step forward, but singly for my own ends, and my own gratification." Meanwhile, this is all a forced condition of thought; and the man who cherishes it, will be perpetually falling back into the cold, heartless convictions he inwardly retains. Self-love is the unwholesome, infectious atmosphere in which he dwells; and, however he may seek to rise, the wings of his soul will eternally be drawn downwards, and he cannot be pervaded, as he might have been, with the free spirit of genuine philanthropy. To be consistent, he ought continually to grow colder and colder; and the romance, which fired his youth, and made him forget the venomous potion he had swallowed, will fade away in age, rendering him careless of all but himself, and indifferent to the adversity and sufferings of all of whom he hears, and all with whom he is connected.

On the other hand, the man who has embraced the creed of disinterested benevolence, will know that it is not his fitting element to "live for himself, or to die for himself." Whether he is under the dominion of family-affection, friendship, patriotism, or a zeal for his brethren of mankind, he will feel that he is at home. The generous man therefore looks forward to the time when the chilling and wretched philosophy of the reign of Louis the Fourteenth shall be forgotten, and a fervent desire for the happiness and improvement of the human species shall reign in all hearts.

I am not especially desirous of sheltering my opinions under the authority of great names: but, in a question of such vital importance to the true welfare of men in society, no fair advantage should be neglected. The author of the system of "self-love the source of all our actions" was La Rochefoucault; and the whole herd of the French philosophers have not been ashamed to follow in the train of their vaunted master. I am grieved to say, that, as I think, the majority of my refining and subtilising countrymen of the present day have enlisted under his banner. But the more noble and generous view of the subject has been powerfully supported by Shaftesbury, Butler, Hutcheson and Hume. On the last of these I particularly pique myself; inasmuch as, though he became naturalised as a Frenchman in a vast variety of topics, the greatness of his intellectual powers exempted him from degradation in this.

That however which I would chiefly urge in the way of authority, is the thing mentioned in the beginning of this Essay, I mean, the sentiments that have animated the authors of religion, that characterise the best ages of Greece and Rome, and that in all cases display themselves when the loftiest and most generous sentiments of the heart are called into action. The opposite creed could only have been engendered in the dregs of a corrupt and emasculated court; and human nature will never shew itself what it is capable of being, till the last remains of a doctrine, invented in the latter part of the seventeenth century, shall have been consigned to the execration they deserve.

ESSAY XII. OF THE LIBERTY OF HUMAN ACTIONS.

The question, which has been attended with so long and obstinate debates, concerning the metaphysical doctrines of liberty and necessity, and the freedom of human actions, is not even yet finally and satisfactorily settled.

The negative is made out by an argument which seems to amount to demonstration, that every event requires a cause, a cause why it is as it is and not otherwise, that the human will is guided by motives, and is consequently always ruled by the strongest motive, and that we can never choose any thing, either without a motive of preference, or in the way of following the weaker, and deserting the stronger motive(26).

(26) Political Justice, Book IV, Chap. VII.

Why is it then that disbelief or doubt should still subsist in a question so fully decided?

For the same reason that compels us to reject many other demonstrations. The human mind is so constituted as to oblige us, if not theoretically, at least practically, to reject demonstration, and adhere to our senses.

The case is thus in the great question of the non-existence of an external world, or of matter. How ever much the understanding may be satisfied of the truth of the proposition by the arguments of Berkeley and others, we no sooner go out into actual life, than we become convinced, in spite of our previous scepticism or unbelief, of the real existence of the table, the chair, and the objects around us, and of the permanence and reality of the persons, both body and mind, with whom we have intercourse. If we were not, we should soon become indifferent to their pleasure and pain, and in no long time reason ourselves into the opinion that the one was not more desirable than the other, and conduct ourselves accordingly.

But there is a great difference between the question of a material world, and the question of liberty and necessity. The most strenuous Berkleian can never say, that there is any contradiction or impossibility in the existence of matter. All that he can consistently and soberly maintain is, that, if the material world exists, we can never perceive it, and that our sensations, and trains of impressions and thinking go on wholly independent of that existence.

But the question of the freedom of human actions is totally of another class. To say that in our choice we reject the stronger motive, and that we choose a thing merely because we choose it, is sheer nonsense and absurdity; and whoever with a sound understanding will fix his mind upon the state of the question will perceive its impossibility.

In the mean time it is not less true, that every man, the necessarian as well as his opponent, acts on the assumption of human liberty, and can never for a moment, when he enters into the scenes of real life, divest himself of this persuasion.

Let us take separately into our consideration the laws of matter and of mind. We acknowledge generally in both an established order of antecedents and consequents, or of causes and effects. This is the sole foundation of human prudence and of all morality. It is because we foresee that certain effects will follow from a certain mode of conduct, that we act in one way rather than another. It is because we foresee that, if the soil is prepared in a certain way, and if seed is properly scattered and covered up in the soil thus prepared, a crop will follow, that we engage in the labours of agriculture. In the same manner, it is because we foresee that, if lessons are properly given, and a young person has them clearly explained to him, certain benefits will result, and because we are apprised of the operation of persuasion, admonition, remonstrance, menace, punishment and reward, that we engage in the labours of education. All the studies of the natural philosopher and the chemist, all our journeys by land and our voyages by sea, and all the systems and science of government, are built upon this principle, that from a certain method of proceeding, regulated by the precepts of wisdom and experience, certain effects may be expected to follow.

Yet, at the same time that we admit of a regular series of cause and effect in the operations both of matter and mind, we never fail, in our reflections upon each, to ascribe to them an essential difference. In the laws by which a falling body descends to the earth, and by which the planets are retained in their orbits, in a word, in all that relates to inanimate nature, we readily assent to the existence of absolute laws, so that, when we have once ascertained the fundamental principles of astronomy and physics, we rely with perfect assurance upon the invariable operation of these laws, yesterday, to-day, and for ever. As long as the system of things, of which we are spectators, and in which we act our several parts, shall remain, so long have the general phenomena of nature gone on unchanged for more years of past ages than we can define, and will in all probability continue to operate for as many ages to come. We admit of no variation, but firmly believe that, if we were perfectly acquainted with all the causes, we could, without danger of error, predict all the effects. We are satisfied that, since first the machine of the universe was set going, every thing in inanimate nature has taken place in a regular course, and nothing has happened and can happen, otherwise than as it actually has been and will be.

But we believe, or, more accurately speaking, we feel, that it is otherwise in the universe of mind. Whoever attentively observes the phenomena of thinking and sentient beings, will be convinced, that men and animals are under the influence of motives, that we are subject to the predominance of the passions, of love and hatred, of desire and aversion, of sorrow and joy, and that the elections we make are regulated by impressions supplied to us by these passions. But we are fully penetrated with the notion, that mind is an arbiter, that it sits on its throne, and decides, as an absolute prince, this may or that; in short, that, while inanimate nature proceeds passively in an eternal chain of cause and effect, mind is endowed with an initiating power, and forms its determinations by an inherent and indefeasible prerogative.

Hence arises the idea of contingency relative to the acts of living and sentient beings, and the opinion that, while, in the universe of matter, every thing proceeds in regular course, and nothing has happened or can happen, otherwise than as it actually has been or will be, in the determinations and acts of living beings each occurrence may be or not be, and waits the mastery of mind to decide whether the event shall be one way or the other, both issues being equally possible till that decision has been made.

Thus, as was said in the beginning, we have demonstration, all the powers of our reasoning faculty, on one side, and the feeling, of our minds, an inward persuasion of which with all our efforts we can never divest ourselves, on the other. This phenomenon in the history of every human creature, had aptly enough been denominated, the "delusive sense of liberty(27)."

(27) The first writer, by whom this proposition was distinctly

enunciated, seems to have been Lord Kaimes, in his Essays on the

Principles of Morality and Natural Religion, published in 1751. But this

ingenious author was afterwards frightened with the boldness of his

own conclusions, and in the subsequent editions of his work endeavoured

ineffectually to explain away what he had said.

And, though the philosopher in his closet will for the most part fully assent to the doctrine of the necessity of human actions, yet this indestructible feeling of liberty, which accompanies us from the cradle to the grave, is entitled to our serious attention, and has never obtained that consideration from the speculative part of mankind, which must by no means be withheld, if we would properly enter into the mysteries of our nature. The necessarian has paid it very imperfect attention to the impulses which form the character of man, if he omits this chapter in the history of mind, while on the other hand the advocate of free will, if he would follow up his doctrine rigorously into all its consequences, would render all speculations on human character and conduct superfluous, put an end to the system of persuasion, admonition, remonstrance, menace, punishment and reward, annihilate the very essence of civil government, and bring to a close all distinction between the sane person and the maniac.

With the disciples of the latter of these doctrines I am by no means specially concerned. I am fully persuaded, as far as the powers of my understanding can carry me, that the phenomena of mind are governed by laws altogether as inevitable as the phenomena of matter, and that the decisions of our will are always in obedience to the impulse of the strongest motive.

The consequences of the principle implanted in our nature, by which men of every creed, when they descend into the scene of busy life, pronounce themselves and their fellow-mortals to be free agents, are sufficiently memorable.

From hence there springs what we call conscience in man, and a sense of praise or blame due to ourselves and others for the actions we perform.

How poor, listless and unenergetic would all our performances be, but for this sentiment! It is in vain that I should talk to myself or others, of the necessity of human actions, of the connection between cause and effect, that all industry, study and mental discipline will turn to account, and this with infinitely more security on the principle of necessity, than on the opposite doctrine, every thing I did would be without a soul. I should still say, Whatever I may do, whether it be right or wrong, I cannot help it; wherefore then should I trouble the master-spirit within me? It is either the calm feeling of self-approbation, or the more animated swell of the soul, the quick beatings of the pulse, the enlargement of the heart, the glory sparkling in the eye, and the blood flushing into the cheek, that sustains me in all my labours. This turns the man into what we conceive of a God, arms him with prowess, gives him a more than human courage, and inspires him with a resolution and perseverance that nothing can subdue.

In the same manner the love or hatred, affection or alienation, we entertain for our fellow-men, is mainly referable for its foundation to the "delusive sense of liberty." "We approve of a sharp knife rather than a blunt one, because its capacity is greater. We approve of its being employed in carving food, rather than in maiming men or other animals, because that application of its capacity is preferable. But all approbation or preference is relative to utility or general good. A knife is as capable as a man, of being employed in purposes of utility; and the one is no more free than the other as to its employment. The mode in which a knife is made subservient to these purposes, is by material impulse. The mode in which a man is made subservient, is by inducement and persuasion. But both are equally the affair of necessity(28)." These are the sentiments dictated to us by the doctrine of the necessity of human actions.

(28) Political Justice, Book IV, Chap. VIII.

But how different are the feelings that arise within us, as soon as we enter into the society of our fellow-creatures! "The end of the commandment is love." It is the going forth of the heart towards those to whom we are bound by the ties of a common nature, affinity, sympathy or worth, that is the luminary of the moral world. Without it there would have been "a huge eclipse of sun and moon;" or at best, as a well-known writer(29) expresses it in reference to another subject, we should have lived in "a silent and drab-coloured creation." We are prepared by the power that made us for feelings and emotions; and, unless these come to diversify and elevate our existence, we should waste our days in melancholy, and scarcely be able to sustain ourselves. The affection we entertain for those towards whom our partiality and kindness are excited, is the life of our life. It is to this we are indebted for all our refinement, and, in the noblest sense of the word, for all our humanity. Without it we should have had no sentiment (a word, however abused, which, when properly defined, comprises every thing that is the crown of our nature), and no poetry.—Love and hatred, as they regard our fellow-creatures, in contradistinction to the complacency, or the feeling of an opposite nature, which is excited in us towards inanimate objects, are entirely the offspring of the delusive sense of liberty.

(29) Thomas Paine.

The terms, praise and blame, express to a great degree the same sentiments as those of love and hatred, with this difference, that praise and blame in their simplest sense apply to single actions, whereas love and hatred are produced in us by the sum of those actions or tendencies, which constitute what we call character. There is also another difference, that love and hatred are engendered in us by other causes as well as moral qualities; but praise and blame, in the sense in which they are peculiarly applied to our fellow-mortals, are founded on moral qualities only. In love and hatred however, when they are intense or are lasting, some reference to moral qualities is perhaps necessarily implied. The love between the sexes, unless in cases where it is of a peculiarly transient nature, always comprises in it a belief that the party who is the object of our love, is distinguished by tendencies of an amiable nature, which we expect to see manifesting themselves in affectionate attentions and acts of kindness. Even the admiration we entertain for the features, the figure, and personal graces of the object of our regard, is mixed with and heightened by our expectation of actions and tones that generate approbation, and, if divested of this, would be of small signification or permanence. In like manner in the ties of affinity, or in cases where we are impelled by the consideration, "He also is a man as well as I," the excitement will carry us but a little way, unless we discover in the being towards whom we are moved some peculiarities which may beget a moral partiality and regard.

And, as towards our fellow-creatures, so in relation to ourselves, our moral sentiments are all involved with, and take their rise in, the delusive sense of liberty. It is in this that is contained the peculiar force of the terms virtue, duty, guilt and desert. We never pronounce these words without thinking of the action to which they refer, as that which might or might not be done, and therefore unequivocally approve or disapprove in ourselves and others. A virtuous man, as the term is understood by all, as soon as we are led to observe upon those qualities, and the exhibition of those qualities in actual life, which constitute our nature, is a man who, being in full possession of the freedom of human action, is engaged in doing those things which a sound judgment of the tendencies of what we do pronounces to be good.

Duty is a term that can scarcely be said to have a meaning, except that which it derives from the delusive sense of liberty. According to the creed of the necessarian, it expresses that mode of action on the part of the individual, which constitutes the best possible application of his capacity to the general benefit(30). In the mean time, if we confine ourselves to this definition, it may as well be taken to describe the best application of a knife, or any other implement proceeding from the hands of the manufacturer, as of the powers of a human being.

But we surely have a very different idea in our minds, when we employ the term duty. It is not agreeable to the use of language that we should use this term, except we speak of a being in the exercise of volition.

(30) Political Justice, Book II, Chap. IV.

Duty then means that which may justly be required of a human creature in the possession of liberty of action. It includes in its proper sense the conception of the empire of will, the notion that mind is an arbiter, that it sits on its throne, and decides, as an absolute prince, this way or that.

Duty is the performance of what is due, the discharge of a debt (debitum). But a knife owes nothing, and can in no sense be said to be held to one sort of application rather than another; the debt can only belong to a human being in possession of his liberty, by whom the knife may be applied laudably or otherwise.

A multitude of terms instantly occur to us, the application of which is limited in the same manner as the term duty is limited: such are, to owe, obligation, debt, bond, right, claim, sin, crime, guilt, merit and desert. Even reward and punishment, however they may be intelligible when used merely in the sense of motives employed, have in general acceptation a sense peculiarly derived from the supposed freedom of the human will.

The mode therefore in which the advocates of the doctrine of necessity have universally talked and written, is one of the most memorable examples of the hallucination of the human intellect. They have at all times recommended that we should translate the phrases in which we usually express ourselves on the hypothesis of liberty, into the phraseology of necessity, that we should talk no other language than that which is in correspondence with the severest philosophy, and that we should exert ourselves to expel all fallacious notions and delusions so much as from our recollection. They did not perceive what a wide devastation and destruction they were proposing of all the terms and phrases that are in use in the communications between man and man in actual life.—They might as well have recommended that we should rigorously bear in mind on the ordinary occasions of life, that there is no such thing as colour, that which we ordinary call by that name having no existence in external objects, but belonging only to our way of perceiving them.

The language which is suggested to us by the conception of the freedom of human actions, moulds the very first articulations of a child, "I will," and "I will not;" and is even distinctly conveyed by his gestures, before he arrives at the power of articulation. This is the explanation and key to his vehement and ungovernable movements, and his rebellion. The petulance of the stripling, the fervent and energetic exertions of the warrior, and the calm and unalterable resolution of the sage, all imply the same thing. Will, and a confidence in its efficiency, "travel through, nor quit us till we die." It is this which inspires us with invincible perseverance, and heroic energies, while without it we should be the most inert and soulless of blocks, the shadows of what history records and poetry immortalises, and not men.

Free will is an integral part of the science of man, and may be said to constitute its most important chapter. We might with as much propriety overlook the intelligence of the senses, that medium which acquaints us with an external world or what we call such, we might as well overlook the consideration of man's reason, his imagination or taste, as fail to dwell with earnest reflection and exposition upon that principle which lies at the foundation of our moral energies, fills us with a moral enthusiasm, prompts all our animated exertions on the theatre of the world, whether upon a wide or a narrow scale, and penetrates us with the most lively and fervent approbation or disapprobation of the acts of ourselves and others in which the forwarding or obstructing human happiness is involved.

But, though the language of the necessarian is at war with the indestructible feelings of the human mind, and though his demonstrations will for ever crumble into dust, when brought to the test of the activity of real life, yet his doctrines, to the reflecting and enlightened, will by no means be without their use. In the sobriety of the closet, we inevitably assent to his conclusions; nor is it easy to conceive how a rational man and a philosopher abstractedly can entertain a doubt of the necessity of human actions. And the number of these persons is perpetually increasing; enlarged and dispassionate views of the nature of man and the laws of the universe are rapidly spreading in the world. We cannot indeed divest ourselves of love and hatred, of the sentiments of praise and blame, and the ideas of virtue, duty, obligation, debt, bond, right, claim, sin, crime, guilt, merit and desert. And, if we could do so, the effects would be most pernicious, and the world be rendered a blank. We shall however unquestionably, as our minds grow enlarged, be brought to the entire and unreserved conviction, that man is a machine, that he is governed by external impulses, and is to be regarded as the medium only through the intervention of which previously existing causes are enabled to produce certain effects. We shall see, according to an expressive phrase, that he "could not help it," and, of consequence, while we look down from the high tower of philosophy upon the scene of human affairs, our prevailing emotion will be pity, even towards the criminal, who, from the qualities he brought into the world, and the various circumstances which act upon him from infancy, and form his character, is impelled to be the means of the evils, which we view with so profound disapprobation, and the existence of which we so entirely regret.

There is an old axiom of philosophy, which counsels us to "think with the learned, and talk with the vulgar;" and the practical application of this axiom runs through the whole scene of human affairs. Thus the most learned astronomer talks of the rising and setting of the sun, and forgets in his ordinary discourse that the earth is not for ever at rest, and does not constitute the centre of the universe. Thus, however we reason respecting the attributes of inanimate matter and the nature of sensation, it never occurs to us, when occupied with the affairs of actual life, that there is no heat in fire, and no colour in the rainbow.

In like manner, when we contemplate the acts of ourselves and our neighbours, we can never divest ourselves of the delusive sense of the liberty of human actions, of the sentiment of conscience, of the feelings of love and hatred, the impulses of praise and blame, and the notions of virtue, duty, obligation, right, claim, guilt, merit and desert. And it has sufficiently appeared in the course of this Essay, that it is not desirable that we should do so. They are these ideas to which the world we live in is indebted for its crowning glory and greatest lustre. They form the highest distinction between men and other animals, and are the genuine basis of self-reverence, and the conceptions of true nobility and greatness, and the reverse of these attributes, in the men with whom we live, and the men whose deeds are recorded in the never-dying page of history.

But, though the doctrine of the necessity of human actions can never form the rule of our intercourse with others, it will still have its use. It will moderate our excesses, and point out to us that middle path of judgment which the soundest philosophy inculcates. We shall learn, according to the apostolic precept, to "be angry, and sin not, neither let the sun go down upon our wrath." We shall make of our fellow-men neither idols to worship, nor demons to be regarded with horror and execration. We shall think of them, as of players, "that strut and fret their hour upon the stage, and then are heard no more." We shall "weep, as though we wept not, and rejoice, as though we rejoiced not, seeing that the fashion of this world passeth away." And, most of all, we shall view with pity, even with sympathy, the men whose frailties we behold, or by whom crimes are perpetrated, satisfied that they are parts of one great machine, and, like ourselves, are driven forward by impulses over which they have no real control.

ESSAY XIII. OF BELIEF.

One of the prerogatives by which man is eminently distinguished from all other living beings inhabiting this globe of earth, consists in the gift of reason.

Beasts reason. They are instructed by experience; and, guided by what they have already known of the series of events, they infer from the sense of what has gone before, an assured expectation of what is to follow. Hence, "beast walks with man, joint tenant of the shade;" and their sagacity is in many instances more unerring than ours, because they have no affectation to mislead them; they follow no false lights, no glimmering intimation of something half-anticipating a result, but trust to the plain, blunt and obvious dictates of their simple apprehension. This however is but the first step in the scale of reason, and is in strictness scarcely entitled to the name.

We set off from the same point from which they commence their career. But the faculty of articulate speech comes in, enabling us to form the crude elements of reason and inference into a code. We digest explanations of things, assigning the particulars in which they resemble other classes, and the particulars by which they are distinguished from whatever other classes have fallen under our notice. We frame propositions, and, detaching ourselves from the immediate impressions of sense, proceed to generalities, which exist only, in a way confused, and not distinctly adverted to, in the conceptions of the animal creation.

It is thus that we arrive at science, and go forward to those subtleties, and that perspicuity of explanation, which place man in a distinct order of being, leaving all the other inhabitants of earth at an immeasurable distance below him. It is thus that we communicate our discoveries to each other, and hand down the knowledge we have acquired, unimpaired and entire, through successive ages, and to generations yet unborn.

But in certain respects we pay a very high price for this distinction. It is to it that we must impute all the follies, extravagances and hallucinations of human intellect. There is nothing so absurd that some man has not affirmed, rendering himself the scorn and laughing-stock of persons of sounder understanding. And, which is worst, the more ridiculous and unintelligible is the proposition he has embraced, the more pertinaciously does he cling to it; so that creeds the most outrageous and contradictory have served as the occasion or pretext for the most impassioned debates, bloody wars, inhuman executions, and all that most deeply blots and dishonours the name of man—while often, the more evanescent and frivolous are the distinctions, the more furious and inexpiable have been the contentions they have produced.

The result of the whole, in the vast combinations of men into tribes and nations, is, that thousands and millions believe, or imagine they believe, propositions and systems, the terms of which they do not fully understand, and the evidence of which they have not considered. They believe, because so their fathers believed before them. No phrase is more commonly heard than, "I was born a Christian;" "I was born a Catholic, or a Protestant."

The priest continues what the nurse began,

And thus the child imposes on the man.

But this sort of belief forms no part of the subject of the present Essay. My purpose is to confine myself to the consideration of those persons, who in some degree, more or less, exercise the reasoning faculty in the pursuit of truth, and, having attempted to examine the evidence of an interesting and weighty proposition, satisfy themselves that they have arrived at a sound conclusion.

It is however the rarest thing in the world, for any one to found his opinion, simply upon the evidence that presents itself to him of the truth of the proposition which comes before him to be examined. Where is the man that breaks loose from all the shackles that in his youth had been imposed upon hills, and says to Truth, "Go on; whithersoever thou leadest, I am prepared to follow?" To weigh the evidence for and against a proposition, in scales so balanced, that the "division of the twentieth part of one poor scruple, the estimation of a hair," shall be recognised and submitted to, is the privilege of a mind of no ordinary fairness and firmness.

The Scriptures say "The heart of man is deceitful above all things." The thinking principle within us is so subtle, has passed through so many forms of instruction, and is under the influence and direction of such a variety of causes, that no man can accurately pronounce by what impulse he has been led to the conclusion in which he finally reposes. Every ingenuous person, who is invited to embrace a certain profession, that of the church for example, will desire, preparatorily to his final determination, to examine the evidences and the merits of the religion he embraces, that he may enter upon his profession under the influence of a sincere conviction, and be inspired with that zeal, in singleness of heart, which can alone prevent his vocation from being disgraceful to him. Yet how many motives are there, constraining him to abide in an affirmative conclusion? His friends expect this from him. Perhaps his own inclination leads him to select this destination rather than any other. Perhaps preferment and opulence wait upon his decision. If the final result of his enquiries lead him to an opposite judgment, to how much obloquy will he be exposed! Where is the man who can say that no unconscious bias has influenced him in the progress of his investigation?

Who shall pronounce that, under very different circumstances, his conclusions would not have been essentially other than they are?

But the enquiry of an active and a searching mind does not terminate on a certain day. He will be for ever revising and reconsidering his first determinations. It is one of the leading maxims of an honourable mind, that we must be, at all times, and to the last hour of our existence, accessible to conviction built upon new evidence, or upon evidence presented in a light in which it had not before been viewed. If then the probationer for the clerical profession was under some bias in his first investigation, how must it be expected to be with him, when he has already taken the vow, and received ordination? Can he with a calm and unaltered spirit contemplate the possibility, that the ground shall be cut away from under him, and that, by dint of irrefragable argument, he shall be stripped of his occupation, and turned out naked and friendless into the world?

But this is only one of the broadest and most glaring instances. In every question of paramount importance there is ever a secret influence urging me earnestly to desire to find one side of the question right and the other wrong. Shall I be a whig or a tory, believe a republic or a mixed monarchy most conducive to the improvement and happiness of mankind, embrace the creed of free will or necessity? There is in all cases a "strong temptation that waketh in the heart." Cowardice urges me to become the adherent of that creed, which is espoused by my nearest friends, or those who are most qualified to serve me. Enterprise and a courageous spirit on the contrary bid me embrace the tenet, the embracing of which shall most conduce to my reputation for extraordinary perspicuity and acuteness, and gain me the character of an intrepid adventurer, a man who dares commit himself to an unknown voyage.

In the question of religion, even when the consideration of the profession of an ecclesiastic does not occur, yet we are taught to believe that there is only one set of tenets that will lead us in the way of salvation. Faith is represented as the first of all qualifications. "If I had not come and spoken unto them, they had not had sin." With what heart then does a man set himself to examine, and scrupulously weigh the evidence on one side and the other, when some undiscerned frailty, some secret bias that all his care cannot detect, may lurk within, and insure for him the "greater condemnation?" I well remember in early life, with what tingling sensation and unknown horror I looked into the books of the infidels and the repositories of unlawful tenets, lest I should be seduced. I held it my duty to "prove all things;" but I knew not how far it might be my fate; to sustain the penalty attendant even upon an honourable and virtuous curiousity.

It is one of the most received arguments of the present day against religious persecution, that the judgments we form are not under the authority of our will, and that, for what it is not in our power to change, it is unjust we should be punished: and there is much truth in this. But it is not true to the fullest extent. The sentiments we shall entertain, are to a considerable degree at the disposal of inticements on the one side, and of menaces and apprehension on the other. That which we wish to believe, we are already greatly in progress to embrace; and that which will bring upon us disgrace and calamity, we are more than half prepared to reject. Persecution however is of very equivocal power: we cannot embrace one faith and reject another at the word of command.

It is a curious question to decide how far punishments and rewards may be made effectual to determine the religion of nations and generations of men. They are often unsuccessful. There is a feeling in the human heart, that prompts us to reject with indignation this species of tyranny. We become more obstinate in clinging to that which we are commanded to discard. We place our honour and our pride in the firmness of our resistance. "The blood of the martyrs is the seed of the church." Yet there is often great efficacy in persecution. It was the policy of the court of Versailles that brought almost to nothing the Huguenots of France. And there is a degree of persecution, if the persecuting party has the strength and the inexorableness to employ it, that it is perhaps beyond the prowess of human nature to stand up against.

The mind of the enquiring man is engaged in a course of perpetual research; and ingenuousness prompts us never to be satisfied with the efforts that we have made, but to press forward. But mind, as well as body, has a certain vis inertiae, and moves only as it is acted upon by impulses from without. With respect to the adopting new opinions, and the discovery of new truths, we must be indebted in the last resort, either to books, or the oral communications of our fellow-men, or to ideas immediately suggested to us by the phenomena of man or nature. The two former are the ordinary causes of a change of judgment to men: they are for the most part minds of a superior class only, that are susceptible of hints derived straight from the external world, without the understandings of other men intervening, and serving as a conduit to the new conceptions introduced. The two former serve, so to express it, for the education of man, and enable us to master, in our own persons, the points already secured, and the wisdom laid up in the great magazine of human knowledge; the last imparts to us the power of adding to the stock, and carrying forward by one step and another the improvements of which our nature is susceptible.

It is much that books, the unchanging records of the thoughts of men in former ages, are able to impart to us. For many of the happiest moments of our lives, for many of the purest and most exalted feelings of the human heart, we are indebted to them. Education is their province; we derive from them civilization and refinement; and we may affirm of literature, what

Otway has said of woman, "We had been brutes without you." It is thus that the acquisitions of the wise are handed down from age to age, and that we are enabled to mount step after step on the ladder of paradise, till we reach the skies.

But, inestimable as is the benefit we derive from books, there is something more searching and soul-stirring in the impulse of oral communication. We cannot shut our ears, as we shut our books; we cannot escape from the appeal of the man who addresses us with earnest speech and living conviction. It is thus, we are told, that, when Cicero pleaded before Caesar for the life of Ligarius, the conqueror of the world was troubled, and changed colour again and again, till at length the scroll prepared for the condemnation of the patriot fell from his hand. Sudden and irresistible conviction is chiefly the offspring of living speech. We may arm ourselves against the arguments of an author; but the strength of reasoning in him who addresses us, takes us at unawares. It is in the reciprocation of answer and rejoinder that the power of conversion specially lies. A book is an abstraction. It is but imperfectly that we feel, that a real man addresses us in it, and that what he delivers is the entire and deep-wrought sentiment of a being of flesh and blood like ourselves, a being who claims our attention, and is entitled to our deference. The living human voice, with a countenance and manner corresponding, constrains us to weigh what is said, shoots through us like a stroke of electricity, will not away from our memory, and haunts our very dreams. It is by means of this peculiarity in the nature of mind, that it has been often observed that there is from time to time an Augustan age in the intellect of nations, that men of superior powers shock with each other, and that light is struck from the collision, which most probably no one of these men would have given birth to, if they had not been thrown into mutual society and communion. And even so, upon a narrower scale, he that would aspire to do the most of which his faculties are susceptible, should seek the intercourse of his fellows, that his powers may be strengthened, and he may be kept free from that torpor and indolence of soul, which, without external excitement, are ever apt to take possession of us.

The man, who lives in solitude, and seldom communicates with minds of the same class as his own, works out his opinions with patient scrutiny, returns to the investigation again and again, imagines that he had examined the question on all sides, and at length arrives at what is to him a satisfactory conclusion. He resumes the view of this conclusion day after day; he finds in it an unalterable validity; he says in his heart, "Thus much I have gained; this is a real advance in the search after truth; I have added in a defined and palpable degree to what I knew before." And yet it has sometimes happened, that this person, after having been shut up for weeks, or for a longer period, in his sanctuary, living, so far as related to an exchange of oral disquisitions with his fellow-men, like Robinson Crusoe in the desolate island, shall come into the presence of one, equally clear-sighted, curious and indefatigable with himself, and shall hear from him an obvious and palpable statement, which in a moment shivers his sightly and glittering fabric into atoms. The statement was palpable and near at hand; it was a thin, an almost imperceptible partition that hid it from him; he wonders in his heart that it never occurred to his meditations. And yet so it is: it was hid from him for weeks, or perhaps for a longer period: it might have been hid from him for twenty years, if it had not been for the accident that supplied it. And he no sooner sees it, than he instantly perceives that the discovery upon which he plumed himself, was an absurdity, of which even a schoolboy might be ashamed.

A circumstance not less curious, among the phenomena which belong to this subject of belief, is the repugnance incident to the most ingenuous minds, which we harbour against the suddenly discarding an opinion we have previously entertained, and the adopting one which comes recommended to us with almost the force of demonstration. Nothing can be better founded than this repugnance. The mind of man is of a peculiar nature. It has been disputed whether we can entertain more than one idea at a time. But certain it is, that the views of the mind at any one time are considerably narrowed. The mind is like the slate of a schoolboy, which can contain only a certain number of characters of a given size, or like a moveable panorama, which places a given scene or landscape before me, and the space assigned, and which comes within the limits marked out to my perception, is full. Many things are therefore almost inevitably shut out, which, had it not been so, might have essentially changed the view of the case, and have taught me that it was a very different conclusion at which I ought to have arrived.

At first sight nothing can appear more unreasonable, than that I should hesitate to admit the seemingly irresistible force of the argument presented to me. An ingenuous disposition would appear to require that, the moment the truth, or what seems to be the truth, is set before me, I should pay to it the allegiance to which truth is entitled. If I do otherwise, it would appear to argue a pusillanimous disposition, a mind not prompt and disengaged to receive the impression of evidence, a temper that loves something else better than the lustre which all men are bound to recognise, and that has a reserve in favour of ancient prejudice, and of an opinion no longer supported by reason.

In fact however I shall act most wisely, and in the way most honourable to my character, if I resolve to adjourn the debate. No matter how complete the view may seem which is now presented to my consideration, or how irresistible the arguments: truth is too majestic a divinity, and it is of too much importance that I should not follow a delusive semblance that may shew like truth, not to make it in the highest degree proper that I should examine again and again, before I come to the conclusion to which I mean to affix my seal, and annex my sanction, "This is the truth." The ancient Goths of Germany, we are told, had a custom of debating every thing of importance to their state twice, once in the high animation of a convivial meeting, and once in the serene stillness of a morning consultation. Philip of Macedon having decided a cause precipitately, the party condemned by him immediately declared his resolution to appeal from the sentence. And to whom, said the king, wilt thou appeal? To Philip, was the answer, in the entire possession of his understanding.

Such is the nature of the human mind—at least, such I find to be the nature of my own—that many trains of thinking, many chains of evidence, the result of accumulated facts, will often not present themselves, at the time when their presence would be of the highest importance. The view which now comes before me is of a substance so close and well-woven, and of colours so brilliant and dazzling, that other matters in a certain degree remote, though of no less intrinsic importance, and equally entitled to influence my judgment in the question in hand, shall be entirely shut out, shall be killed, and fail to offer themselves to my perceptions.

It is a curious circumstance which Pope, a man of eminent logical power and acuteness, relates, that, having at his command in his youth a collection of all the tracts that had been written on both sides in the reign of James the Second, he applied himself with great assiduity to their perusal, and the consequence was, that he was a Papist and Protestant by turns, according to the last book he read(31).

(31) Correspondence with Atterbury, Letter IV.

This circumstance in the structure of the human understanding is well known, and is the foundation of many provisions that occur in the constitution of political society. How each man shall form his creed, and arrange those opinions by which his conduct shall be regulated, is of course a matter exclusively subjected to his own discretion. But, when he is called upon to act in the name of a community, and to decide upon a question in which the public is interested, he of necessity feels himself called upon to proceed with the utmost caution. A judge on the bench, a chancellor, is not contented with that sudden ray of mental illumination to which an ingenuous individual is often disposed to yield in an affair of abstract speculation. He feels that he is obliged to wait for evidence, the nature of which he does not yet anticipate, and to adjourn his decision. A deliberative council or assembly is aware of the necessity of examining a question again and again. It is upon this principle that the two houses of the English parliament are required to give a first, a second and a third reading, together with various other forms and technicalities, to the provision that is brought before them, previously to its passing into a law. And there is many a fundamental dogma and cornerstone of the sentiments that I shall emphatically call my own, that is of more genuine importance to the individual, than to a nation is a number of those regulations, which by courtesy we call acts of parliament.

Nothing can have a more glaring tendency to subvert the authority of my opinion among my fellow-men, than instability. "What went ye out into the wilderness to see" said Jesus Christ: "a reed shaken with the wind?" We ought at all times to be open to conviction. We ought to be ever ready to listen to evidence. But, conscious of our human frailty, it is seldom that we ought immediately to subscribe to the propositions, however specious, that are now for the first time presented to us. It is our duty to lay up in our memory the suggestions offered upon any momentous question, and not to suffer them to lose their inherent weight and impressiveness; but it is only through the medium of consideration and reconsideration, that they can become entitled to our full and unreserved assent.

The nature of belief, or opinion, has been well illustrated by Lord Shaftesbury(32). There are many notions or judgments floating in the mind of every man, which are mutually destructive of each other. In this sense men's opinions are governed by high and low spirits, by the state of the solids and fluids of the human body, and by the state of the weather. But in a paramount sense that only can be said to be a man's opinion which he entertains in his clearest moments, and from which, when he is most himself, he is least subject to vary. In this emphatical sense, I should say, a man does not always know what is his real opinion. We cannot strictly be said to believe any thing, in cases where we afterwards change our opinion without the introduction of some evidence that was unknown to us before. But how many are the instances in which we can be affirmed to be in the adequate recollection of all the evidences and reasonings which have at some time occurred to us, and of the opinions, together with the grounds on which they rested, which we conceived we had justly and rationally entertained?

The considerations here stated however should by no means be allowed to inspire us with indifference in matters of opinion. It is the glory and lustre of our nature, that we are capable of receiving evidence, and weighing the reasons for and against any important proposition in the balance of an impartial and enlightened understanding. The only effect that should be produced in us, by the reflection that we can at last by no means be secure that we have attained to a perfect result, should be to teach us a wholesome diffidence and humility, and induce us to confess that, when we have done all, we are ignorant, dim-sighted and fallible, that our best reasonings may betray, and our wisest conclusions deceive us.

(32) Enquiry concerning Virtue, Book 1, Part 1, Section ii.

ESSAY XIV. OF YOUTH AND AGE.

Magna debetur pueris reverentia.

Quintilian.

I am more doubtful in writing the following Essay than in any of those which precede, how far I am treating of human nature generally, or to a certain degree merely recording my own feelings as an individual. I am guided however in composing it, by the principle laid down in my Preface, that the purpose of my book in each instance should be to expand some new and interesting truth, or some old truth viewed under a new aspect, which had never by any preceding writer been laid before the public.

Education, in the conception of those whose office it is to direct it, has various engines by means of which it is to be made effective, and among these are reprehension and chastisement.

The philosophy of the wisest man that ever existed, is mainly derived from the act of introspection. We look into our own bosoms, observe attentively every thing that passes there, anatomise our motives, trace step by step the operations of thought, and diligently remark the effects of external impulses upon our feelings and conduct. Philosophers, ever since the time in which Socrates flourished, to carry back our recollections no further, have found that the minds of men in the most essential particulars are framed so far upon the same model, that the analysis of the individual may stand in general consideration for the analysis of the species. Where this principle fails, it is not easy to suggest a proceeding that shall supply the deficiency. I look into my own breast; I observe steadily and with diligence what passes there; and with all the parade of the philosophy of the human mind I can do little more than this.

In treating therefore of education in the point of view in which it has just been proposed, I turn my observation upon myself, and I proceed thus.—If I do not stand as a competent representative for the whole of my species, I suppose I may at least assume to be the representative of no inconsiderable number of them.

I find then in myself, for as long a time as I can trace backward the records of memory, a prominent vein of docility. Whatever it was proposed to teach me, that was in any degree accordant with my constitution and capacity, I was willing to learn. And this limit is sufficient for the topic I am proposing to treat. I do not intend to consider education of any other sort, than that which has something in it of a liberal and ingenuous nature. I am not here discussing the education of a peasant, an artisan, or a slave.

In addition to this vein of docility, which easily prompted me to learn whatever was proposed for my instruction and improvement, I felt in myself a sentiment of ambition, a desire to possess the qualifications which I found to be productive of esteem, and that should enable me to excel among my contemporaries. I was ambitious to be a leader, and to be regarded by others with feelings of complacency. I had no wish to rule by brute force and compulsion; but I was desirous to govern by love, and honour, and "the cords of a man."

I do not imagine that, when I aver thus much of myself, I am bringing forward any thing unprecedented, or that multitudes of my fellow-men do not largely participate with me.

The question therefore I am considering is, through what agency, and with what engines, a youth thus disposed, and with these qualifications, is to be initiated in all liberal arts.

I will go back no further than to the commencement of the learning of Latin. All before was so easy to me, as never to have presented the idea of a task. I was immediately put into the accidence. No explanation was attempted to be given why Latin was to be of use to me, or why it was necessary to commit to memory the cases of nouns and the tenses of verbs. I know not whether this was owing to the unwillingness of my instructor to give himself the trouble, or to my supposed incapacity to apprehend the explanation. The last of these I do not admit. My docility however came to my aid, and I did not for a moment harbour any repugnance to the doing what was required of me. At first, and unassisted in the enquiry, I felt a difficulty in supposing that the English language, all the books in my father's library, did not contain every thing that it would be necessary for me to know. In no long time however I came to experience a pleasure in turning the thoughts expressed in an unknown tongue into my own; and I speedily understood that I could never be on a level with those eminent scholars whom it was my ambition to rival, without the study of the classics.

What then were the obstacles, that should in any degree counteract my smooth and rapid progress in the studies suggested to me? I can conceive only two.

First, the versatility and fickleness which in a greater or less degree beset all human minds, particularly in the season of early youth. However docile we may be, and willing to learn, there will be periods, when either some other object powerfully solicits us, or satiety creeps in, and makes us wish to occupy our attention with any thing else rather than with the task prescribed us. But this is no powerful obstacle. The authority of the instructor, a grave look, and the exercise of a moderate degree of patience will easily remove it in such a probationer as we are here considering.

Another obstacle is presumption. The scholar is willing to conceive well of his own capacity. He has a vanity in accomplishing the task prescribed him in the shortest practicable time. He is impatient to go away from the business imposed upon him, to things of his own election, and occupations which his partialities and his temper prompt him to pursue. He has a pride in saying to himself, "This, which was a business given to occupy me for several hours, I can accomplish in less than one." But the presumption arising out of these views is easily subdued. If the pupil is wrong in his calculation, the actual experiment will speedily convince him of his error. He is humbled by and ashamed of his mistake. The merely being sent back to study his lesson afresh, is on the face of the thing punishment enough.

It follows from this view of the matter, that an ingenuous youth, endowed with sufficient capacity for the business prescribed him, may be led on in the path of intellectual acquisition and improvement with a silken cord. It will demand a certain degree of patience on the part of the instructor. But Heaven knows, that this patience is sufficiently called into requisition when the instructor shall be the greatest disciplinarian that ever existed. Kind tones and encouragement will animate the learner amidst many a difficult pass. A grave remark may perhaps sometimes be called for. And, if the preceptor and the pupil have gone on like friends, a grave remark, a look expressive of rebuke, will be found a very powerful engine. The instructor should smooth the business of instruction to his pupil, by appealing to his understanding, developing his taste, and assisting him to remark the beauties of the composition on which he is occupied.

I come now then to the consideration of the two engines mentioned in the commencement of this Essay, reprehension and chastisement.

And here, as in what went before, I am reduced to the referring to my own experience, and looking back into the history of my own mind.

I say then, that reprehension and reprimand can scarcely ever be necessary. The pupil should undoubtedly be informed when he is wrong. He should be told what it is that he ought to have omitted, and that he ought to have done. There should be no reserve in this. It will be worthy of the highest censure, if on these points the instructor should be mealy-mouthed, or hesitate to tell the pupil in the plainest terms, of his faults, his bad habits, and the dangers that beset his onward and honourable path.

But this may be best, and most beneficially done, and in a way most suitable to the exigence, and to the party to be corrected, in a few words. The rest is all an unwholsome tumour, the disease of speech, and not the sound and healthful substance through which its circulation and life are conveyed.

There is always danger of this excrescence of speech, where the speaker is the umpire, and feels himself at liberty, unreproved, to say what he pleases. He is charmed with the sound of his own voice. The periods flow numerous from his tongue, and he gets on at his ease. There is in all this an image of empire; and the human mind is ever prone to be delighted in the exercise of unrestricted authority. The pupil in this case stands before his instructor in an attitude humble, submissive, and bowing to the admonition that is communicated to him. The speaker says more than it was in his purpose to say; and he knows not how to arrest himself in his triumphant career. He believes that he is in no danger of excess, and recollects the old proverb that "words break no bones."

But a syllable more than is necessary and justly measured, is materially of evil operation to ingenuous youth. The mind of such a youth is tender and flexible, and easily swayed one way or the other. He believes almost every thing that he is bid to believe; and the admonition that is given him with all the symptoms of friendliness and sincerity he is prompt to subscribe to. If this is wantonly aggravated to him, he feels the oppression, and is galled with the injustice. He knows himself guiltless of premeditated wrong. He has not yet learned that his condition is that of a slave; and he feels a certain impatience at his being considered as such, though he probably does not venture to express it. He shuts up the sense of this despotism in his own bosom; and it is his first lesson of independence and rebellion and original sin.

It is one of the grossest mistakes of which we can be guilty, if we confound different offences and offenders together. The great and the small alike appear before us in the many-coloured scene of human society, and, if we reprehend bitterly and rate a juvenile sinner for the fault, which he scarcely understood, and assuredly had not premeditated, we break down at once a thousand salutary boundaries, and reduce the ideas of right and wrong in his mind to a portentous and terrible chaos. The communicator of liberal knowledge assuredly ought not to confound his office with that of a magistrate at a quarter-sessions, who though he does not sit in judgment upon transgressions of the deepest and most atrocious character, yet has brought before him in many cases defaulters of a somewhat hardened disposition, whose lot has been cast among the loose and the profligate, and who have been carefully trained to a certain audacity of temper, taught to look upon the paraphernalia of justice with scorn, and to place a sort of honour in sustaining hard words and the lesser visitations of punishment with unflinching nerve.

If this is the judgment we ought to pass upon the bitter and galling and humiliating terms of reprehension apt to be made use of by the instructor to his pupil, it is unnecessary to say a word on the subject of chastisement. If such an expedient is ever to be had recourse to, it can only be in cases of contumaciousness and rebellion; and then the instructor cannot too unreservedly say to himself, "This is matter of deep humiliation to me: I ought to have succeeded by an appeal to the understanding and ingenuous feelings of youth; but I am reduced to a confession of my impotence."

But the topic which, most of all, I was desirous to bring forward in this Essay, is that of the language so customarily employed by the impatient and irritated preceptor, "Hereafter, in a state of mature and ripened judgment, you will thank me for the severity I now exercise towards you."

No; it may safely be answered: that time will never arrive.

As, in one of my earlier Essays(33), I undertook to shew that there is not so much difference between the talents of one man and another as has often been apprehended, so we are guilty of a gross error in the way in which we divide the child from the man, and consider him as if he belonged to a distinct species of beings.

(33) Essay II.

I go back to the recollections of my youth, and can scarcely find where to draw the line between ineptness and maturity. The thoughts that occurred to me, as far back as I can recollect them, were often shrewd; the suggestions ingenious; the judgments not seldom acute. I feel myself the same individual all through.

Sometimes I was unreasonably presumptuous, and sometimes unnecessarily distrustful. Experience has taught me in various instances a sober confidence in my decisions; but that is all the difference. So to express it, I had then the same tools to work with as now; but the magazine of materials upon which I had to operate was scantily supplied. Like the apothecary in Romeo and Juliet, the faculty, such as it was, was within me; but my shelves contained but a small amount of furniture:

A beggarly account of empty boxes,

Remnants of packthread, and old cakes of roses,

Which, thinly scattered, served to make a shew.

In speaking thus of the intellectual powers of my youth, I am however conceding too much. It is true, "Practice maketh perfect." But it is surprising, in apt and towardly youth, how much there is to commend in the first essays. The novice, who has his faculties lively and on the alert, will strike with his hammer almost exactly where the blow ought to be placed, and give nearly the precisely right force to the act. He will seize the thread it was fitting to seize; and, though he fail again and again, will shew an adroitness upon the whole that we scarcely know how to account for. The man whose career shall ultimately be crowned with success, will demonstrate in the beginning that he was destined to succeed.

There is therefore no radical difference between the child and the man. His flesh becomes more firm and sinewy; his bones grow more solid and powerful; his joints are more completely strung. But he is still essentially the same being that he was. When a genuine philosopher holds a new-born child in his arms, and carefully examines it, he perceives in it various indications of temper and seeds of character. It was all there, though folded up and confused, and not obtruding itself upon the remark of every careless spectator. It continues with the child through life, grows with his growth, and never leaves him till he is at last consigned to the tomb. How absurd then by artful rules and positive institutions to undertake to separate what can never be divided! The child is occasionally grave and reflecting, and deduces well-founded inferences; he draws on the past, and plunges into the wide ocean of the future. In proportion as the child advances into the youth, his intervals of gravity increase, and he builds up theories and judgments, some of which no future time shall suffice to overturn. It is idle to suppose that the first activity of our faculties, when every thing is new and produces an unbated impression, when the mind is uncumbered, and every interest and every feeling bid us be observing and awake, should pass for nothing. We lay up stores then, which shall never be exhausted. Our minds are the reverse of worn and obtuse. We bring faculties into the world with us fresh from the hands of the all-bounteous giver; they are not yet moulded to a senseless routine; they are not yet corrupted by the ill lessons of effrontery, impudence and vice. Childhood is beautiful; youth is ingenuous; and it can be nothing but a principle which is hostile to all that most adorns this sublunary scene, that would with violence and despotic rule mar the fairest flower that creation has to boast.

It happens therefore almost unavoidably that, when the man mature looks back upon the little incidents of his youth, he sees them to a surprising degree in the same light, and forms the same conclusions respecting them, as he did when they were actually passing. "The forgeries of opinion," says Cicero, "speedily pass away; but the rules and decisions of nature are strengthened." Bitter reproaches and acts of violence are the offspring of perturbation engendered upon imbecility, and therefore can never be approved upon a sober and impartial revision. And, if they are to be impeached in the judgment of an equal and indifferent observer, we may be sure they will be emphatically condemned by the grave and enlightened censor who looks back upon the years of his own nonage, and recollects that he was himself the victim of the intemperance to be pronounced upon. The interest that he must necessarily take in the scenes in which he once had an engrossing concern, will supply peculiar luminousness to his views. He taxes himself to be just. The transaction is over now, and is passed to the events that preceded the universal deluge. He holds the balance with a steadiness, which sets at defiance all attempts to give it a false direction one way or the other. But the judgment he made on the case at the time, and immediately after the humiliation he suffered, remains with him. It was the sentiment of his ripening youth; it was the opinion of his opening manhood; and it still attends him, when he is already fast yielding to the incroachments and irresistible assaults of declining years.

ESSAY XV. OF LOVE AND FRIENDSHIP.

Who is it that says, "There is no love but among equals?" Be it who it may, it is a saying universally known, and that is in every one's mouth. The contrary is precisely the truth, and is the great secret of every thing that is admirable in our moral nature.

By love it is my intention here to understand, not a calm, tranquil, and, as it were, half-pronounced feeling, but a passion of the mind. We may doubtless entertain an approbation of other men, without adverting to the question how they stand in relation to ourselves, as equals or otherwise. But the sentiment I am here considering, is that where the person in whom it resides most strongly sympathises with the joys and sorrows of another, desires his gratification, hopes for his welfare, and shrinks from the anticipation of his being injured; in a word, is the sentiment which has most the spirit of sacrifice in it, and prepares the person in whom it dwells, to postpone his own advantage to the advantage of him who is the object of it.

Having placed love among the passions, which is no vehement assumption, I then say, there can be no passion, and by consequence no love, where there is not imagination. In cases where every thing is understood, and measured, and reduced to rule, love is out of the question. Whenever this sentiment prevails, I must have my attention fixed more on the absent than the present, more upon what I do not see than on what I do see. My thoughts will be taken up with the future or the past, with what is to come or what has been. Of the present there is necessarily no image. Sentiment is nothing, till you have arrived at a mystery and a veil, something that is seen obscurely, that is just hinted at in the distance, that has neither certain outline nor colour, but that is left for the mind to fill up according to its pleasure and in the best manner it is able.

The great model of the affection of love in human beings, is the sentiment which subsists between parents and children.

Let not this appear a paradox. There is another relation in human society to which this epithet has more emphatically been given: but, if we analyse the matter strictly, we shall find that all that is most sacred and beautiful in the passion between the sexes, has relation to offspring. What Milton calls, "The rites mysterious of connubial love," would have little charm in them in reflection, to a mind one degree above the brutes, were it not for the mystery they include, of their tendency to give existence to a new human creature like ourselves. Were it not for this circumstance, a man and a woman would hardly ever have learned to live together; there scarcely could have been such a thing as domestic society; but every intercourse of this sort would have been "casual, joyless, unendeared;" and the propensity would have brought along with it nothing more of beauty, lustre and grace, than the pure animal appetites of hunger and thirst. Bearing in mind these considerations, I do not therefore hesitate to say, that the great model of the affection of love in human beings, is the sentiment which subsists between parents and children.

The original feature in this sentiment is the conscious feeling of the protector and the protected. Our passions cannot subsist in lazy indolence; passion and action must operate on each other; passion must produce action, and action give strength to the tide of passion. We do not vehemently desire, where we can do nothing. It is in a very faint way that I entertain a wish to possess the faculty of flying; and an ordinary man can scarcely be said to desire to be a king or an emperor. None but a madman, of plebeian rank, falls in love with a princess. But shew me a good thing within my reach; convince me that it is in my power to attain it; demonstrate to me that it is fit for me, and I am fit for it; then begins the career of passion. In the same manner, I cannot love a person vehemently, and strongly interest myself in his miscarriages or success, till I feel that I can be something to him. Love cannot dwell in a state of impotence. To affect and be affected, this is the common nature I require; this is the being that is like unto myself; all other likeness resides in the logic and the definition, but has nothing to do with feeling or with practice.

What can be more clear and sound in explanation, than the love of a parent to his child? The affection he bears and its counterpart are the ornaments of the world, and the spring of every thing that makes life worth having. Whatever besides has a tendency to illustrate and honour our nature, descends from these, or is copied from these, grows out of them as the branches of a tree from the trunk, or is formed upon them as a model, and derives from them its shape, its character, and its soul. Yet there are men so industrious and expert to strip the world we live in of all that adorns it, that they can see nothing glorious in these affections, but find the one to be all selfishness, and the other all prejudice and superstition.

The love of the parent to his child is nursed and fostered by two plain considerations; first, that the subject is capable of receiving much, and secondly, that my power concerning it is great and extensive.

When an infant is presented to my observation, what a wide field of sentiment and reflection is opened to me! Few minds are industrious and ductile enough completely to compass this field, if the infant is only accidentally brought under their view. But, if it is an infant with which I begin to be acquainted to-day, and my acquaintance with which shall not end perhaps till one of us ceases to exist, how is it possible that the view of its little figure should not lead me to the meditation of its future history, the successive stages of human life, and the various scenes and mutations and vicissitudes and fortunes through which it is destined to pass? The Book of

Fate lies open before me. This infant, powerless and almost impassive now, is reserved for many sorrows and many joys, and will one day possess a power, formidable and fearful to afflict those within its reach, or calculated to diffuse blessings, wisdom, virtue, happiness, to all around. I conceive all the various destinations of which man is susceptible; my fancy at least is free to select that which pleases me best; I unfold and pursue it in all its directions, observe the thorns and difficulties with which it is beset, and conjure up to my thoughts all that it can boast of inviting, delightful and honourable.

But if the infant that is near to me lays hold of my imagination and affections at the moment in which he falls under my observation, how much more do I become interested in him, as he advances from year to year! At first, I have the blessing of the gospel upon me, in that, "having not seen, yet I believe." But, as his powers expand, I understand him better. His little eye begins to sparkle with meaning; his tongue tells a tale that may be understood; his very tones, and gestures, and attitudes, all inform me concerning what he shall be. I am like a florist, who has received a strange plant from a distant country. At first he sees only the stalk, and the leaves, and the bud having yet no other colour than that of the leaves. But as he watches his plant from day to day, and from hour to hour, the case which contains the flower divides, and betrays first one colour and then another, till the shell gradually subsides more and more towards the stalk, and the figure of the flower begins now to be seen, and its radiance and its pride to expand itself to the ravished observer.—Every lesson that the child leans, every comment that he makes upon it, every sport that he pursues, every choice that he exerts, the demeanour that he adopts to his playfellows, the modifications and character of his little fits of authority or submission, all make him more and more an individual to me, and open a wider field for my sagacity or my prophecy, as to what he promises to be, and what he may be made.

But what gives, as has already been observed, the point and the finish to all the interest I take respecting him, lies in the vast power I possess to influence and direct his character and his fortune. At first it is abstract power, but, when it has already been exerted (as the writers on politics as a science have observed of property), the sweat of my brow becomes mingled with the apple I have gathered, and my interest is greater. No one understands my views and projects entirely but myself, and the scheme I have conceived will suffer, if I do not complete it as I began.

And there are men that say, that all this mystery, the most beautiful attitude of human nature, and the crown of its glory, is pure selfishness!

Let us now turn from the view of the parental, to that of the filial affection.

The great mistake that has been made on this subject, arises from the taking it nakedly and as a mere abstraction. It has been sagely remarked, that when my father did that which occasioned me to come into existence, he intended me no benefit, and therefore I owe him no thanks. And the inference which has been made from this wise position is, that the duty of children to parents is a mere imposture, a trick, employed by the old to defraud the young out of their services.

I grant most readily, that the mere material ligament that binds together the father and the child, by itself is worthless, and that he who owes nothing more than this to his father, owes him nothing. The natural, unanimated relationship is like the grain of mustard-seed in the discourses of Jesus Christ, "which indeed is the least of all seeds; but, when it is unfolded and grows up, it becomes a mighty tree, so that the birds of the air may come and lodge in its branches."

The hard and insensible man may know little of the debt he owes to his father; but he that is capable of calling up the past, and beholding the things that are not as if they now were, will see the matter in a very different light. Incalculable are the privations (in a great majority of instances), the toils, the pains, the anxieties, that every child imposes on his father from the first hour of his existence. If he could know the ceaseless cares, the tender and ardent feelings, the almost incredible efforts and exertions, that have accompanied him in his father's breast through the whole period of his growth, instead of thinking that he owed his parent nothing, he would stand still and wonder that one human creature could do so much for another.

I grant that all this may be done for a child by a stranger, and that then in one sense the obligation would be greater. It is however barely possible that all this should be done. The stranger wants the first exciting cause, the consideration, "This creature by the great scheme of nature belongs to me, and is cast upon my care." And, as the tie in the case of the stranger was not complete in the beginning, so neither can it be made so in the sequel. The little straggler is like the duckling hatched in the nest of a hen; there is danger every day, that as the nursling begins to be acquainted with its own qualities, it may plunge itself into another element, and swim away from its benefactor.

Even if we put all these considerations out of the question, still the affection of the child to its parent of adoption, wants the kernel, and, if I may so speak, the soul, of the connection which has been formed and modelled by the great hand of nature. If the mere circumstance of filiation and descent creates no debt, it however is the principle of a very close connection. One of the most memorable mysteries of nature, is how, out of the slightest of all connections (for such, literally speaking, is that between father and child), so many coincidences should arise. The child resembles his parent in feature, in temperament, in turn of mind, and in class of disposition, while at the same time in many particulars, in these same respects, he is a new and individual creature. In one view therefore the child is merely the father multiplied and repeated. Now one of the indefeasible principles of affection is the partaking of a common nature; and as man is a species by himself, so to a certain degree is every nation and every family; and this consideration, when added to the moral and spiritual ties already treated of, undoubtedly has a tendency to give them their zest and perfection.

But even this is not the most agreeable point of view in which we may consider the filial affection. I come back to my first position, that where there is no imagination, there can be no passion, and by consequence no love. No parent ever understood his child, and no child ever understood his parent. We have seen that the affectionate parent considers his child like a flower in the bud, as a mine of power that is to be unfolded, as a creature that is to act and to pass through he knows not what, as a canvas that "gives ample room and verge enough," for his prophetic soul to hang over in endless visions, and his intellectual pencil to fill up with various scenes and fortunes. And, if the parent does not understand his child, certainly as little does the child understand his parent. Wherever this relation subsists in its fairest form, the parent is as a God, a being qualified with supernatural powers, to his offspring. The child consults his father as an oracle; to him he proposes all his little questions; from him he learns his natural philosophy, his morals, his rules of conduct, his religion, and his creed. The boy is uninformed on every point; and the father is a vast Encyclopedia, not merely of sciences, but of feelings, of sagacity, of practical wisdom, and of justice, which the son consults on all occasions, and never consults in vain. Senseless and inexpert is that parent, who endeavours to govern the mind by authority, and to lay down rugged and peremptory dogmas to his child; the child is fully and unavoidably prepared to receive every thing with unbounded deference, and to place total reliance in the oracle which nature has assigned him. Habits, how beautiful! Inestimable benefit of nature, that has given me a prop against which to sustain my unripened strength, and has not turned me loose to wander with tottering steps amidst the vast desert of society!

But it is not merely for contemplative wisdom that the child honours his parent; he sees in him a vast fund of love, attachment and sympathy. That he cannot mistake; and it is all a mystery to him. He says, What am I, that I should be the object of this? and whence comes it? He sees neither the fountain from which it springs, nor the banks that confine it. To him it is an ocean, unfathomable, and without a shore.

To the bounty of its operations he trusts implicitly. The stores of judgment and knowledge he finds in his father, prompt him to trust it. In many instances where it appeared at first obscure and enigmatical, the event has taught him to acknowledge its soundness. The mutinousness of passion will sometimes excite a child to question the decrees of his parent; it is very long before his understanding, as such, comes to set up a separate system, and teaches him to controvert the decisions of his father.

Perhaps I ought earlier to have stated, that the filial connection we have here to consider, does not include those melancholy instances where some woful defect or utter worthlessness in the parent counteracts the natural course of the affections, but refers only to cases, where the character of father is on the whole sustained with honour, and the principle of the connection is left to its true operation. In such cases the child not only observes for himself the manifestations of wisdom and goodness in his parent, but is also accustomed to hear well of him from all around. There is a generous conspiracy in human nature, not to counteract the honour borne by the offspring to him from whom he sprung, and the wholesome principle of superiority and dependence which is almost indispensible between persons of different ages dwelling under the same roof. And, exclusively of this consideration, the men who are chiefly seen by the son are his father's friends and associates; and it is the very bent, and, as it were, law of our nature, that we do not associate much, but with persons whom we favour, and who are prepared to mention us with kindness and honour.

Thus every way the child is deeply imbued with veneration for his parent, and forms the habit of regarding him as his book of wisdom, his philosopher and guide. He is accustomed to hear him spoken of as a true friend, an active ally, and a pattern of justice and honour; and he finds him so. Now these are the true objects of affection,—wisdom and beneficence; and the human heart loves this beneficence better when it is exercised towards him who loves, first, because inevitably in almost all instances we are best pleased with the good that is done to ourselves, and secondly, because it can scarcely happen but that we in that case understand it best, both in its operation and its effects.

The active principles of religion are all moulded upon this familiar and sensible relation of father and child: and to understand whet the human heart is capable to conceive on this subject, we have only to refer to the many eloquent and glowing treatises that have been written upon the love of God to his creatures, and the love that the creature in return owes to his God. I am not now considering religion in a speculative point of view, or enquiring among the different sects and systems of religion what it is that is true; but merely producing religion as an example of what have been the conceptions of the human mind in successive ages of the world on the subject of love.

This All that we behold, the immensity of the universe, the admirable harmony and subtlety of its structure, as they appear in the vastest and the minutest bodies, is considered by religion, as the emanation of pure love, a mighty impulse and ardour in its great author to realise the idea existing in his mind, and to produce happiness. The Providence that watches over us, so that not a sparrow dies unmarked, and that "the great Sensorium of the world vibrates, if a hair of our head but falls to the ground in the remotest desert of his creation," is still unremitted, never-satiated love. And, to go from this to the peculiarities of the Christian doctrine, "Greater love hath no man than this, that a man lay down his life for his friends: God so loved the world, that he gave his only-begotten Son to suffer, to be treated contumeliously, and to die with ignominy, that we might live."

If on the other hand we consider the love which the creature must naturally pay to his creator, we shall find that the affection we can suppose the most ingenuous child to bear to the worthiest parent, is a very faint image of the passion which may be expected to grow out of this relation. In God, as he is represented to us in the books of the worthiest divines, is every thing that can command love; wisdom to conceive, power to execute, and beneficence actually to carry into effect, whatever is excellent and admirable. We are lost in contemplating the depth and immensity of his perfections. "Every good and every perfect gift is from the universal Father, with whom is no variableness, neither shadow of turning." The most soothing and gratifying of all sentiments, is that of entire confidence in the divine goodness, a reliance which no adversity can shake, and which supports him that entertains it under every calamity, that sees the finger of God in every thing that comes to pass, that says, "It is good for me to be afflicted," believes, that "all things work together for blessings" to the pious and the just, and is intimately persuaded that "our light affliction, which is but for a moment, is the means and the earnest of a far more exceeding and eternal weight of glory."

If we descend from these great archetypes, the love between parent and child, and between the creator and his creature, we shall still find the same inequality the inseparable attendant upon the most perfect ties of affection. The ancients seem to have conceived the truest and most exalted ideas on the subject of friendship. Among the most celebrated instances are the friendship of Achilles and Patroclus, Orestes and Pylades, Aeneas and Achates, Cyrus and Araspes, Alexander and Hephaestion, Scipio and Laelius. In each of these the parties are, the true hero, the man of lofty ambition, the magnificent personage in whom is concentred every thing that the historian or the poet was able to realise of excellence, and the modest and unpretending individual in whom his confidence was reposed. The grand secret of the connection is unfolded in the saying of the Macedonian conqueror, "Craterus loves the king, but Hephaestion loves Alexander." Friendship is to the loftier mind the repose, the unbending of the soul. The great man (whatever may be the department in which his excellence consists) has enough of his greatness, when he stands before the world, and receives the homage that is paid to his merits. Ever and anon he is anxious to throw aside this incumbrance, and be as a man merely to a man. He wishes to forget the "pride, pomp, and circumstance" of greatness, and to be that only which he is himself. He desires at length to be sure, that he receives no adulation, that he is accosted with no insincerity, and that the individual to whose society he has thought proper to withdraw, has no by-ends, no sinister purposes in all his thoughts. What he seeks for, is a true friend, a being who sincerely loves, one who is attached to him, not for the accidents that attend him, but for what most strictly belongs to him, and of which he cannot be divested. In this friend there is neither interested intention nor rivalry.

Such are the characteristic features of the superior party in these exemplars of friendship among the ancients. Of the unpretending, unassuming party Homer, the great master of the affections and emotions in remoter ages, has given us the fullest portrait in the character of Patroclus. The distinguishing feature of his disposition is a melting and affectionate spirit, the concentred essence of tenderness and humanity. When Patroclus comes from witnessing the disasters of the Greeks, to collect a report of which he had been sent by Achilles, he is "overwhelmed with floods of tears, like a spring which pours down its waters from the steep edge of a precipice." It is thus that Jupiter characterises him when he lies dead in the field of battle:

Thou (addressing himself in his thoughts to Hector) hast slain the friend of Achilles, not less memorable for the blandness of his temper, than the bravery of his deeds.

It is thus that Menelaus undertakes to excite the Grecian chiefs to rescue his body:

Let each man recollect the sweetness of his disposition for, as long as he lived, he was unremitted in kindness to all. When Achilles proposes the games at the funeral, he says, "On any other occasion my horses should have started for the prize, but now it cannot be. They have lost their incomparable groom, who was accustomed to refresh their limbs with water, and anoint their flowing manes; and they are inconsolable." Briseis also makes her appearance among the mourners, avowing that, "when her husband had been slain in battle, and her native city laid in ashes, this generous man prevented her tears, averring to her, that she should be the wife of her conqueror, and that he would himself spread the nuptial banquet for her in the hero's native kingdom of Phthia."

The reciprocity which belongs to a friendship between unequals may well be expected to give a higher zest to their union. Each party is necessary to the other. The superior considers him towards whom he pours out his affection, as a part of himself.

The head is not more native to the heart,

The hand more instrumental to the mouth.

He cannot separate himself from him, but at the cost of a fearful maim. When the world is shut out by him, when he retires into solitude, and falls back upon himself, then his unpretending friend is most of all necessary to him. He is his consolation and his pleasure, the safe coffer in which he reposits all his anxieties and sorrows. If the principal, instead of being a public man, is a man of science, this kind of unbending becomes certainly not the less welcome to him. He wishes occasionally to forget the severity of his investigations, neither to have his mind any longer wound up and stretched to the height of meditation, nor to feel that he needs to be any way on his guard, or not completely to give the rein to all his sallies and the sportiveness of his soul. Having been for a considerable time shut up in sequestered reflection, he wishes, it may be, to have the world, the busy impassioned world, brought to his ears, without his being obliged to enter into its formalities and mummeries. If he desires to speak of the topics which had so deeply engaged him, he can keep as near the edge as he pleases, and drop or resume them as his fancy may prompt. And it seems useless to say, how much his modest and unassuming friend will be gratified in being instrumental to relieve the labours of his principal, in feeling that he is necessary to him, and in meditating on the delight he receives in being made the chosen companion and confident of him whom he so ardently admires. It was precisely in this spirit, that Fulke Greville, two hundred years ago, directed that it should be inscribed on his tomb, "Here lies the friend of Sir Philip Sidney." Tenderness on the one part, and a deep feeling of honour and respect on the other, give a completeness to the union which it must otherwise for ever want. "There is no limit, none," to the fervour with which the stronger goes forward to protect the weak; while in return the less powerful would encounter a thousand deaths rather than injury should befall the being to whom in generosity and affection he owes so much.

In the mean time, though inequality is necessary to give this completeness to friendship, the inequality must not be too great.

The inferior party must be able to understand and appreciate the sense and the merits of him to whom he is thus bound. There must be no impediment to hinder the communications of the principal from being fully comprehended, and his sentiments entirely participated. There must be a boundless confidence, without apprehension that the power of the stronger party can by the remotest possibility be put forth ungenerously. "Perfect love casteth out fear." The evangelist applies this aphorism even to the love of the creature to his creator. "The Lord spake unto Moses, face to face, as a man speaketh unto his friend." In the union of which I am treating the demonstrative and ordinary appearance will be that of entire equality, which is heightened by the inner, and for the greater part unexplained and undeveloped, impression of a contrary nature. There is in either party a perfect reliance, an idea of inequality with the most entire assurance that it can never operate unworthily in the stronger party, or produce insincerity or servility in the weaker. There will in reality always be some reserve, some shadow of fear between equals, which in the friendship of unequals, if happily assorted, can find no place. There is a pouring out of the heart on the one side, and a cordial acceptance on the other, which words are inadequate to describe.

To proceed. If from friendship we go forward to that which in all languages is emphatically called love, we shall still find ourselves dogged and attended by inequality. Nothing can be more certain, however we may seek to modify and abate it, than the inequality of the sexes. Let us attend to it as it stands in Milton:

For contemplation he and velour formed

For softness she and sweet attractive grace;

He for God only, she for God in him.

Thus it is painted to us as having been in Paradise; and with similar inequality have the sexes subsisted in all ages and nations since. If it were possible to take from the fair sex its softness and attractive grace, and endow it instead with audacious, masculine and military qualities, there is scarcely any one that does not perceive, with whatever advantages it might be attended in other respects, that it would be far from tending to cherish and increase the passion of love.

It is in reality obvious, that man and woman, as they come from the hands of nature, are so much upon a par with each other, as not to afford the best subjects between whom to graft a habit of entire, unalterable affection. In the scenes of vulgar and ordinary society, a permanent connection between persons of opposite sexes is too apt to degenerate into a scene of warfare, where each party is for ever engaged in a struggle for superiority, and neither will give way. A penetrating observer, with whom in former days I used intimately to converse, was accustomed to say, that there was generally more jarring and ill blood between the two parties in the first year of their marriage, than during all the remainder of their lives. It is at length found necessary, as between equally matched belligerents on the theatre of history, that they should come to terms, make a treaty of peace, or at least settle certain laws of warfare, that they may not waste their strength in idle hostilities.

The nations of antiquity had a way of settling this question in a very summary mode. As certain Oriental tribes have determined that women have no souls, and that nothing can be more proper than to shut them up, like singing birds in cages, so the Greeks and Romans for the most part excluded their females from the society of the more martial sex. Marriage with them was a convenience merely; and the husband and wife were in reality nothing more than the master and the slave. This point once settled as a matter of national law, there was certainly in most cases little danger of any vexatious rivalship and struggle for power.

But there is nothing in which the superiority of modern times over the ancient has been more conspicuous, than in our sentiments and practices on this subject. This superiority, as well as several other of our most valuable acquisitions, took its rise in what we call the dark ages. Chivalry was for the most part the invention of the eleventh century. Its principle was built upon a theory of the sexes, giving to each a relative importance, and assigning to both functions full of honour and grace. The knights (and every gentleman during that period in due time became a knight) were taught, as the main features of their vocation, the "love of God and the ladies." The ladies in return were regarded as the genuine censors of the deeds of knighthood. From these principles arose a thousand lessons of humanity. The ladies regarded it as their glory to assist their champions to arm and to disarm, to perform for them even menial services, to attend them in sickness, and to dress their wounds. They bestowed on them their colours, and sent them forth to the field hallowed with their benedictions. The knights on the other hand considered any slight towards the fair sex as an indelible stain to their order; they contemplated the graceful patronesses of their valour with a feeling that partook of religious homage and veneration, and esteemed it as perhaps the first duty of their profession, to relieve the wrongs, and avenge the injuries of the less powerful sex.

This simple outline as to the relative position of the one sex and the other, gave a new face to the whole scheme and arrangements of civil society. It is like those admirable principles in the order of the material universe, or those grand discoveries brought to light from time to time by superior genius, so obvious and simple, that we wonder the most common understanding could have missed them, yet so pregnant with results, that they seem at once to put a new life and inspire a new character into every part of a mighty and all-comprehensive mass.

The passion between the sexes, in its grosser sense, is a momentary impulse merely; and there was danger that, when the fit and violence of the passion was over, the whole would subside into inconstancy and a roving disposition, or at least into indifference and almost brutal neglect. But the institutions of chivalry immediately gave a new face to this. Either sex conceived a deep and permanent interest in the other. In the unsettled state of society which characterised the period when these institutions arose, the defenceless were liable to assaults of multiplied kinds, and the fair perpetually stood in need of a protector and a champion. The knights on the other hand were taught to derive their fame and their honour from the suffrages of the ladies. Each sex stood in need of the other; and the basis of their union was mutual esteem.

The effect of this was to give a hue of imagination to all their intercourse. A man was no longer merely a man, nor a woman merely a woman. They were taught mutual deference. The woman regarded her protector as something illustrious and admirable; and the man considered the smiles and approbation of beauty as the adequate reward of his toils and his dangers. These modes of thinking introduced a nameless grace into all the commerce of society. It was the poetry of life. Hence originated the delightful narratives and fictions of romance; and human existence was no longer the bare, naked train of vulgar incidents, which for so many ages of the world it had been accustomed to be. It was clothed in resplendent hues, and wore all the tints of the rainbow. Equality fled and was no more; and love, almighty, perdurable love, came to supply its place.

By means of this state of things the vulgar impulse of the sexes towards each other, which alone was known to the former ages of the world, was transformed into somewhat of a totally different nature. It became a kind of worship. The fair sex looked upon their protectors, their fathers, their husbands, and the whole train of their chivalry, as something more than human. There was a grace in their motions, a gallantry in their bearing, and a generosity in their spirit of enterprise, that the softness of the female heart found irresistible. Nor less on the other hand did the knights regard the sex to whose service and defence they were sworn, as the objects of their perpetual deference. They approached them with a sort of gallant timidity, listened to their behests with submission, and thought the longest courtship and devotion nobly recompensed by the final acceptance of the fair.

The romance and exaggeration characteristic of these modes of thinking have gradually worn away in modern times; but much of what was most valuable in them has remained. Love has in later ages never been divested of the tenderness and consideration, which were thus rendered some of its most estimable features. A certain desire in each party to exalt the other, and regard it as worthy of admiration, became inextricably interwoven with the simple passion. A sense of the honour that was borne by the one to the other, had the happiest effect in qualifying the familiarity and unreserve in the communion of feelings and sentiments, without which the attachment of the sexes cannot subsist. It is something like what the mystic divines describe of the beatific vision, where entire wonder and adoration are not judged to be incompatible with the most ardent affection, and all meaner and selfish regards are annihilated.

From what has been thus drawn together and recapitulated it seems clearly to follow, as was stated in the beginning, that love cannot exist in its purest form and with a genuine ardour, where the parties are, and are felt by each other to be, on an equality; but that in all cases it is requisite there should be a mutual deference and submission, agreeably to the apostolic precept, "Likewise all of you be subject one to the other." There must be room for the imagination to exercise its powers; we must conceive and apprehend a thousand things which we do not actually witness; each party must feel that it stands in need of the other, and without the other cannot be complete; each party must be alike conscious of the power of receiving and conferring benefit; and there must be the anticipation of a distant future, that may every day enhance the good to be imparted and enjoyed, and cause the individuals thus united perpetually to become more sensible of the fortunate event which gave them to each other, and has thus entailed upon each a thousand advantages in which they could otherwise never have shared.

ESSAY XVI. OF FRANKNESS AND RESERVE.

Animals are divided into the solitary and the are gregarious: the former being only occasionally associated with its mate, and perhaps engaged in the care of its offspring; the latter spending their lives in herds and communities. Man is of this last class or division.

Where the animals of any particular species live much in society, it seems requisite that in some degree they should be able to understand each other's purposes, and to act with a certain portion of concert.

All other animals are exceedingly limited in their powers of communication. But speech renders that being whom we justly entitle the lord of the creation, capable of a boundless interchange of ideas and intentions. Not only can we communicate to each other substantively our elections and preferences: we can also exhort and persuade, and employ reasons and arguments to convince our fellows, that the choice we have made is also worthy of their adoption. We can express our thoughts, and the various lights and shades, the bleedings, of our thoughts. Language is an instrument capable of being perpetually advanced in copiousness, perspicuity and power.

No principle of morality can be more just, than that which teaches us to regard every faculty we possess as a power intrusted to us for the benefit of others as well as of ourselves, and which therefore we are bound to employ in the way which shall best conduce to the general advantage.

"Speech was given us, that by it we might express our thoughts(34);" in other words, our impressions, ideas and conceptions. We then therefore best fulfil the scope of our nature, when we sincerely and unreservedly communicate to each other our feelings and apprehensions. Speech should be to man in the nature of a fair complexion, the transparent medium through which the workings of the mind should be made legible.

(34) Moliere.

I think I have somewhere read of Socrates, that certain of his friends expostulated with him, that the windows of his house were so constructed that every one who went by could discover all that passed within. "And wherefore not?" said the sage. "I do nothing that I would wish to have concealed from any human eye. If I knew that all the world observed every thing I did, I should feel no inducement to change my conduct in the minutest particular."

It is not however practicable that frankness should be carried to the extent above mentioned. It has been calculated that the human mind is capable of being impressed with three hundred and twenty sensations in a second of time. At all events we well know that, even "while I am speaking, a variety of sensations are experienced by me, without so much as interrupting, that is, without materially diverting, the train of my ideas. My eye successively remarks a thousand objects that present themselves, and my mind wanders to the different parts of my body, without occasioning the minutest obstacle to my discourse, or my being in any degree distracted by the multiplicity of these objects(35)." It is therefore beyond the reach of the faculty of speech, for me to communicate all the sensations I experience; and I am of necessity reduced to a selection.

(35) See above, Essay 7.

Nor is this the whole. We do not communicate all that we feel, and all that we think; for this would be impertinent. We owe a certain deference and consideration to our fellow-men; we owe it in reality to ourselves. We do not communicate indiscriminately all that passes within us. The time would fail us; and "the world would not contain the books that might be written." We do not speak merely for the sake of speaking; otherwise the communication of man with his fellow would be but one eternal babble. Speech is to be employed for some useful purpose; nor ought we to give utterance to any thing that shall not promise to be in some way productive of benefit or amusement.

Frankness has its limits, beyond which it would cease to be either advantageous or virtuous. We are not to tell every thing: but we are not to conceal any thing, that it would be useful or becoming in us to utter. Our first duty regarding the faculty of speech is, not to keep back what it would be beneficial to our neighbour to know. But this is a negative sincerity only. If we would acquire a character for frankness, we must be careful that our conversation is such, as to excite in him the idea that we are open, ingenuous and fearless. We must appear forward to speak all that will give him pleasure, and contribute to maintain in him an agreeable state of being. It must be obvious that we are not artificial and on our guard.—After all, it is difficult to lay down rules on this subject: the spring of whatever is desirable respecting it, must be in the temper of the man with whom others have intercourse. He must be benevolent, sympathetic and affectionate. His heart must overflow with good-will; and he must be anxious to relieve every little pain, and to contribute to the enjoyment and complacent feelings, of those with whom he is permanently or accidentally connected. "Out of the abundance of the heart the mouth speaketh."

There are two considerations by which we ought to be directed in the exercise of the faculty of speech.

The first is, that we should tell our neighbour all that it would be useful to him to know. We must have no sinister or bye ends. "No man liveth to himself." We are all of us members of the great congregation of mankind.

The same blood should circulate through every limb and every muscle. Our pulses should beat time to each other; and we should have one common sensorium, vibrating throughout, upon every material accident that occurs, and when any object is at stake essentially affecting the welfare of our fellow-beings. We should forget ourselves in the interest that we feel for the happiness of others; and, if this were universal, each man would be a gainer, inasmuch as he lost himself, and was cared and watched for by many.

In all these respects we must have no reserve. We should only consider what it is that it would be beneficial to have declared.

We must not look back to ourselves, and consult the dictates of a narrow and self-interested prudence. The whole essence of communication is adulterated, if, instead of attending to the direct effects of what suggests itself to our tongue, we are to consider how by a circuitous route it may react upon our own pleasures and advantage.

Nor only are we bound to communicate to our neighbour all that it will be useful to him to know. We have many neighbours, beside those to whom we immediately address ourselves. To these our absent fellow-beings, we owe a thousand duties. We are bound to defend those whom we hear aspersed, and who are spoken unworthily of by the persons whom we incidentally encounter. We should be the forward and spontaneous advocates of merit in every shape and in every individual in whom we know it to exist. What a character would that man make for himself, of whom it was notorious that he consecrated his faculty of speech to the refuting unjust imputations against whomsoever they were directed, to the contradicting all false and malicious reports, and to the bringing forth obscure and unrecognised worth from the shades in which it lay hid! What a world should we live in, if all men were thus prompt and fearless to do justice to all the worth they knew or apprehended to exist! Justice, simple justice, if it extended no farther than barely to the faculty of speech, would in no long time put down all misrepresentation and calumny, bring all that is good and meritorious into honour, and, so to speak, set every man in his true and rightful position. But whoever would attempt this, must do it in all honour, without parade, and with no ever-and-anon looking back upon his achievement, and saying, See to how much credit I am entitled!—as if he laid more stress upon himself, the doer of this justice, than upon justice in its intrinsic nature and claims.

But we not only owe something to the advantage and interest of our neighbours, but something also to the sacred divinity of Truth. I am not only to tell my neighbour whatever I know that may be beneficial to him, respecting his position in society, his faults, what other men appear to contemplate that may conduce to his advantage or injury, and to advise him how the one may best be forwarded, or the other defeated and brought to nothing: I am bound also to consider in what way it may be in my power so to act on his mind, as shall most enlarge his views, confirm and animate his good resolutions, and meliorate his dispositions and temper. We are all members of one great community: and we shall never sufficiently discharge our duty in that respect, till, like the ancient Spartans, the love of the whole becomes our predominant passion, and we cease to imagine that we belong to ourselves, so much as to the entire body of which we are a part. There are certain views in morality, in politics, and various other important subjects, the general prevalence of which will be of the highest benefit to the society of which we are members; and it becomes us in this respect, with proper temperance and moderation, to conform ourselves to the zealous and fervent precept of the apostle, to "promulgate the truth and be instant, in season and out of season," that we may by all means leave some monument of our good intentions behind us, and feel that we have not lived in vain.

There is a maxim extremely in vogue in the ordinary intercourses of society, which deserves to be noticed here, for the purpose of exposing it to merited condemnation. It is very common between friends, or persons calling themselves such, to say, "Do not ask my advice in a certain crisis of your life; I will not give it; hereafter, if the thing turns out wrong, you will reflect on me, and say that it was at my suggestion that you were involved in calamity." This is a dastardly excuse, and shews a pitiful selfishness in the man that urges it.

It is true, that we ought ever to be on the alert, that we may not induce our friend into evil. We should be upon our guard, that we may not from overweening arrogance and self-conceit dictate to another, overpower his more sober judgment, and assume a rashness for him, in which perhaps we would not dare to indulge for ourselves. We should be modest in our suggestions, and rather supply him with materials for decision, than with a decision absolutely made. There may however be cases where an opposite proceeding is necessary. We must arrest our friend, nay, even him who is merely our fellow-creature, with a strong arm, when we see him hovering on the brink of a precipice, or the danger is so obvious, that nothing but absolute blindness could conceal it from an impartial bystander.

But in all cases our best judgment should always be at the service of our brethren of mankind. "Give to him that asketh thee; and from him that would borrow of thee turn not thou away."

This may not always be practicable or just, when applied to the goods of fortune: but the case of advice, information, and laws of conduct, comes within that of Ennius, to suffer our neighbour to light his candle at our lamp. To do so will enrich him, without making us a jot the poorer. We should indeed respect the right of private judgment, and scarcely in any case allow our will to supersede his will in his own proper province. But we should on no account suffer any cowardly fears for ourselves, to induce us to withhold from him any assistance that our wider information or our sounder judgment might supply to him.

The next consideration by which we should be directed in the exercise of the faculty of speech, is that we should employ it so as should best conduce to the pleasure of our neighbour. Man is a different creature in the savage and the civilised state. It has been affirmed, and it may be true, that the savage man is a stranger to that disagreeable frame of mind, known by the name of ennui. He can pore upon the babbling stream, or stretch himself upon a sunny bank, from the rising to the setting of the sun, and be satisfied. He is scarcely roused from this torpid state but by the cravings of nature. If they can be supplied without effort, he immediately relapses into his former supineness; and, if it requires search, industry and exertion to procure their gratification, he still more eagerly embraces the repose, which previous fatigue renders doubly welcome.

But, when the mind has once been wakened up from its original lethargy, when we have overstepped the boundary which divides the man from the beast, and are made desirous of improvement, while at the same moment the tumultuous passions that draw us in infinitely diversified directions are called into act, the case becomes exceedingly different. It might be difficult at first to rouse man from his original lethargy: it is next to impossible that he should ever again be restored to it. The appetite of the mind being once thoroughly awakened in society, the human species are found to be perpetually craving after new intellectual food. We read, we write, we discourse, we ford rivers, and scale mountains, and engage in various pursuits, for the pure pleasure that the activity and earnestness of the pursuit afford us. The day of the savage and the civilised man are still called by the same name. They may be measured by a pendulum, and will be found to be of the same duration. But in all other points of view they are inexpressibly different.

Hence therefore arises another duty that is incumbent upon us as to the exercise of the faculty of speech. This duty will be more or less urgent according to the situation in which we are placed.

If I sit down in a numerous assembly, if I become one of a convivial party of ten or twelve persons, I may unblamed be for the greater part, or entirely silent, if I please. I must appear to enter into their sentiments and pleasures, or, if I do not, I shall be an unwelcome guest; but it may scarcely be required for me to clothe my feelings with articulate speech.

But, when my society shall be that of a few friends only, and still more if the question is of spending hours or days in the society of a single friend, my duty becomes altered, and a greater degree of activity will be required from me. There are cases, where the minor morals of the species will be of more importance than those which in their own nature are cardinal. Duties of the highest magnitude will perhaps only be brought into requisition upon extraordinary occasions; but the opportunities we have of lessening the inconveniences of our neighbour, or of adding to his accommodations and the amount of his agreeable feelings, are innumerable. An acceptable and welcome member of society therefore will not talk, only when he has something important to communicate. He will also study how he may amuse his friend with agreeable narratives, lively remarks, sallies of wit, or any of those thousand nothings, which' set off with a wish to please and a benevolent temper, will often entertain more and win the entire good will of the person to whom they are addressed, than the wisest discourse, or the vein of conversation which may exhibit the powers and genius of the speaker to the greatest advantage.

Men of a dull and saturnine complexion will soon get to an end of all they felt it incumbent on them to say to their comrades. But the same thing will probably happen, though at a much later period, between friends of an active mind, of the largest stores of information, and whose powers have been exercised upon the greatest variety of sentiments, principles, and original veins of thinking. When two such men first fall into society, each will feel as if he had found a treasure. Their communications are without end; their garrulity is excited, and converts into a perennial spring. The topics upon which they are prompted to converse are so numerous, that one seems to jostle out the other.

It may proceed thus from day to day, from month to month, and perhaps from year to year. But, according to the old proverb, "It is a long lane that has no turning." The persons here described will have a vast variety of topics upon which they are incited to compare their opinions, and will lay down these topics and take them up again times without number. Upon some, one of the parties will feel himself entirely at home while the other is comparatively a novice, and, in others, the advantage will be with the other; so that the gain of both, in this free and unrestrained opening of the soul, will be incalculable. But the time will come, like as in perusing an author of the most extraordinary genius and the most versatile powers, that the reading of each other's minds will be exhausted. They know so much of each other's tone of thinking, that all that can be said will be anticipated. The living voice, the sparkling eye, and the beaming countenance will do much to put off the evil day, when we shall say, I have had enough. But the time will come in which we shall feel that this after all is but little, and we shall become sluggish, ourselves to communicate, or to excite the dormant faculties of our friend, when the spring, the waters of which so long afforded us the most exquisite delight, is at length drawn dry.

I remember in my childish years being greatly struck with that passage in the Bible, where it is written, "But I say unto you, that, for every idle word that men shall speak, they shall give an account in the day of judgment:" and, as I was very desirous of conforming myself to the directions of the sacred volume, I was upon the point of forming a sort of resolution, that I would on no account open my mouth to speak, without having a weighty reason for uttering the thing I felt myself prompted to say.

But practical directions of this sort are almost in all cases of ambiguous interpretation. From the context of this passage it is clear, that by "idle words" we are to understand vicious words, words tending to instil into the mind unauthorised impulses, that shew in the man who speaks "a will most rank, foul disproportion, thoughts unnatural," and are calculated to render him by whom they are listened to, light and frivolous of temper, and unstrung for the graver duties of human life.

But idle words, in the sense of innocent amusement, are not vicious. "There is a time for all things." Amusement must not encroach upon or thrust aside the real business, the important engagements, and the animated pursuits of man. But it is entitled to take its turn unreproved. Human life is so various, and the disposition and temper of the mind of so different tones and capacity, that a wise man will "frame his face to all occasions." Playfulness, if not carried to too great an extreme, is an additional perfection in human nature. We become relieved from our more serious cares, and better fitted to enter on them again after an interval. To fill up the days of our lives with various engagements, to make one occupation succeed to another, so as to liberate us from the pains of ennui, and the dangers of what may in an emphatical sense be called idleness, is no small desideratum. That king may in this sense be admitted to have formed no superficial estimate of our common nature, who is said to have proclaimed a reward to the individual that should invent a new amusement.

And, to consider the question as it stands in relation to the subject of the present Essay, a perpetual gravity and a vigilant watch to be placed on the door of our lips, would be eminently hostile to that frankness which is to be regarded as one of the greatest ornaments of our nature. "It is meet, that we should make merry and be glad." A formal countenance, a demure, careful and unaltered cast of features, is one of the most disadvantageous aspects under which human nature can exhibit itself. The temper must be enterprising and fearless, the manner firm and assured, and the correspondence between the heart and the tongue prompt and instantaneous, if we desire to have that view of man that shall do him the most credit, and induce us to form the most honourable opinion respecting him. On our front should sit fearless confidence and unsubdued hilarity. Our limbs should be free and unfettered, a state of the animal which imparts a grace infinitely more winning than that of the most skilful dancer. The very sound of our voice should be full, firm, mellow, and fraught with life and sensibility; of that nature, at the hearing of which every bosom rises, and every eye is lighted up. It is thus that men come to understand and confide in each other. This is the only frame that can perfectly conduce to our moral improvement, the awakening of our faculties, the diffusion of science, and the establishment of the purest notions and principles of civil and political liberty.

ESSAY XVII. OF BALLOT.

The subject of the preceding Essay leads by an obvious transition to the examination of a topic, which at present occupies to a considerable extent the attention of those who are anxious for the progress of public improvement, and the placing the liberties of mankind on the securest basis: I mean, the topic of the vote by ballot.

It is admitted that the most beneficial scheme for the government of nations, is a government by representation: that is, that there shall be in every nation, or large collection of men, a paramount legislative assembly, composed of deputies chosen by the people in their respective counties, cities, towns, or departments. In what manner then shall these deputies be elected?

The argument in favour of the election by ballot is obvious.

In nearly all civilised countries there exists more or less an inequality of rank and property: we will confine our attention principally to the latter.

Property necessarily involves influence. Mankind are but too prone to pay a superior deference to those who wear better clothes, live in larger houses, and command superior accommodations to those which fall to the lot of the majority.

One of the main sources of wealth in civilised nations is the possession of land. Those who have a considerable allotment of land in property, for the most part let it out in farms on lease or otherwise to persons of an inferior rank, by whom it is cultivated. In this case a reciprocal relation is created between the landlord and the tenant: and, if the landlord conducts himself towards his tenant agreeably to the principles of honour and liberality, it is impossible that the tenant should not feel disposed to gratify his landlord, so far as shall be compatible with his own notions of moral rectitude, or the paramount interests of the society of which he is a member.

If the proprietor of any extensive allotment of land does not let it out in farms, but retains it under his own direction, he must employ a great number of husbandmen and labourers; and over them he must be expected to exercise the same sort of influence, as under the former statement we supposed him to exercise over his tenants.

The same principle will still operate wherever any one man in society is engaged in the expenditure of a considerable capital. The manufacturer will possess the same influence over his workmen, as the landed proprietor over his tenants or labourers. Even the person who possesses considerable opulence, and has no intention to engage in the pursuits of profit or accumulation, will have an ample retinue, and will be enabled to use the same species of influence over his retainers and trades-people, as the landlord exercises over his tenants and labourers, and the manufacturer over his workmen.

A certain degree of this species of influence in society, is perhaps not to be excepted against. The possessor of opulence in whatever form, may be expected to have received a superior education, and, being placed at a certain distance from the minuter details and the lesser wheels in the machine of society, to have larger and more expansive views as to the interests of the whole. It is good that men in different ranks of society should be brought into intercourse with each other; it will subtract something from the prejudices of both, and enable each to obtain some of the advantages of the other. The division of rank is too much calculated to split society into parties having a certain hostility to each other. In a free state we are all citizens: it is desirable that we should all be friends.

But this species of influence may be carried too far. To a certain extent it is good. Inasmuch as it implies the enlightening one human understanding by the sparks struck out from another, or even the communication of feelings between man and man, this is not to be deprecated. Some degree of courteous compliance and deference of the ignorant to the better informed, is inseparable from the existence of political society as we behold it; such a deference as we may conceive the candid and conscientious layman to pay to the suggestions of his honest and disinterested pastor.

Every thing however that is more than this, is evil. There should be no peremptory mandates, and no threat or apprehension of retaliation and mischief to follow, if the man of inferior station or opulence should finally differ in opinion from his wealthier neighbour. We may admit of a moral influence; but there must be nothing, that should in the smallest degree border on compulsion.

But it is unfortunately in the very nature of weak, erring and fallible mortals, to make an ill use of the powers that are confided to their discretion. The rich man in the wantonness of his authority will not stop at moral influence, but, if he is disappointed of his expectation by what he will call my wilfulness and obstinacy, will speedily find himself impelled to vindicate his prerogative, and to punish my resistance. In every such disappointment he will discern a dangerous precedent, and will apprehend that, if I escape with impunity, the whole of that ascendancy, which he has regarded as one of the valuable privileges contingent to his station, will be undermined.

Opulence has two ways of this grosser sort, by which it may enable its possessor to command the man below him,—punishment and reward. As the holder, for example, of a large landed estate, or the administrator of an ample income, may punish the man who shews himself refractory to his will, so he may also reward the individual who yields to his suggestions. This, in whatever form it presents itself, may be classed under the general head of bribery.

The remedy for all this therefore, real or potential, mischief, is said to lie in the vote by ballot, a contrivance, by means of which every man shall be enabled to give his vote in favour of or against any candidate that shall be nominated, in absolute secrecy, without it being possible for any one to discover on which side the elector decided,—nay, a contrivance, by which the elector is invited to practise mystery and concealment, inasmuch as it would seem an impertinence in him to speak out, when the law is expressly constructed to bid him act and be silent. If he speaks, he is guilty of a sort of libel on his brother-electors, who are hereby implicitly reproached by him for their impenetrableness and cowardice.

We are told that the institution of the ballot is indispensible to the existence of a free state, in a country where the goods of fortune are unequally distributed. In England, as the right of sending members to parliament is apportioned at the time I am writing, the power of electing is bestowed with such glaring inequality, and the number of electors in many cases is so insignificant, as inevitably to give to the noble and the rich the means of appointing almost any representatives they think fit, so that the house of commons may more justly be styled the nominees of the upper house, than the deputies of the nation. And it is further said, Remedy this inequality as much as you please, and reform the state of the representation to whatever degree, still, so long as the votes at elections are required to be given openly, the reform will be unavailing, and the essential part of the mischief will remain. The right of giving our votes in secrecy, is the only remedy that can cut off the ascendancy of the more opulent members of the community over the rest, and give us the substance of liberty, instead of cheating us with the shadow.

On the other side I would beg the reader to consider, that the vote by ballot, in its obvious construction, is not the symbol of liberty, but of slavery. What is it, that presents to every eye the image of liberty, and compels every heart to confess, This is the temple where she resides? An open front, a steady and assured look, an habitual and uninterrupted commerce between the heart and the tongue. The free man communicates with his neighbour, not in corners and concealed places, but in market-places and scenes of public resort; and it is thus that the sacred spark is caught from man to man, till all are inspired with a common flame. Communication and publicity are of the essence of liberty; it is the air they breathe; and without it they die.

If on the contrary I would characterise a despotism, I should say, It implied a certain circumference of soil, through whose divisions and districts every man suspected his neighbour, where every man was haunted with the terror that "walls have ears," and only whispered his discontent, his hopes and his fears, to the trees of the forest and the silent streams. If the dwellers on this soil consulted together, it would be in secret cabals and with closed doors; engaging in the sacred cause of public welfare and happiness, as if it were a thing of guilt, which the conspirator scarcely ventured to confess to his own heart.

A shrewd person of my acquaintance the other day, to whom I unadvisedly proposed a question as to what he thought of some public transaction, instantly replied with symptoms of alarm, "I beg to say that I never disclose my opinions upon matters either of religion or politics to any one." What did this answer imply as to the political government of the country where it was given?

Is it characteristic of a free state or a tyranny?

One of the first and highest duties that falls to the lot of a human creature, is that which he owes to the aggregate of reasonable beings inhabiting what he calls his country. Our duties are then most solemn and elevating, when they are calculated to affect the well being of the greatest number of men; and of consequence what a patriot owes to his native soil is the noblest theatre for his moral faculties. And shall we teach men to discharge this debt in the dark? Surely every man ought to be able to "render a reason of the hope that is in him," and give a modest, but an assured, account of his political conduct. When he approaches the hustings at the period of a public election, this is his altar, where he sacrifices in the face of men to that deity, which is most worth his adoration of all the powers whose single province is our sublunary state.

But the principle of the institution of ballot is to teach men to perform their best actions under the cloke of concealment. When I return from giving my vote in the choice of a legislative representative, I ought, if my mode of proceeding were regulated by the undebauched feelings of our nature, to feel somewhat proud that I had discharged this duty, uninfluenced, uncorrupted, in the sincere frame of a conscientious spirit. But the institution of ballot instigates me carefully to conceal what I have done. If I am questioned respecting it, the proper reply which is as it were put into my mouth is, "You have no right to ask me; and I shall not tell." But, as every man does not recollect the proper reply at the moment it is wanted, and most men feel abashed, when a direct question is put to them to which they know they are not to return a direct answer, many will stammer and feel confused, will perhaps insinuate a falshood, while at the same time their manner to a discerning eye will, in spite of all their precautions, disclose the very truth.

The institution of ballot not only teaches us that our best actions are those which we ought most steadily to disavow, but carries distrust and suspicion into all our most familiar relations. The man I want to deceive, and throw out in the keenness of his hunting, is my landlord. But how shall I most effectually conceal the truth from him? May I be allowed to tell it to my wife or my child? I had better not. It is a known maxim of worldly prudence, that the truth which may be a source of serious injury to me, is safest, when it is shut up in my own bosom. If I once let it out, there is no saying where the communication may stop. "Day unto day uttereth speech; and night unto night sheweth forth knowledge."

And is this the proud attitude of liberty, to which we are so eager to aspire? After all, there will be some ingenuous men in the community, who will not know how for ever to suppress what is dearest to their hearts. But at any rate this institution holds out a prize to him that shall be most secret and untraceable in his proceedings, that shall "shoe his horses with felt," and proceed in all his courses with silence and suspicion.

The first principle of morality to social man is, that we act under the eye of our fellows. The truly virtuous man would do as he ought, though no eye observed him. Persons, it is true, who deport themselves merely as "men-pleasers," for ever considering how the by-standers will pronounce of their conduct, are entitled to small commendation. The good man, it is certain, will see

> To do what virtue would, though sun and moon
>
> Were in the flat sea sunk.

But, imperfect creatures as we mortals usually are, these things act and react upon each other. A man of honourable intentions will demean himself justly, from the love of right. But he is confirmed in his just dealing by the approbation of his fellows; and, if he were tempted to step awry, he would be checked by the anticipation of their censure. Such is the nature of our moral education. It is with virtue, as it is with literary fame. If I write well, I can scarcely feel secure that I do so, till I obtain the suffrage of some competent judges, confirming the verdict which I was before tempted to pronounce in my own favour.

This acting as in a theatre, where men and Gods are judges of my conduct, is the true destination of man; and we cannot violate the universal law under which we were born, without having reason to fear the most injurious effects.

And is this mysterious and concealed way of proceeding one of the forms through which we are to pass in the school of liberty? The great end of all liberal institutions is, to make a man fearless, frank as the day, acting from a lively and earnest impulse, which will not be restrained, disdains all half-measures, and prompts us, as it were, to carry our hearts in our hands, for all men to challenge, and all men to comment on. It is true, that the devisers of liberal institutions will have foremost in their thoughts, how men shall be secure in their personal liberty, unrestrained in the execution of what their thoughts prompt them to do, and uncontrolled in the administration of the fruits of their industry. But the moral end of all is, that a man shall be worthy of the name, erect, independent of mind, spontaneous of decision, intrepid, overflowing with all good feelings, and open in the expression of the sentiments they inspire. If man is double in his weightiest purposes, full of ambiguity and concealment, and not daring to give words to the impulses of his soul, what matters it that he is free? We may pronounce of this man, that he is unworthy of the blessing that has fallen to his lot, and will never produce the fruits that should be engendered in the lap of liberty.

There is however, it should seem, a short answer to all this. It is in vain to expatiate to us upon the mischiefs of lying, hypocrisy and concealment, since it is only through them, as the way by which we are to march, that nations can be made free.

This certainly is a fearful judgment awarded upon our species: but is it true?

We are to begin, it seems, with concealing from our landlord, or our opulent neighbour, our political determinations; and so his corrupt influence will be broken, and the humblest individual will be safe in doing that which his honest and unbiased feelings may prompt him to do.

No: this is not the way in which the enemy of the souls of men is to be defeated. We must not begin with the confession of our faint-heartedness and our cowardice. A quiet, sober, unaltered frame of judgment, that insults no one, that has in it nothing violent, brutal and defying, is the frame that becomes us. If I would teach another man, my superior in rank, how he ought to construe and decide upon the conduct I hold, I must begin by making that conduct explicit.

It is not in morals, as it is in war. There stratagem is allowable, and to take the enemy by surprise. "Who enquires of an enemy, whether it is by fraud or heroic enterprise that he has gained the day?" But it is not so that the cause of liberty is to be vindicated in the civil career of life.

The question is of reducing the higher ranks of society to admit the just immunities of their inferiors. I will not allow that they shall be cheated into it. No: no man was ever yet recovered to his senses in a question of morals, but by plain, honest, soul-commanding speech. Truth is omnipotent, if we do not violate its majesty by surrendering its outworks, and giving up that vantage-ground, of which if we deprive it, it ceases to be truth. It finds a responsive chord in every human bosom. Whoever hears its voice, at the same time recognises its power. However corrupt he may be, however steeped in the habits of vice, and hardened in the practices of tyranny, if it be mildly, distinctly, emphatically enunciated, the colour will forsake his cheek, his speech will alter and be broken, and he will feel himself unable to turn it off lightly, as a thing of no impression and validity. In this way the erroneous man, the man nursed in the house of luxury, a stranger to the genuine, unvarnished state of things, stands a fair chance of being corrected.

But, if an opposite, and a truer way of thinking than that to which he is accustomed, is only brought to his observation by the reserve of him who entertains it, and who, while he entertains it, is reluctant to hold communion with his wealthier neighbour, who regards him as his adversary, and hardly admits him to be of the same common nature, there will be no general improvement. Under this discipline the two ranks of society will be perpetually more estranged, view each other with eye askance, and will be as two separate and hostile states, though inhabiting the same territory. Is this the picture we desire to see of genuine liberty, philanthropic, desirous of good to all, and overflowing with all generous emotions?

I hate where vice can bolt her arguments,

And virtue has no tongue to check her pride.

The man who interests himself for his country and its cause, who acts bravely and independently, and knows that he runs some risk in doing so, must have a strange opinion of the sacredness of truth, if the very consciousness of having done nobly does not supply him with courage, and give him that simple, unostentatious firmness, which shall carry immediate conviction to the heart. It is a bitter lesson that the institution of ballot teaches, while it says, "You have done well; therefore be silent; whisper it not to the winds; disclose it not to those who are most nearly allied to you; adopt the same conduct which would suggest itself to you, if you had perpetrated an atrocious crime."

In no long time after the commencement of the war of the allies against France, certain acts were introduced into the English parliament, declaring it penal by word or writing to utter any thing that should tend to bring the government into contempt; and these acts, by the mass of the adversaries of despotic power, were in way of contempt called the Gagging Acts. Little did I and my contemporaries of 1795 imagine, when we protested against these acts in the triumphant reign of William Pitt, that the soi-disant friends of liberty and radical reformers, when their turn of triumph came, would propose their Gagging Acts, recommending to the people to vote agreeably to their consciences, but forbidding them to give publicity to the honourable conduct they had been prevailed on to adopt!

But all this reasoning is founded in an erroneous, and groundlessly degrading, opinion of human nature. The improvement of the general institutions of society, the correction of the gross inequalities of our representation, will operate towards the improvement of all the members of the community. While ninety-nine in an hundred of the inhabitants of England are carried forward in the scale of intellect and virtue, it would be absurd to suppose that the hundredth man will stand still, merely because he is rich. Patriotism is a liberal and a social impulse; its influence is irresistible; it is contagious, and is propagated by the touch; it is infectious, and mixes itself with the air that we breathe.

Men are governed in their conduct in a surprising degree by the opinion of others. It was all very well, when noblemen were each of them satisfied of the equity and irresistible principle of their ascendancy, when the vulgar population felt convinced that passive obedience was entailed on them from their birth, when we were in a manner but just emancipated (illusorily emancipated!) from the state of serfs and villains. But a memorable melioration of the state of man will carry some degree of conviction to the hearts of all. The most corrupt will be made doubtful: many who had not gone so far in ill, will desert the banners of oppression.

We see this already. What a shock was propagated through the island, when, the other day, a large proprietor, turning a considerable cluster of his tenants out of the houses and lands they occupied, because they refused to vote for a representative in parliament implicitly as he bade them, urged in his own justification, "Shall I not do what I will with my own?" This was all sound morals and divinity perhaps at the period of his birth. Nobody disputed it; or, if any one did, he was set down by the oracles of the vicinage as a crackbrained visionary. This man, so confident in his own prerogatives, had slept for the last twenty years, and awoke totally unconscious of what had been going on in almost every corner of Europe in the interval. A few more such examples; and so broad and sweeping an assumption will no more be heard of, and it will remain in the records of history, as a thing for the reality of which we have sufficient evidence, but which common sense repudiates, and which seems to demand from us a certain degree of credulity to induce us to admit that it had ever been.

The manners of society are by no means so unchanged and unalterable as many men suppose. It is here, as in the case of excessive drinking, which I had lately occasion to mention(36). In rude and barbarous times men of the highest circles piqued themselves upon their power of swallowing excessive potations, and found pleasure in it. It is in this as in so many other vices, we follow implicitly where our elders lead the way. But the rage of drinking is now gone by; and you will with difficulty find a company of persons of respectable appearance, who assemble round a table for the purpose of making beasts of themselves. Formerly it was their glory; now, if any man unhappily retains the weakness, he hides it from his equals, as he would a loathsome disease. The same thing will happen as to parliamentary corruption, and the absolute authority that was exercised by landlords over the consciences of their tenants. He that shall attempt to put into act what is then universally condemned, will be a marked man, and will be generally shunned by his fellows. The eye of the world will be upon him, as the murderer fancies himself followed by the eye of omnipotence; and he will obey the general voice of the community, that he may be at peace with himself.

(36) See above, Essay 9.

Let us not then disgrace a period of memorable improvement, by combining it with an institution that should mark that we, the great body of the people, regard the more opulent members of the community as our foes. Let us hold out to them the right hand of fellowship; and they will meet us. They will be influenced, partly by ingenuous shame for the unworthy conduct which they and their fathers had so long pursued, and partly by sympathy for the genuine joy and expansion of heart that is spreading itself through the land. Scarcely any one can restrain himself from participating in the happiness of the great body of his countrymen; and, if they see that we treat them with generous confidence, and are unwilling to recur to the memory of former grievances, and that a spirit of philanthropy and unlimited good-will is the sentiment of the day, it can scarcely happen but that their conversion will be complete, and the harmony be made entire(37).

(37) The subject of this Essay is resumed in the close of the following.

ESSAY XVIII. OF DIFFIDENCE.

The following Essay will be to a considerable degree in the nature of confession, like the Confessions of St. Augustine or of Jean Jacques Rousseau. It may therefore at first sight appear of small intrinsic value, and scarcely worthy of a place in the present series. But, as I have had occasion more than once to remark, we are all of us framed in a great measure on the same model, and the analysis of the individual may often stand for the analysis of a species. While I describe myself therefore, I shall probably at the same time be describing no inconsiderable number of my fellow-beings.

It is true, that the duty of man under the head of Frankness, is of a very comprehensive nature. We ought all of us to tell to our neighbour whatever it may be of advantage to him to know, we ought to be the sincere and zealous advocates of absent merit and worth, and we are bound by every means in our power to contribute to the improvement of others, and to the diffusion of salutary truths through the world.

From the universality of these precepts many readers might be apt to infer, that I am in my own person the bold and unsparing preacher of truth, resolutely giving to every man his due, and, agreeably to the apostle's direction, "instant in season, and out of season." The individual who answers to this description will often be deemed troublesome, often annoying; he will produce a considerable sensation in the circle of those who know him; and it will depend upon various collateral circumstances, whether he shall ultimately be judged a rash and intemperate disturber of the contemplations of his neighbours, or a disinterested and heroic suggester of new veins of thinking, by which his contemporaries and their posterity shall be essentially the gainers.

I have no desire to pass myself upon those who may have any curiosity respecting me for better than I am; and I will therefore here put down a few particulars, which may tend to enable them to form an equitable judgment.

One of the earliest passions of my mind was the love of truth and sound opinion. "Why should I," such was the language of my solitary meditations, "because I was born in a certain degree of latitude, in a certain century, in a country where certain institutions prevail, and of parents professing a certain faith, take it for granted that all this is right?—This is matter of accident. 'Time and chance happeneth to all:' and I, the thinking principle within me, might, if such had been the order of events, have been born under circumstances the very reverse of those under which I was born. I will not, if I can help it, be the creature of accident; I will not, like a shuttle-cock, be at the disposal of every impulse that is given me." I felt a certain disdain for the being thus directed; I could not endure the idea of being made a fool of, and of taking every ignis fatuus for a guide, and every stray notion, the meteor of the day, for everlasting truth. I am the person, spoken of in a preceding Essay(38), who early said to Truth, "Go on: whithersoever thou leadest, I am prepared to follow."

(38) See above, Essay XIII.

During my college-life therefore, I read all sorts of books, on every side of any important question, that were thrown in my way, or that I could hear of. But the very passion that determined me to this mode of proceeding, made me wary and circumspect in coming to a conclusion. I knew that it would, if any thing, be a more censurable and contemptible act, to yield to every seducing novelty, than to adhere obstinately to a prejudice because it had been instilled into me in youth. I was therefore slow of conviction, and by no means "given to change." I never willingly parted with a suggestion that was unexpectedly furnished to me; but I examined it again and again, before I consented that it should enter into the set of my principles.

In proportion however as I became acquainted with truth, or what appeared to me to be truth, I was like what I have read of Melancthon, who, when he was first converted to the tenets of Luther, became eager to go into all companies, that he might make them partakers of the same inestimable treasures, and set before them evidence that was to him irresistible. It is needless to say, that he often encountered the most mortifying disappointment.

Young and eager as I was in my mission, I received in this way many a bitter lesson. But the peculiarity of my temper rendered this doubly impressive to me. I could not pass over a hint, let it come from what quarter it would, without taking it into some consideration, and endeavouring to ascertain the precise weight that was to be attributed to it. It would however often happen, particularly in the question of the claims of a given individual to honour and respect, that I could see nothing but the most glaring injustice in the opposition I experienced. In canvassing the character of an individual, it is not for the most part general, abstract or moral, principles that are called into question: I am left in possession of the premises which taught me to admire the man whose character is contested; and conformably to those premises I see that his claim to the honour I have paid him is fully made out.

In my communications with others, in the endeavour to impart what I deemed to be truth, I began with boldness: but I often found that the evidence that was to me irresistible, was made small account of by others; and it not seldom happened, as candour was my principle, and a determination to receive what could be strewn to be truth, let it come from what quarter it would, that suggestions were presented to me, materially calculated to stagger the confidence with which I had set out. If I had been divinely inspired, if I had been secured by an omniscient spirit against the danger of error, my case would have been different. But I was not inspired. I often encountered an opposition I had not anticipated, and was often presented with objections, or had pointed out to me flaws and deficiencies in my reasonings, which, till they were so pointed out, I had not apprehended. I had not lungs enabling me to drown all contradiction; and, which was still more material, I had not a frame of mind, which should determine me to regard whatever could be urged against me as of no value. I therefore became cautious. As a human creature, I did not relish the being held up to others' or to myself, as rash, inconsiderate and headlong, unaware of difficulties the most obvious, embracing propositions the most untenable, and "against hope believing in hope." And, as an apostle of truth, I distinctly perceived that a reputation for perspicacity and sound judgment was essential to my mission. I therefore often became less a speaker, than a listener, and by no means made it a law with myself to defend principles and characters I honoured, on every occasion on which I might hear them attacked.

A new epoch occurred in my character, when I published, and at the time I was writing, my Enquiry concerning Political Justice. My mind was wrought up to a certain elevation of tone; the speculations in which I was engaged, tending to embrace all that was most important to man in society, and the frame to which I had assiduously bent myself, of giving quarter to nothing because it was old, and shrinking from nothing because it was startling and astounding, gave a new bias to my character. The habit which I thus formed put me more on the alert even in the scenes of ordinary life, and gave me a boldness and an eloquence more than was natural to me. I then reverted to the principle which I stated in the beginning, of being ready to tell my neighbour whatever it might be of advantage to him to know, to shew myself the sincere and zealous advocate of absent merit and worth, and to contribute by every means in my power to the improvement of others and to the diffusion of salutary truth through the world. I desired that every hour that I lived should be turned to the best account, and was bent each day to examine whether I had conformed myself to this rule. I held on this course with tolerable constancy for five or six years: and, even when that constancy abated, it failed not to leave a beneficial effect on my subsequent conduct.

But, in pursuing this scheme of practice, I was acting a part somewhat foreign to my constitution. I was by nature more of a speculative than an active character, more inclined to reason within myself upon what I heard and saw, than to declaim concerning it. I loved to sit by unobserved, and to meditate upon the panorama before me. At first I associated chiefly with those who were more or less admirers of my work; and, as I had risen (to speak in the slang phrase) like "a star" upon my contemporaries without being expected, I was treated generally with a certain degree of deference, or, where not with deference and submission, yet as a person whose opinions and view of things were to be taken into the account. The individuals who most strenuously opposed me, acted with a consciousness that, if they affected to despise me, they must not expect that all the bystanders would participate in that feeling.

But this was to a considerable degree the effect of novelty. My lungs, as I have already said, were not of iron; my manner was not overbearing and despotic; there was nothing in it to deter him who differed from me from entering the field in turn, and telling the tale of his views and judgments in contradiction to mine. I descended into the arena, and stood on a level with the rest. Beyond this, it occasionally happened that, if I had not the stentorian lungs, and the petty artifices of rhetoric and conciliation, that should carry a cause independently of its merits, my antagonists were not deficient in these respects. I had nothing in my favour to balance this, but a sort of constitutional equanimity and imperturbableness of temper, which, if I was at any time silenced, made me not look like a captive to be dragged at the chariot-wheels of my adversary.

All this however had a tendency to subtract from my vocation as a missionary. I was no longer a knight-errant, prepared on all occasions by dint of arms to vindicate the cause of every principle that was unjustly handled, and every character that was wrongfully assailed. Meanwhile I returned to the field, occasionally and uncertainly. It required some provocation and incitement to call me out: but there was the lion, or whatever combative animal may more justly prefigure me, sleeping, and that might be awakened.

There is another feature necessary to be mentioned, in order to make this a faithful representation. There are persons, it should seem, of whom it may be predicated, that they are semper parati. This has by no means been my case. My genius often deserted me. I was far from having the thought, the argument, or the illustration at all times ready, when it was required. I resembled to a certain degree the persons we read of, who are said to be struck as if with a divine judgment. I was for a moment changed into one of the mere herd, de grege porcus. My powers therefore were precarious, and I could not always be the intrepid and qualified advocate of truth, if I vehemently desired it. I have often, a few minutes afterwards, or on my return to my chambers, recollected the train of thinking, which world have strewn me off to advantage, and memorably done me honour, if I could have had it at my command the moment it was wanted.

And so much for confession. I am by no means vindicating myself.

I honour much more the man who is at all times ready to tell his neighbour whatever it may be of advantage to him to know, to shew himself the sincere and untemporising advocate of absent merit and worth, and to contribute by every means in his power to the improvement of others, and to the diffusion of salutary truths through the world.

This is what every man ought to be, and what the best devised scheme of republican institutions would have a tendency to make us all.

But, though the man here described is to a certain degree a deserter of his true place in society, and cannot be admitted to have played his part in all things well, we are by no means to pronounce upon him a more unfavourable judgment than he merits. Diffidence, though, where it disqualifies us in any way from doing justice to truth, either as it respects general principle or individual character, a defect, yet is on no account to be confounded in demerit with that suppression of truth, or misrepresentation, which grows out of actual craft and design.

The diffident man, in some cases seldomer, and in some oftener and in a more glaring manner, deserts the cause of truth, and by that means is the cause of misrepresentation, and indirectly the propagator of falshood. But he is constant and sincere as far as he goes; he never lends his voice to falshood, or intentionally to sophistry; he never for an instant goes over to the enemy's standard, or disgraces his honest front by strewing it in the ranks of tyranny or imposture. He may undoubtedly be accused, to a certain degree, of dissimulation, or throwing into shade the thing that is, but never of simulation, or the pretending the thing to be that is not. He is plain and uniform in every thing that he professes, or to which he gives utterance; but, from timidity or irresolution, he keeps back in part the offering which he owes at the shrine where it is most honourable and glorious for man to worship.

And this brings me back again to the subject of the immediately preceding Essay, the propriety of voting by ballot.

The very essence of this scheme is silence. And this silence is not merely like that which is prompted by a diffident temper, which by fits is practiced by the modest and irresolute man, and by fits disappears before the sun of truth and through the energies of a temporary fortitude. It is uniform. It is not brought into act only, when the individual unhappily does not find in himself the firmness to play the adventurer. It becomes matter of system, and is felt as being recommended to us for a duty.

Nor does the evil stop there. In the course of my ordinary communications with my fellow-men, I speak when I please, and I am silent when I please, and there is nothing specially to be remarked either way. If I speak, I am perhaps listened to; and, if I am silent, it is likely enough concluded that it is because I have nothing of importance to say. But in the question of ballot the case is far otherwise. There it is known that the voter has his secret. When

I am silent upon a matter occurring in the usual intercourses of life where I might speak, nay, where we will suppose I ought to speak, I am at least guilty of dissimulation only. But the voter by ballot is strongly impelled to the practice of the more enormous sin of simulation. It is known, as I have said, that he has his secret. And he will often be driven to have recourse to various stratagems, that he may elude the enquirer, or that he may set at fault the sagacity of the silent observer. He has something that he might tell if he would, and he distorts himself in a thousand ways, that he may not betray the hoard which he is known to have in his custody. The institution of ballot is the fruitful parent of ambiguities, equivocations and lies without number.

ESSAY XIX. OF SELF-COMPLACENCY.

The subject of this Essay is intimately connected with those of Essays XI and XII, perhaps the most important of the series.

It has been established in the latter, that human creatures are constantly accompanied in their voluntary actions with the delusive sense of liberty, and that our character, our energies, and our conscience of moral right and wrong, are mainly dependent upon this feature in our constitution.

The subject of my present disquisition relates to the feeling of self-approbation or self-complacency, which will be found inseparable from the most honourable efforts and exertions in which mortal men can be engaged.

One of the most striking of the precepts contained in what are called the Golden Verses of Pythagoras, is couched in the words, "Reverence thyself."

The duties which are incumbent on man are of two sorts, negative and positive. We are bound to set right our mistakes, and to correct the evil habits to which we are prone; and we are bound also to be generously ambitious, to aspire after excellence, and to undertake such things as may reflect honour on ourselves, and be useful to others.

To the practice of the former of these classes of duties we may be instigated by prohibitions, menaces and fear, the fear of mischiefs that may fall upon us conformably to the known series of antecedents and consequents in the course of nature, or of mischiefs that may be inflicted on us by the laws of the country in which we live, or as results of the ill will and disapprobation felt towards us by individuals. There is nothing that is necessarily generous or invigorating in the practice of our negative duties. They amount merely to a scheme for keeping us within bounds, and restraining us from those sallies and escapes, which human nature, undisciplined and left to itself, might betray us into. But positive enterprise, and great actual improvement cannot be expected by us in this way. All this is what the apostle refers to, when he speaks of "the law as a schoolmaster to bring us to liberty," after which he advises us "not to be again entangled with the yoke of bondage."

On the other hand, if we would enter ourselves in the race of positive improvement, if we would become familiar with generous sentiments, and the train of conduct which such sentiments inspire, we must provide ourselves with the soil in which such things grow, and engage in the species of husbandry by which they are matured; in other words, we must be no strangers to self-esteem and self-complacency.

The truth of this statement may perhaps be most strikingly illustrated, if we take for our example the progress of schoolboys under a preceptor. A considerable proportion of these are apt, diligent, and desirous to perform the tasks in which they are engaged, so as to satisfy the demands of their masters and parents, and to advance honourably in the path that is recommended to them. And a considerable proportion put themselves on the defensive, and propose to their own minds to perform exactly as much as shall exempt them from censure and punishment, and no more.

Now I say of the former, that they cannot accomplish the purpose they have conceived, unless so far as they are aided by a sentiment of self-reverence.

The difference of the two parties is, that the latter proceed, so far as their studies are concerned, as feeling themselves under the law of necessity, and as if they were machines merely, and the former as if they were under what the apostle calls "the law of liberty."

We cannot perform our tasks to the best of our power, unless we think well of our own capacity.

But this is the smallest part of what is necessary. We must also be in good humour with ourselves. We must say, I can do that which I shall have just occasion to look back upon with satisfaction. It is the anticipation of this result, that stimulates our efforts, and carries us forward. Perseverance is an active principle, and cannot continue to operate but under the influence of desire. It is incompatible with languor and neutrality. It implies the love of glory, perhaps of that glory which shall be attributed to us by others, or perhaps only of that glory which shall be reaped by us in the silent chambers of the mind. The diligent scholar is he that loves himself, and desires to have reason to applaud and love himself. He sits down to his task with resolution, he approves of what he does in each step of the process, and in each enquires, Is this the thing I purposed to effect?

And, as it is with the unfledged schoolboy, after the same manner it is with the man mature. He must have to a certain extent a good opinion of himself, he must feel a kind of internal harmony, giving to the circulations of his frame animation and cheerfulness, or he can never undertake and execute considerable things.

The execution of any thing considerable implies in the first place previous persevering meditation. He that undertakes any great achievement will, according to the vulgar phrase, "think twice," before he buckles up his resolution, and plunges into the ocean, which he has already surveyed with anxious glance while he remained on shore. Let our illustration be the case of Columbus, who, from the figure of the earth, inferred that there must be a way of arriving at the Indies by a voyage directly west, in distinction from the very complicated way hitherto practiced, by sailing up the Mediterranean, crossing the isthmus of Suez, and so falling down the Red Sea into the Indian Ocean. He weighed all the circumstances attendant on such an undertaking in his mind. He enquired into his own powers and resources, imaged to himself the various obstacles that might thwart his undertaking, and finally resolved to engage in it. If Columbus had not entertained a very good opinion of himself, it is impossible that he should have announced such a project, or should have achieved it.

Again. Let our illustration be, of Homer undertaking to compose the Iliad. If he had not believed himself to be a man of very superior powers to the majority of the persons around him, he would most assuredly never have attempted it. What an enterprise! To describe in twenty-four books, and sixteen thousand verses, the perpetual warfare and contention of two great nations, all Greece being armed for the attack, and all the western division of Asia Minor for the defence: the war carried on by two vast confederacies, under numerous chiefs, all sovereign and essentially independent of each other. To conceive the various characters of the different leaders, and their mutual rivalship. To engage all heaven, such as it was then understood, as well as what was most respectable on earth, in the struggle. To form the idea, through twenty-four books, of varying the incidents perpetually, and keeping alive the attention of the reader or hearer without satiety or weariness. For this purpose, and to answer to his conception of a great poem, Homer appears to have thought it necessary that the action should be one; and he therefore took the incidental quarrel of Achilles and the commander in chief, the resentment of Achilles, and his consequent defection from the cause, till, by the death of Patroclus, and then of Hector, all traces of the misunderstanding first, and then of its consequences, should be fully obliterated.

There is further an essential difference between the undertaking of Columbus and that of Homer. Once fairly engaged, there was for Columbus no drawing back. Being already at sea on the great Atlantic Ocean, he could not retrace his steps. Even when he had presented his project to the sovereigns of Spain, and they had accepted it, and still more when the ships were engaged, and the crews mustered, he must go forward, or submit to indelible disgrace.

It is not so in writing a poem. The author of the latter may stop whenever he pleases. Of consequence, during every day of its execution, he requires a fresh stimulus. He must look back on the past, and forward on what is to come, and feel that he has considerable reason to be satisfied. The great naval discoverer may have his intervals of misgiving and discouragement, and may, as Pope expresses it, "wish that any one would hang him." He goes forward; for he has no longer the liberty to choose. But the author of a mighty poem is not in the same manner entangled, and therefore to a great degree returns to his work each day, "screwing his courage to the sticking-place." He must feel the same fortitude and elasticity, and be as entirely the same man of heroic energy, as when he first arrived at the resolution to engage. How much then of self-complacency and self-confidence do his undertaking and performance imply!

I have taken two of the most memorable examples in the catalogue of human achievements: the discovery of a New World, and the production of the Iliad. But all those voluntary actions, or rather series and chains of actions, which comprise energy in the first determination, and honour in the execution, each in its degree rests upon self-complacency as the pillar upon which its weight is sustained, and without which it must sink into nothing.

Self-complacency then being the indispensible condition of all that is honourable in human achievements, hence we may derive a multitude of duties, and those of the most delicate nature, incumbent on the preceptor, as well as a peculiar discipline to be observed by the candidate, both while he is "under a schoolmaster," and afterwards when he is emancipated, and his plan of conduct is to be regulated by his own discretion.

The first duty of the preceptor is encouragement.

Not that his face is to be for ever dressed in smiles, and that his tone is to be at all times that of invitation and courtship. The great theatre of the world is of a mingled constitution, made up of advantages and sufferings; and it is perhaps best that so should be the different scenes of the drama as they pass. The young adventurer is not to expect to have every difficulty smoothed for him by the hand of another. This were to teach him a lesson of effeminacy and cowardice. On the contrary it is necessary that he should learn that human life is a state of hardship, that the adversary we have to encounter does not always present himself with his fangs sheathed in the woolly softness which occasionally renders them harmless, and that nothing great or eminently honourable was ever achieved but through the dint of resolution, energy and struggle. It is good that the winds of heaven should blow upon him, that he should encounter the tempest of the elements, and occasionally sustain the inclemency of the summer's heat and winter's cold, both literally and metaphorically.

But the preceptor, however he conducts himself in other respects, ought never to allow his pupil to despise himself, or to hold himself as of no account. Self-contempt can never be a discipline favourable to energy or to virtue. The pupil ought at all times to judge himself in some degree worthy, worthy and competent now to attempt, and hereafter to accomplish, things deserving of commendation. The preceptor must never degrade his pupil in his own eyes, but on the contrary must teach him that nothing but resolution and perseverance are necessary, to enable him to effect all that the judicious director can expect from him. He should be encouraged through every step of his progress, and specially encouraged when he has gained a certain point, and arrived at an important resting-place. It is thus we are taught the whole circle of what are called accomplishments, dancing, music, fencing, and the rest; and it is surely a strange anomaly, if those things which are most essential in raising the mind to its true standard, cannot be communicated with equal suavity and kindness, be surrounded with allurements, and regarded as sources of pleasure and genuine hilarity.

In the mean time it is to be admitted that every human creature, especially in the season of youth, and not being the victim of some depressing disease either of body or mind, has in him a good obstinate sort of self-complacency, which cannot without much difficulty be eradicated. "Though he falleth seven times, yet will he rise again." And, when we have encountered various mortifications, and have been many times rebuked and inveighed against, we nevertheless recover our own good opinion, and are ready to enter into a fresh contention for the prize, if not in one kind, then in another.

It is in allusion to this feature in the human character, that we have an expressive phrase in the English language,—"to break the spirit." The preceptor may occasionally perhaps prescribe to the pupil a severe task; and the young adventurer may say, Can I be expected to accomplish this? But all must be done in kindness. The generous attempter must be reminded of the powers he has within him, perhaps yet unexercised; with cheering sounds his progress must be encouraged; and, above all, the director of the course must take care not to tax him beyond his strength. And, be it observed, that the strength of a human creature is to be ascertained by two things; first, the abstract capacity, that the thing required is not beyond the power of a being so constituted to perform; and, secondly, we must take into the account his past achievements, the things he has already accomplished, and not expect that he is at once to overleap a thousand obstacles.

For there is such a thing as a broken spirit. I remember a boy who was my schoolfellow, that, having been treated with uncalled for severity, never appeared afterwards in the scene of instruction, but with a neglected appearance, and the articles of his dress scarcely half put on. I was very young at the time, and viewed only the outside of things. I cannot tell whether he had any true ambition previously to his disgrace, but I am sure he never had afterwards.

How melancholy an object is the man, who, "for the privilege to breathe, bears up and down the city

A discontented and repining spirit

Burthensome to itself,"

incapable of enterprise, listless, with no courage to undertake, and no anticipation of the practicability of success and honour! And this spectacle is still more affecting, when the subject shall be a human creature in the dawn of youth, when nature opens to him a vista of beauty and fruition on every side, and all is encouraging, redolent of energy and enterprise!

To break the spirit of a man, bears a considerable resemblance to the breaking the main spring, or principal movement, of a complicated and ingeniously constructed machine. We cannot tell when it is to happen; and it comes at last perhaps at the time that it is least expected. A judicious superintendent therefore will be far from trying consequences in his office, and will, like a man walking on a cliff whose extremes are ever and anon crumbling away and falling into the ocean, keep much within the edge, and at a safe distance from the line of danger.

But this consideration has led me much beyond the true subject of this Essay. The instructor of youth, as I have already said, is called upon to use all his skill, to animate the courage, and maintain the cheerfulness and self-complacency of his pupil. And, as such is the discipline to be observed to the candidate, while he is "under a schoolmaster," so, when he is emancipated, and his plan of conduct is to be regulated by his own discretion, it is necessary that he should carry forward the same scheme, and cultivate that tone of feeling, which should best reconcile him to himself, and, by teaching him to esteem himself and bear in mind his own value, enable him to achieve things honourable to his character, and memorably useful to others. Melancholy, and a disposition anticipating evil are carefully to be guarded against, by him who is desirous to perform his part well on the theatre of society. He should habitually meditate all cheerful things, and sing the song of battle which has a thousand times spurred on his predecessors to victory. He should contemplate the crown that awaits him, and say to himself, I also will do my part, and endeavour to enrol myself in the select number of those champions, of whom it has been predicated that they were men, of whom, compared with the herd of ordinary mortals, "the world," the species among whom they were rated, "was not worthy."

Another consideration is to be recollected here. Without self-complacency in the agent no generous enterprise is to be expected, and no train of voluntary actions, such as may purchase honour to the person engaged in them.

But, beside this, there is no true and substantial happiness but for the self-complacent. "The good man," as Solomon says, "is satisfied from himself." The reflex act is inseparable from the constitution of the human mind. How can any one have genuine happiness, unless in proportion as he looks round, and, "behold! every thing is very good?" This is the sunshine of the soul, the true joy, that gives cheerfulness to all our circulations, and makes us feel ourselves entire and complete. What indeed is life, unless so far as it is enjoyed? It does not merit the name. If I go into a school, and look round on a number of young faces, the scene is destitute of its true charm, unless so far as I see inward peace and contentment on all sides. And, if we require this eminently in the young, neither can it be less essential, when in growing manhood we have the real cares of the world to contend with, or when in declining age we need every auxiliary to enable us to sustain our infirmities.

But, before I conclude my remarks on this subject, it is necessary that I should carefully distinguish between the thesis, that self-complacency is the indispensible condition of all that is honourable in human achievements, and the proposition contended against in Essay XI, that "self-love is the source of all our actions." Self-complacency is indeed the feeling without which we cannot proceed in an honourable course; but is far from being the motive that impels us to act. The motive is in the real nature and absolute properties of the good thing that is proposed to our choice: we seek the happiness of another, because his happiness is the object of our desire. Self-complacency may be likened to the bottle-holder in one of those contentions for bodily prowess, so characteristic of our old English manners. The bottle-holder is necessary to supply the combatant with refreshment, and to encourage him to persist; but it would be most unnatural to regard him as the cause of the contest. No: the parties have found reason for competition, they apprehend a misunderstanding or a rivalry impossible to be settled but by open contention, and the putting forth of mental and corporeal energy; and the bottle-holder is an auxiliary called in afterwards, his interference implying that the parties have already a motive to act, and have thrown down the gauntlet in token of the earnest good-will which animates them to engage.

ESSAY XX. OF PHRENOLOGY.

The following remarks can pretend to be nothing more than a few loose and undigested thoughts upon a subject, which has recently occupied the attention of many men, and obtained an extraordinary vogue in the world. It were to be wished, that the task had fallen into the hands of a writer whose studies were more familiar with all the sciences which bear more or less on the topic I propose to consider: but, if abler and more competent men pass it by, I feel disposed to plant myself in the breach, and to offer suggestions which may have the fortune to lead others, better fitted for the office than myself, to engage in the investigation. One advantage I may claim, growing out of my partial deficiency. It is known not to be uncommon for a man to stand too near to the subject of his survey, to allow him to obtain a large view of it in all its bearings. I am no anatomist: I simply take my stand upon the broad ground of the general philosophy of man.

It is a very usual thing for fanciful theories to have their turn amidst the eccentricities of the human mind, and then to be heard of no more. But it is perhaps no ill occupation, now and then, for an impartial observer, to analyse these theories, and attempt to blow away the dust which will occasionally settle on the surface of science. If phrenology, as taught by Gall and Spurzheim, be a truth, I shall probably render a service to that truth, by endeavouring to shew where the edifice stands in need of more solid supports than have yet been assigned to it. If it be a falshood, the sooner it is swept away to the gulph of oblivion the better. Let the inquisitive and the studious fix their minds on more substantial topics, instead of being led away by gaudy and deceitful appearances. The human head, that crowning capital of the column of man, is too interesting a subject, to be the proper theme of every dabbler. And it is obvious, that the professors of this so called discovery, if they be rash and groundless in their assertions, will be in danger of producing momentous errors, of exciting false hopes never destined to be realised, and of visiting with pernicious blasts the opening buds of excellence, at the time when they are most exposed to the chance of destruction.

I shall set out with acknowledging, that there is, as I apprehend, a science in relation to the human head, something like what Plato predicates of the statue hid in a block of marble. It is really contained in the block; but it is only the most consummate sculptor, that can bring it to the eyes of men, and free it from all the incumbrances, which, till he makes application of his art to it, surround the statue, and load it with obscurities and disfigurement. The man, who, without long study and premeditation, rushes in at once, and expects to withdraw the curtain, will only find himself disgraced by the attempt.

There is a passage in an acute writer(39), whose talents singularly fitted him, even when he appeared totally immerged in mummery and trifles, to illustrate the most important truths, that is applicable to the point I am considering.

(39) Sterne, Tristram Shandy, Vol. 1.

"Pray, what was that man's name,—for I write in such a hurry, I have no time to recollect or look for it,—who first made the observation, 'That there was great inconstancy in our air and climate?' Whoever he was, it was a just and good observation in him. But the corollary drawn from it, namely, 'That it is this which has furnished us with such a variety of odd and whimsical characters;'—that was not his;—it was found out by another man, at least a century and a half after him. Then again, that this copious storehouse of original materials is the true and natural cause that our comedies are so much better than those of France, or any others that have or can be wrote upon the continent;—that discovery was not fully made till about the middle of king William's reign, when the great Dryden, in writing one of his long prefaces (if I mistake not), most fortunately hit upon it. Then, fourthly and lastly, that this strange irregularity in our climate, producing so strange an irregularity in our characters, cloth thereby in some sort make us amends, by giving us somewhat to make us merry with, when the weather will not suffer us to go out of doors,—that observation is my own; and was struck out by me this very rainy day, March 26, 1759, and betwixt the hour of nine and ten in the morning.

"Thus—thus, my fellow-labourers and associates in this great harvest of our learning, now ripening before our eyes; thus it is, by slow steps of casual increase, that our knowledge physical, metaphysical, physiological, polemical, nautical, mathematical, aenigmatical, technical, biographical, romantical, chemical, and obstetrical, with fifty other branches of it, (most of them ending, as these do, in ical,) has, for these two last centuries and more, gradually been creeping upwards towards that acme of their perfections, from which, if we may form a conjecture from the advantages of these last seven years, we cannot possibly be far off."

Nothing can be more true, than the proposition ludicrously illustrated in this passage, that real science is in most instances of slow growth, and that the discoveries which are brought to perfection at once, are greatly exposed to the suspicion of quackery. Like the ephemeron fly, they are born suddenly, and may be expected to die as soon.

Lavater, the well known author of Essays on Physiognomy, appears to have been born seventeen years before the birth of Gall. He attempted to reduce into a system the indications of human character that are to be found in the countenance. Physiognomy, as a subject of ingenious and probable conjecture, was well known to the ancients. But the test, how far any observations that have been made on the subject are worthy the name of a science, will lie in its application by the professor to a person respecting whom he has had no opportunity of previous information. Nothing is more easy, when a great warrior, statesman, poet, philosopher or philanthropist is explicitly placed before us, than for the credulous inspector or fond visionary to examine the lines of his countenance, and to point at the marks which should plainly shew us that he ought to have been the very thing that he is. This is the very trick of gipsies and fortune-tellers. But who ever pointed to an utter stranger in the street, and said, I perceive by that man's countenance that he is one of the great luminaries of the world? Newton, or Bacon, or Shakespear would probably have passed along unheeded. Instances of a similar nature occur every day. Hence it plainly appears that, whatever may hereafter be known on the subject, we can scarcely to the present time be said to have overstepped the threshold. And yet nothing can be more certain than that there is a science of physiognomy, though to make use of an illustration already cited, it has not to this day been extricated out of the block of marble in which it is hid. Human passions, feelings and modes of thinking leave their traces on the countenance: but we have not, thus far, left the dame's school in this affair, and are not qualified to enter ourselves in the free-school for more liberal enquiries.

The writings of Lavater on the subject of physiognomy are couched in a sort of poetic prose, overflowing with incoherent and vague exclamations, and bearing small resemblance to a treatise in which the elements of science are to be developed. Their success however was extraordinary; and it was probably that success, which prompted Gall first to turn his attention from the indications of character that are to be found in the face of man, to the study of the head generally, as connected with the intellectual and moral qualities of the individual.

It was about four years before the commencement of the present century, that Gall appears to have begun to deliver lectures on the structure and external appearances of the human head. He tells us, that his attention was first called to the subject in the ninth year of his age (that is, in the year 1767), and that he spent thirty years in the private meditation of his system, before he began to promulgate it. Be that as it will, its most striking characteristic is that of marking out the scull into compartments, in the same manner as a country delineated on a map is divided into districts, and assigning a different faculty or organ to each. In the earliest of these diagrams that has fallen under my observation, the human scull is divided into twenty-seven compartments.

I would say of craniology, as I have already said of physiognomy, that there is such a science attainable probably by man, but that we have yet made scarcely any progress in the acquiring it. As certain lines in the countenance are indicative of the dispositions of the man, so it is reasonable to believe that a certain structure of the head is in correspondence with the faculties and propensities of the individual.

Thus far we may probably advance without violating a due degree of caution. But there is a wide distance between this general statement, and the conduct of the man who at once splits the human head into twenty-seven compartments.

The exterior appearance of the scull is affirmed to correspond with the structure of the brain beneath. And nothing can be more analogous to what the deepest thinkers have already confessed of man, than to suppose that there is one structure of the brain better adapted for intellectual purposes than another. There is probably one structure better adapted than another, for calculation, for poetry, for courage, for cowardice, for presumption, for diffidence, for roughness, for tenderness, for self-control and the want of it. Even as some have inherently a faculty adapted for music or the contrary(40).

(40) See above, Essay II.

But it is not reasonable to believe that we think of calculation with one portion of the brain, and of poetry with another.

It is very little that we know of the nature of matter; and we are equally ignorant as to the substance, whatever it is, in which the thinking principle in man resides. But, without adventuring in any way to dogmatise on the subject, we find so many analogies between the thinking principle, and the structure of what we call the brain, that we cannot but regard the latter as in some way the instrument of the former.

Now nothing can be more certain respecting the thinking principle, than its individuality. It has been said, that the mind can entertain but one thought at one time; and certain it is, from the nature of attention, and from the association of ideas, that unity is one of the principal characteristics of mind. It is this which constitutes personal identity; an attribute that, however unsatisfactory may be the explanations which have been given respecting it, we all of us feel, and that lies at the foundation of all our voluntary actions, and all our morality.

Analogous to this unity of thought and mind, is the arrangement of the nerves and the brain in the human body. The nerves all lead up to the brain; and there is a centrical point in the brain itself, in which the reports of the senses terminate, and at which the action of the will may be conceived to begin. This, in the language of our fathers, was called the "seat of the soul."

We may therefore, without departing from the limits of a due caution and modesty, consider this as the throne before which the mind holds its court. Hither the senses bring in their reports, and hence the sovereign will issues his commands. The whole system appears to be conducted through the instrumentality of the nerves, along whose subtle texture the feelings and impressions are propagated. Between the reports of the senses and the commands of the will, intervenes that which is emphatically the office of the mind, comprising meditation, reflection, inference and judgment. How these functions are performed we know not; but it is reasonable to believe that the substance of the brain or of some part of the brain is implicated in them.

Still however we must not lose sight of what has been already said, that in the action of the mind unity is an indispensible condition. Our thoughts can only hold their council and form their decrees in a very limited region. This is their retreat and strong hold; and the special use and functions of the remoter parts of the brain we are unable to determine; so utterly obscure and undefined is our present knowledge of the great ligament which binds together the body and the thinking principle.

Enough however results from this imperfect view of the ligament, to demonstrate the incongruity and untenableness of a doctrine which should assign the indications of different functions, exercises and propensities of the mind to the exterior surface of the scull or the brain. This is quackery, and is to be classed with chiromancy, augury, astrology, and the rest of those schemes for discovering the future and unknown, which the restlessness and anxiety of the human mind have invented, built upon arbitrary principles, blundered upon in the dark, and having no resemblance to the march of genuine science. I find in sir Thomas Browne the following axioms of chiromancy: "that spots in the tops of the nails do signifie things past; in the middle, things present; and at the bottom, events to come: that white specks presage our felicity; blue ones our misfortunes: that those in the nails of the thumb have significations of honour, in the forefinger, of riches, and so respectively in the rest."

Science, to be of a high and satisfactory character, ought to consist of a deduction of causes and effects, shewing us not merely that a thing is so, but why it is as it is, and cannot be otherwise. The rest is merely empirical; and, though the narrowness of human wit may often drive us to this; yet it is essentially of a lower order and description. As it depends for its authority upon an example, or a number of examples, so examples of a contrary nature may continually come in, to weaken its force, or utterly to subvert it. And the affair is made still worse, when we see, as in the case of craniology, that all the reasons that can be deduced (as here from the nature of mind) would persuade us to believe, that there can be no connection between the supposed indications, and the things pretended to be indicated.

Craniology, or phrenology, proceeds exactly in the same train, as chiromancy, or any of those pretended sciences which are built merely on assumption or conjecture. The first delineations presented to the public, marked out, as I have said, the scull into compartments, in the same manner as a country delineated on a map is divided into districts. Geography is a real science, and accordingly, like other sciences, has been slow and gradual in its progress. At an early stage travellers knew little more than the shores and islands of the Mediterranean. Afterwards, they passed the straits of Hercules, and entered into the Atlantic. At length the habitable world was distributed into three parts, Europe, Asia, and Africa. More recently, by many centuries, came the discovery of America. It is but the other day comparatively, that we found the extensive island of New Holland in the Southern Ocean. The ancient geographers placed an elephant or some marine monster in the vacant parts of their maps, to signify that of these parts they knew nothing. Not so Dr. Gall. Every part of his globe of the human Scull, at least with small exceptions, is fully tenanted; and he, with his single arm, has conquered a world.

The majority of the judgments that have been divulged by the professors of this science, have had for their subjects the sculls of men, whose habits and history have been already known. And yet with this advantage the errors and contradictions into which their authors have fallen are considerably numerous. Thus I find, in the account of the doctor's visit to the House of Correction and the Hospital of Torgau in July 1805, the following examples.

"Every person was desirous to know what Dr. Gall would say about T—, who was known in the house as a thief full of cunning, and who, having several times made his escape, wore an additional iron. It was surprising, that he saw in him far less of the organ of cunning, than in many of the other prisoners. However it was proved, that examples, and conversation with other thieves in the house, had suggested to him the plan for his escape, and that the stupidity which he possesses was the cause of his being retaken."

"We were much surprised to be told, that M., in whom Dr. Gall had not discovered the organ of representation, possessed extraordinary abilities in imitating the voice of animals; but we were convinced after enquiries, that his talent was not a natural one, but acquired by study. He related to us that, when he was a Prussian soldier garrisoned at Berlin, he used to deceive the waiting women in the Foundling Hospital by imitating the voice of exposed infants, and sometimes counterfeited the cry of a wild drake, when the officers were shooting ducks."

"Of another Dr. Gall said, His head is a pattern of inconstancy and confinement, and there appears not the least mark of the organ of courage. This rogue had been able to gain a great authority among his fellow-convicts. How is this to be reconciled with the want of constancy which his organisation plainly indicates? Dr. Gall answered, He gained his ascendancy not by courage, but by cunning."

It is well known, that in Thurtel, who was executed for one of the most cold-blooded and remorseless murders ever heard of, the phrenologists found the organ of benevolence uncommonly large.

In Spurzheim's delineation of the human head I find six divisions of organs marked out in the little hemisphere over the eye, indicating six different dispositions. Must there not be in this subtle distribution much of what is arbitrary and sciolistic?

It is to be regretted, that no person skilful in metaphysics, or the history of the human mind, has taken a share in this investigation. Many errors and much absurdity would have been removed from the statements of these theorists, if a proper division had been made between those attributes and propensities, which by possibility a human creature may bring into the world with him, and those which, being the pure growth of the arbitrary institutions of society, must be indebted to those institutions for their origin. I have endeavoured in a former Essay(41) to explain this distinction, and to shew how, though a human being cannot be born with an express propensity towards any one of the infinite pursuits and occupations which may be found in civilised society, yet that he may be fitted by his external or internal structure to excel in some one of those pursuits rather than another. But all this is overlooked by the phrenologists. They remark the various habits and dispositions, the virtues and the vices, that display themselves in society as now constituted, and at once and without consideration trace them to the structure that we bring into the world with us.

(41) See above, Essay II.

Certainly many of Gall's organs are a libel upon our common nature. And, though a scrupulous and exact philosopher will perhaps confess that he has little distinct knowledge as to the design with which "the earth and all that is therein" were made, yet he finds in it so much of beauty and beneficent tendency, as will make him extremely reluctant to believe that some men are born with a decided propensity to rob, and others to murder. Nor can any thing be more ludicrous than this author's distinction of the different organs of memory—of things, of places, of names, of language, and of numbers: organs, which must be conceived to be given in the first instance long before names or language or numbers had an existence. The followers of Gall have in a few instances corrected this: but what their denominations have gained in avoiding the grossest absurdities of their master, they have certainly lost in explicitness and perspicuity.

There is a distinction, not unworthy to be attended to, that is here to be made between Lavater's system of physiognomy, and Gall's of craniology, which is much in favour of the former. The lines and characteristic expressions of the face which may so frequently be observed, are for the most part the creatures of the mind. This is in the first place a mode of observation more agreeable to the pride and conscious elevation of man, and is in the next place more suitable to morality, and the vindication of all that is most admirable in the system of the universe. It is just, that what is most frequently passing in the mind, and is entertained there with the greatest favour, should leave its traces upon the countenance. It is thus that the high and exalted philosopher, the poet, and the man of benevolence and humanity are sometimes seen to be such by the bystander and the stranger. While the malevolent, the trickish, and the grossly sensual, give notice of what they are by the cast of their features, and put their fellow-creatures upon their guard, that they may not be made the prey of these vices.

But the march of craniology or phrenology, by whatever name it is called, is directly the reverse of this. It assigns to us organs, as far as the thing is explained by the professors either to the public or to their own minds, which are entailed upon us from our birth, and which are altogether independent, or nearly so, of any discipline or volition that can be exercised by or upon the individual who drags their intolerable chain. Thus I am told of one individual that he wants the organ of colour; and all the culture in the world can never supply that defect, and enable him to see colour at all, or to see it as it is seen by the rest of mankind. Another wants the organ of benevolence; and his case is equally hopeless. I shrink from considering the condition of the wretch, to whom nature has supplied the organs of theft and murder in full and ample proportions. The case is like that of astrology

(Their stars are more in fault than they),

with this aggravation, that our stars, so far as the faculty of prediction had been supposed to be attained, swayed in few things; but craniology climbs at once to universal empire; and in her map, as I have said, there are no vacant places, no unexplored regions and happy wide-extended deserts.

It is all a system of fatalism. Independently of ourselves, and far beyond our control, we are reserved for good or for evil by the predestinating spirit that reigns over all things. Unhappy is the individual who enters himself in this school. He has no consolation, except the gratified wish to know distressing truths, unless we add to this the pride of science, that he has by his own skill and application purchased for himself the discernment which places him in so painful a preeminence. The great triumph of man is in the power of education, to improve his intellect, to sharpen his perceptions, and to regulate and modify his moral qualities. But craniology reduces this to almost nothing, and exhibits us for the most part as the helpless victims of a blind and remorseless destiny.

In the mean time it is happy for us, that, as this system is perhaps the most rigorous and degrading that was ever devised, so it is in almost all instances founded upon arbitrary assumptions and confident assertion, totally in opposition to the true spirit of patient and laborious investigation and sound philosophy.

It is in reality very little that we know of the genuine characters of men. Every human creature is a mystery to his fellow. Every human character is made up of incongruities. Of nearly all the great personages in history it is difficult to say what was decidedly the motive in which their actions and system of conduct originated. We study what they did, and what they said; but in vain. We never arrive at a full and demonstrative conclusion. In reality no man can be certainly said to know himself. "The heart of man is deceitful above all things."

But these dogmatists overlook all those difficulties, which would persuade a wise man to suspend his judgment, and induce a jury of philosophers to hesitate for ever as to the verdict they would pronounce. They look only at the external character of the act by which a man honours or disgraces himself. They decide presumptuously and in a lump, This man is a murderer, a hero, a coward, the slave of avarice, or the votary of philanthropy; and then, surveying the outside of his head, undertake to find in him the configuration that should indicate these dispositions, and must be found in all persons of a similar character, or rather whose acts bear the same outward form, and seem analogous to his.

Till we have discovered the clue that should enable us to unravel the labyrinth of the human mind, it is with small hopes of success that we should expect to settle the external indications, and decide that this sort of form and appearance, and that class of character, will always be found together.

But it is not to be wondered at, that these disorderly fragments of a shapeless science should become the special favourites of the idle and the arrogant. Every man (and every woman), however destitute of real instruction, and unfitted for the investigation of the deep or the sublime mysteries of our nature, can use his eyes and his hands. The whole boundless congregation of mankind, with its everlasting varieties, is thus at once subjected to the sentence of every pretender:

And fools rush in, where angels fear to tread.

Nothing is more delightful to the headlong and presumptuous, than thus to sit in judgment on their betters, and pronounce ex cathedra on those, "whose shoe-latchet they are not worthy to stoop down and unloose." I remember, after lord George Gordon's riots, eleven persons accused were set down in one indictment for their lives, and given in charge to one jury. But this is a mere shadow, a nothing, compared with the wholesale and indiscriminating judgment of the vulgar phrenologist.

ESSAY XXI. OF ASTRONOMY.

SECTION I.

It can scarcely be imputed to me as profane, if I venture to put down a few sceptical doubts on the science of astronomy. All branches of knowledge are to be considered as fair subjects of enquiry: and he that has never doubted, may be said, in the highest and strictest sense of the word, never to have believed.

The first volume that furnished to me the groundwork of the following doubts, was the book commonly known by the name of Guthrie's Geographical Grammar, many parts and passages of which engaged my attention in my own study, in the house of a rural schoolmaster, in the year 1772. I cannot therefore proceed more fairly than by giving here an extract of certain passages in that book, which have relation to the present subject. I know not how far they have been altered in the edition of Guthrie which now lies before me, from the language of the book then in my possession; but I feel confident that in the main particulars they continue the same(42).

(42) *The article Astronomy, in this book, appears to have been written*

by the well known James Ferguson.

"In passing rapidly over the heavens with his new telescope, the universe increased under the eye of Herschel; 44,000 stars, seen in the space of a few degrees, seemed to indicate that there were seventy-five millions in the heavens. But what are all these, when compared with those that fill the whole expanse, the boundless field of aether?

"The immense distance of the fixed stars from our earth, and from each other, is of all considerations the most proper for raising our ideas of the works of God. Modern discoveries make it probable that each of these stars is a sun, having planets and comets revolving round it, as our sun has the earth and other planets revolving round him.—A ray of light, though its motion is so quick as to be commonly thought instantaneous, takes up more time in travelling from the stars to us, than we do in making a West-India voyage. A sound, which, next to light, is considered as the quickest body we are acquainted with, would not arrive to us from thence in 50,000 years. And a cannon-ball, flying at the rate of 480 miles an hour, would not reach us in 700,000 years.

"From what we know of our own system, it may be reasonably concluded, that all the rest are with equal wisdom contrived, situated, and provided with accommodations for rational inhabitants.

"What a sublime idea does this suggest to the human imagination, limited as are its powers, of the works of the Creator! Thousands and thousands of suns, multiplied without end, and ranged all around us, at immense distances from each other, attended by ten thousand times ten thousand worlds, all in rapid motion, yet calm, regular and harmonious, invariably keeping the paths prescribed them: and these worlds peopled with myriads of intelligent beings, formed for endless progression in perfection and felicity!"

The thought that would immediately occur to a dispassionate man in listening to this statement, would be, What a vast deal am I here called on to believe!

Now the first rule of sound and sober judgment, in encountering any story, is that, in proportion to the magnitude and seemingly incredible nature of the propositions tendered to our belief, should be the strength and impregnable nature of the evidence by which those propositions are supported.

It is not here, as in matters of religion, that we are called upon by authority from on high to believe in mysteries, in things above our reason, or, as it may be, contrary to our reason. No man pretends to a revelation from heaven of the truths of astronomy. They have been brought to light by the faculties of the human mind, exercised upon such facts and circumstances as our industry has set before us.

To persons not initiated in the rudiments of astronomical science, they rest upon the great and high-sounding names of Galileo, Kepler, Halley and Newton. But, though these men are eminently entitled to honour and gratitude from their fellow-mortals, they do not stand altogether on the same footing as Matthew, Mark, Luke and John, by whose pens has been recorded "every word that proceedeth out of the mouth of God."

The modest enquirer therefore, without pretending to put himself on an equality with these illustrious men, may be forgiven, when he permits himself to suggest a few doubts, and presumes to examine the grounds upon which he is called upon to believe all that is contained in the above passages.

Now the foundations upon which astronomy, as here delivered, is built, are, first, the evidence of our senses, secondly, the calculations of the mathematician, and, in the third place, moral considerations. These have been denominated respectively, practical astronomy, scientific, and theoretical.

As to the first of these, it is impossible for us on this occasion not to recollect what has so often occurred as to have grown into an every-day observation, of the fallibility of our senses.

It may be doubted however whether this is a just statement. We are not deceived by our senses, but deceived in the inference we make from our sensations. Our sensations respecting what we call the external world, are chiefly those of length, breadth and solidity, hardness and softness, heat and cold, colour, smell, sound and taste. The inference which the generality of mankind make in relation to these sensations is, that there is something out of ourselves corresponding to the impressions we receive; in other words, that the causes of our sensations are like to the sensations themselves. But this is, strictly speaking, an inference; and, if the cause of a sensation is not like the sensation, it cannot precisely be affirmed that our senses deceive us. We know what passes in the theatre of the mind; but we cannot be said absolutely to know any thing, more.

Modern philosophy has taught us, in certain cases, to controvert the position, that the causes of our sensations are like to the sensations themselves. Locke in particular has called the attention of the reasoning part of mankind to the consideration, that heat and cold, sweet and bitter, and odour offensive or otherwise, are perceptions, which imply a percipient being, and cannot exist in inanimate substances. We might with equal propriety ascribe pain to the whip that beats us, or pleasure to the slight alternation of contact in the person or thing that tickles us, as suppose that heat and cold, or taste, or smell are any thing but sensations.

The same philosophers who have called our attention to these remarks, have proceeded to shew that the causes of our sensations of sound and colour have no precise correspondence, do not tally with the sensations we receive. Sound is the result of a percussion of the air. Colour is produced by the reflection of the rays of light; so that the same object, placed in a position, different as to the spectator, but in itself remaining unaltered, will produce in him a sensation of different colours, or shades of colour, now blue, now green, now brown, now black, and so on. This is the doctrine of Newton, as well as of Locke.

It follows that, if there were no percipient being to receive these sensations, there would be no heat or cold, no taste, no smell, no sound, and no colour.

Aware of this difference between our sensations in certain cases and the causes of these sensations, Locke has divided the qualities of substances in the material universe into primary and secondary, the sensations we receive of the primary representing the actual qualities of material substances, but the sensations we receive of what he calls the secondary having no proper resemblance to the causes that produce them.

Now, if we proceed in the spirit of severe analysis to examine the primary qualities of matter, we shall not perhaps find so marked a distinction between those and the secondary, as the statement of Locke would have led us to imagine.

The Optics of Newton were published fourteen years later than Locke's Essay concerning Human Understanding.

In endeavouring to account for the uninterrupted transmission of rays of light through transparent substances, however hard they may be found to be, Newton has these observations.

"Bodies are much more rare and porous, than is commonly believed. Water is nineteen times lighter, and by consequence nineteen times rarer, than gold; and gold is so rare, as very readily, and without the least opposition, to transmit the magnetic effluvia, and easily to admit quicksilver into its pores, and to let water pass through it. From all which we may conclude, that gold has more pores than solid parts, and by consequence that water has above forty times more pores than parts. And he that shall find out an hypothesis, by which water may be so rare, and yet not capable of compression by force, may doubtless, by the same hypothesis, make gold, and water, and all other bodies, as much rarer as he pleases, so that light may find a ready passage through transparent substances(43)."

(43) Newton, Optics, Book II, Part III, Prop. viii.

Again: "The colours of bodies arise from the magnitude of the particles that reflect them. Now, if we conceive these particles of bodies to be so disposed among themselves, that the intervals, or empty spaces between them, may be equal in magnitude to them all; and that these particles may be composed of other particles much smaller, which have as much empty space between them as equals all the magnitudes of these smaller particles; and that in like manner these smaller particles are again composed of others much smaller, all which together are equal to all the pores, or empty spaces, between them; and so on perpetually till you come to solid particles, such as have no pores, or empty spaces within them: and if in any gross body there be, for instance, three such degrees of particles, the least of which are solid; this body will have seven times more pores than solid parts. But if there be four such degrees of particles, the least of which are solid, the body will have fifteen times more pores than solid parts. If there be five degrees, the body will have one and thirty times more pores than solid parts. If six degrees, the body will have sixty and three times more pores than solid parts. And so on perpetually(44)."

(44) Ibid.

In the Queries annexed to the Optics, Newton further suggests an opinion, that the rays of light are repelled by bodies without immediate contact. He observes that:

"Where attraction ceases, there a repulsive virtue ought to succeed. And that there is such a virtue, seems to follow from the reflexions and inflexions of the rays of light. For the rays are repelled by bodies, in both these cases, without the immediate contact of the reflecting or inflecting body. It seems also to follow from the emission of light; the ray, so soon as it is shaken off from a shining body by the vibrating motion of the parts of the body, and gets beyond the reach of attraction, being driven away with exceeding great velocity. For that force, which is sufficient to turn it back in reflexion, may be sufficient to emit it. It seems also to follow from the production of air and vapour: the particles, when they are shaken off from bodies by heat or fermentation, so soon as they are beyond the reach of the attraction of the body, receding from it and also from one another, with great strength; and keeping at a distance, so as sometimes to take up a million of times more space than they did before, in the form of a dense body."

Newton was of opinion that matter was made up, in the last resort, of exceedingly small solid particles, having no pores, or empty spaces within them. Priestley, in his Disquisitions relating to Matter and Spirit, carries the theory one step farther; and, as Newton surrounds his exceedingly small particles with spheres of attraction and repulsion, precluding in all cases their actual contact, Priestley is disposed to regard the centre of these spheres as mathematical points only. If there is no actual contact, then by the very terms no two particles of matter were ever so near to each other, but that they might be brought nearer, if a sufficient force could be applied for that purpose. You had only another sphere of repulsion to conquer; and, as there never is actual contact, the whole world is made up of one sphere of repulsion after another, without the possibility of ever arriving at an end.

"The principles of the Newtonian philosophy," says our author, "were no sooner known, than it was seen how few in comparison, of the phenomena of nature, were owing to solid matter, and how much to powers, which were only supposed to accompany and surround the solid parts of matter. It has been asserted, and the assertion has never been disproved, that for any thing we know to the contrary, all the solid matter in the solar system might be contained within a nutshell(45)."

(45) Priestley, Disquisitions, Section II. I know not by whom this

illustration was first employed. Among other authors, I find, in

Fielding (Joseph Andrews, Book II, Chap. II), a sect of philosophers

spoken of, who "can reduce all the matter of the world into a nutshell."

It is then with senses, from the impressions upon which we are impelled to draw such false conclusions, and that present us with images altogether unlike any thing that exists out of ourselves, that we come to observe the phenomena of what we call the universe. The first observation that it is here incumbent on us to make, and which we ought to keep ever at hand, to be applied as occasion may offer, is the well known aphorism of Socrates, that "we know only this, that we know nothing." We have no compass to guide

us through the pathless waters of science; we have no revelation, at least on the subject of astronomy, and of the unnumbered inhabitable worlds that float in the ocean of ether; and we are bound therefore to sail, as the mariners of ancient times sailed, always within sight of land. One of the earliest maxims of ordinary prudence, is that we ought ever to correct the reports of one sense by the assistance of another sense. The things we here speak of are not matters of faith; and in them therefore it is but reason, that we should imitate the conduct of Didymus the apostle, who said, "Except I put my fingers into the prints of the nails, and thrust my hand into his side, I will not believe." My eyes report to me an object, as having a certain magnitude, texture, and roughness or smoothness; but I require that my hands should confirm to me the evidence of my eyes. I see something that appears to be an island at an uncertain distance from the shore; but, if I am actuated by a laudable curiosity, and wish to possess a real knowledge, I take a boat, and proceed to ascertain by nearer inspection, whether that which I imagined to be an island is an island or no.

There are indeed many objects with which we are conversant, that are in so various ways similar to each other, that, after having carefully examined a few, we are satisfied upon slighter investigation to admit the dimensions and character of others. Thus, having measured with a quadrant the height of a tower, and found on the narrowest search and comparison that the report of my instrument was right, I yield credit to this process in another instance, without being at the trouble to verify its results in any more elaborate method.

The reason why we admit the inference flowing from our examination in the second instance, and so onward, with less scrupulosity and scepticism than in the first, is that there is a strict resemblance and analogy in the two cases. Experience is the basis of our conclusions and our conduct. I strike against a given object, a nail for example, with a certain degree of force, because I have remarked in myself and others the effect of such a stroke. I take food and masticate it, because I have found that this process contributes to the sound condition of my body and mind. I scatter certain seeds in my field, and discharge the other functions of an agriculturist, because I have observed that in due time the result of this industry is a crop. All the propriety of these proceedings depends upon the exact analogy between the old case and the new one. The state of the affair is still the same, when my business is merely that of an observer and a traveller. I know water from earth, land from sea, and mountains from vallies, because I have had experience of these objects, and confidently infer that, when certain appearances present themselves to my organs of sight, I shall find the same results to all my other senses, as I found when such appearances occurred to me before.

But the interval that divides the objects which occur upon and under the earth, and are accessible in all ways to our examination, on the one hand, and the lights which are suspended over our heads in the heavens on the other, is of the broadest and most memorable nature. Human beings, in the infancy of the world, were contented reverently to behold these in their calmness and beauty, perhaps to worship them, and to remark the effects that they produced, or seemed to produce, upon man and the subjects of his industry. But they did not aspire to measure their dimensions, to enquire into their internal frame, or to explain the uses, far removed from our sphere of existence, which they might be intended to serve.

It is however one of the effects of the improvement of our intellect, to enlarge our curiosity. The daringness of human enterprise is one of the prime glories of our nature. It is our boast that we undertake to "measure earth, weigh air, and state the tides." And, when success crowns the boldness of our aspirations after what vulgar and timorous prudence had pronounced impossible, it is then chiefly that we are seen to participate of an essence divine.

What has not man effected by the boldness of his conceptions and the adventurousness of his spirit? The achievements of human genius have appeared so incredible, till they were thoroughly examined, and slowly established their right to general acceptance, that the great heroes of intellect were universally regarded by their contemporaries as dealers in magic, and implements of the devil. The inventor of the art of printing, that glorious instrument for advancing the march of human improvement, and the discoverer of the more questionable art of making gunpowder, alike suffered under this imputation. We have rendered the seas and the winds instruments of our pleasure, "exhausted the old world, and then discovered a new one," have drawn down lightning from heaven, and exhibited equal rights and independence to mankind. Still however it is incumbent on us to be no less wary and suspicious than we are bold, and not to imagine, because we have done much, that we are therefore able to effect every thing.

As was stated in the commencement of this Essay, we know our own sensations, and we know little more. Matter, whether in its primary or secondary qualities, is certainly not the sort of thing the vulgar imagine it to be. The illustrious Berkeley has taught many to doubt of its existence altogether; and later theorists have gone farther than this, and endeavoured to shew, that each man, himself while he speaks on the subject, and you and I while we hear, have no conclusive evidence to convince us, that we may not, each of us, for aught we know, be the only thing that exists, an entire universe to ourselves.

We will not however follow these ingenious persons to the startling extreme to which their speculations would lead us. But, without doing so, it will not misbecome us to be cautious, and to reflect what we do, before we take a leap into illimitable space.

SECTION II.

"The sun," we are told, "is a solid body, ninety-five millions of miles distant from the earth we inhabit, one million times larger in cubic measurement, and to such a degree impregnated with heat, that a comet, approaching to it within a certain distance, was by that approximation raised to a heat two thousand times greater than that of red-hot iron."

It will be acknowledged, that there is in this statement much to believe; and we shall not be exposed to reasonable blame, if we refuse to subscribe to it, till we have received irresistible evidence of its truth.

It has already been observed, that, for the greater part of what we imagine we know on the surface or in the bowels of the earth, we have, or may have if we please, the evidence of more than one of our senses, combining to lead to the same conclusion. For the propositions of astronomy we have no sensible evidence, but that of sight, and an imperfect analogy, leading from those visible impressions which we can verify, to a reliance upon those which we cannot.

The first cardinal particular we meet with in the above statement concerning the sun, is the term, distance. Now, all that, strictly speaking, we can affirm respecting the sun and other heavenly bodies, is that we have the same series of impressions respecting them, that we have respecting terrestrial objects near or remote, and that there is an imperfect analogy between the one case and the other.

Before we affirm any thing, as of our own knowledge and competence, respecting heavenly bodies which are said to be millions of millions of miles removed from us, it would not perhaps be amiss that we should possess ourselves of a certain degree of incontestible information, as to the things which exist on the earth we inhabit. Among these, one of the subjects attended with a great degree of doubt and obscurity, is the height of the mountains with which the surface of the globe we inhabit is diversified. It is affirmed in the received books of elementary geography, that the Andes are the highest mountains in the world. Morse, in his American Gazetteer, third edition, printed at Boston in 1810(46), says, "The height of Chimborazzo, the most elevated point of the vast chain of the Andes, is 20,280 feet above the level of the sea, which is 7102 feet higher than any other mountain in the known world:" thus making the elevation of the mountains of Thibet, or whatever other rising ground the compiler had in his thought, precisely 13,178 feet above the level of the sea, and no more. This decision however has lately been contradicted. Mr. Hugh Murray, in an Account of Discoveries and Travels in Asia, published in 1820, has collated the reports of various recent travellers in central Asia; and he states the height of Chumularee, which he speaks of as the most elevated point of the mountains of Thibet, as nearly 30,000 feet above the level of the sea.

(46) Article, Andes.

The elevation of mountains, till lately, was in no way attempted to be ascertained but by the use of the quadrant, and their height was so generally exaggerated, that Riccioli, one of the most eminent astronomers of the seventeenth century, gives it as his opinion that mountains, like the Caucasus, may have a perpendicular elevation of fifty Italian miles(47). Later observers have undertaken to correct the inaccuracy of these results through the application of the barometer, and thus, by informing themselves of the weight of the air at a certain elevation, proceeding to infer the height of the situation.

(47) Rees, Encyclopedia; article, Mountains.

There are many circumstances, which are calculated to induce a circumspect enquirer to regard the affirmative positions of astronomy, as they are delivered by the most approved modern writers, with considerable diffidence.

They are founded, as has already been said, next to the evidence of our senses, upon the deductions of mathematical knowledge.

Mathematics are either pure or mixed.

Pure mathematics are concerned only with abstract propositions, and have nothing to do with the realities of nature. There is no such thing in actual existence as a mathematical point, line or surface. There is no such thing as a circle or square. But that is of no consequence. We can define them in words, and reason about them. We can draw a diagram, and suppose that line to be straight which is not really straight, and that figure to be a circle which is not strictly a circle. It is conceived therefore by the generality of observers, that mathematics is the science of certainty.

But this is not strictly the case. Mathematics are like those abstract and imaginary existences about which they are conversant. They may constitute in themselves, and in the apprehension of an infallible being, a science of certainty. But they come to us mixed and incorporated with our imperfections. Our faculties are limited; and we may be easily deceived, as to what it is that we see with transparent and unerring clearness, and what it is that comes to us through a crooked medium, refracting and distorting the rays of primitive truth. We often seem clear, when in reality the twilight of undistinguishing night has crept fast and far upon us. In a train of deductions, as in the steps of an arithmetical process, an error may have insinuated itself imperceptibly at a very early stage, rendering all the subsequent steps a wandering farther and farther from the unadulterated truth. Human mathematics, so to speak, like the length of life, are subject to the doctrine of chances. Mathematics may be the science of certainty to celestial natures, but not to man.

But, if in the case of pure mathematics, we are exposed to the chances of error and delusion, it is much worse with mixed mathematics. The moment we step out of the high region of abstraction, and apply ourselves to what we call external nature, we have forfeited that sacred character and immunity, which we seemed entitled to boast, so long as we remained inclosed in the sanctuary of unmingled truth. As has already been said, we know what passes in the theatre of the mind; but we cannot be said absolutely to know any thing more. In our speculations upon actual existences we are not only subject to the disadvantages which arise from the limited nature of our faculties, and the errors which may insensibly creep upon us in the process. We are further exposed to the operation of the unevennesses and irregularities that perpetually occur in external nature, the imperfection of our senses, and of the instruments we construct to assist our observations, and the discrepancy which we frequently detect between the actual nature of the things about us and our impressions respecting them.

This is obvious, whenever we undertake to apply the processes of arithmetic to the realities of life. Arithmetic, unsubjected to the impulses of passion and the accidents of created nature, holds on its course; but, in the phenomena of the actual world, "time and chance happeneth to them all."

Thus it is, for example, in the arithmetical and geometrical ratios, set up in political economy by the celebrated Mr. Malthus. His numbers will go on smoothly enough, 1, 2, 4, 8, 16, 32, as representing the principle of population among mankind, and 1, 2, 3, 4, 5, 6, the means of subsistence; but restiff and uncomplying nature refuses to conform herself to his dicta.

Dr. Price has calculated the produce of one penny, put out at the commencement of the Christian era to five per cent. compound interest, and finds that in the year 1791 it would have increased to a greater sum than would be contained in three hundred millions of earths, all solid gold. But what has this to do with the world in which we live? Did ever any one put out his penny to interest in this fashion for eighteen hundred years? And, if he did, where was the gold to be found, to satisfy his demand?

Morse, in his American Gazetteer, proceeding on the principles of Malthus, tells us that, if the city of New York goes on increasing for a century in a certain ratio, it will by that time contain 5,257,493 inhabitants. But does any one, for himself or his posterity, expect to see this realised?

Blackstone, in his Commentaries on the Laws of England, has observed that, as every man has two ancestors in the first ascending degree, and four in the second, so in the twentieth degree he has more than a million, and in the fortieth the square of that number, or upwards of a million millions. This statement therefore would have a greater tendency to prove that mankind in remote ages were numerous, almost beyond the power of figures to represent, than the opposite doctrine of Malthus, that they have a perpetual tendency to such increase as would infallibly bring down the most tremendous calamities on our posterity.

Berkeley, whom I have already referred to on another subject, and who is admitted to be one of our profoundest philosophers, has written a treatise(48) to prove, that the mathematicians, who object to the mysteries supposed to exist in revealed religion, "admit much greater mysteries, and even falshoods in science, of which he alleges the doctrine of fluxions as an eminent example(49)." He observes, that their conclusions are established by virtue of a twofold error, and that these errors, being in contrary directions, are supposed to compensate each other, the expounders of the doctrine thus arriving at what they call truth, without being able to shew how, or by what means they have arrived at it.

(48) The Analyst.

(49) Life of Berkeley, prefixed to his Works.

It is a memorable and a curious speculation to reflect, upon how slight grounds the doctrine of "thousands and thousands of suns, multiplied without end, and ranged all around us, at immense distances from each other, and attended by ten thousand times ten thousand worlds," mentioned in the beginning of this Essay, is built. It may be all true. But, true or false, it cannot be without its use to us, carefully to survey the road upon which we are advancing, the pier which human enterprise has dared to throw out into the vast ocean of Cimmerian darkness. We have constructed a pyramid, which throws into unspeakable contempt the vestiges of ancient Egyptian industry: but it stands upon its apex; it trembles with every breeze; and momentarily threatens to overwhelm in its ruins the fearless undertakers that have set it up.

It gives us a mighty and sublime idea of the nature of man, to think with what composure and confidence a succession of persons of the greatest genius have launched themselves in illimitable space, with what invincible industry they have proceeded, wasting the midnight oil, racking their faculties, and almost wearing their organs to dust, in measuring the distance of Sirius and the other fixed stars, the velocity of light, and "the myriads of intelligent beings formed for endless progression in perfection and felicity," that people the numberless worlds of which they discourse. The illustrious names of

Copernicus, Galileo, Gassendi, Kepler, Halley and Newton impress us with awe; and, if the astronomy they have opened before us is a romance, it is at least a romance more seriously and perseveringly handled than any other in the annals of literature.

A vulgar and a plain man would unavoidably ask the astronomers, How came you so familiarly acquainted with the magnitude and qualities of the heavenly bodies, a great portion of which, by your own account, are millions of millions of miles removed from us? But, I believe, it is not the fashion of the present day to start so rude a question. I have just turned over an article on Astronomy in the Encyclopaedia Londinensis, consisting of one hundred and thirty-three very closely printed quarto pages, and in no corner of this article is any evidence so much as hinted at. Is it not enough? Newton and his compeers have said it.

The whole doctrine of astronomy rests upon trigonometry, a branch of the science of mathematics which teaches us, having two sides and one angle, or two angles and one side, of a triangle given us, to construct the whole. To apply this principle therefore to the heavenly bodies, it is necessary for us to take two stations, the more remote from each other the better, from which our observations should be made. For the sake of illustration we will suppose them to be taken at the extremes of the earth's diameter, in other words, nearly eight thousand miles apart from each other, the thing itself having never been realised to that extent. From each of these stations we will imagine a line to be drawn, terminating in the sun. Now it seems easy, by means of a quadrant, to find the arch of a circle (in other words, the angle) included between these lines terminating in the sun, and the base formed by a right line drawn from one of these stations to the other, which in this case is the length of the earth's diameter. I have therefore now the three particulars required to enable me to construct my triangle. And, according to the most approved astronomical observations hitherto made, I have an isosceles triangle, eight thousand miles broad at its base, and ninety-five millions of miles in the length of each of the sides reaching from the base to the apex.

It is however obvious to the most indifferent observer, that the more any triangle, or other mathematical diagram, falls within the limits which our senses can conveniently embrace, the more securely, when our business is practical, and our purpose to apply the result to external objects, can we rely on the accuracy of our results. In a case therefore like the present, where the base of our isosceles triangle is to the other two sides as eight units to twelve thousand, it is impossible not to perceive that it behoves us to be singularly diffident as to the conclusion at which we have arrived, or rather it behoves us to take for granted that we are not unlikely to fall into the most important error. We have satisfied ourselves that the sides of the triangle including the apex, do not form an angle, till they have arrived at the extent of ninety-five millions of miles. How are we sure that they do then? May not lines which have reached to so amazing a length without meeting, be in reality parallel lines? If an angle is never formed, there can be no result. The whole question seems to be incommensurate to our faculties.

It being obvious that this was a very unsatisfactory scheme for arriving at the knowledge desired, the celebrated Halley suggested another method, in the year 1716, by an observation to be taken at the time of the transit of Venus over the sun(50).

(50) *Philosophical Transactions, Vol. XXIX, p. 454.*

It was supposed that we were already pretty accurately acquainted with the distance of the moon from the earth, it being so much nearer to us, by observing its parallax, or the difference of its place in the heavens as seen from the surface of the earth, from that in which it would appear if seen from its centre(51). But the parallax of the sun is so exceedingly small, as scarcely to afford the basis of a mathematical calculation(52). The parallax of Venus is however almost four times as great as that of the sun; and there must therefore be a very sensible difference between the times in which Venus may be seen passing over the sun from different parts of the earth. It was on this account apprehended, that the parallax of the sun, by means of observations taken from different places at the time of the transit of Venus in 1761 and 1769, might be ascertained with a great degree of precision(53).

(51) *Bonnycastle, Astronomy, 7th edition, p. 262, et seq.*

(52) *Ibid, p. 268.*

(53) *Phil. Transactions, Vol. XXIX, p. 457.*

But the imperfectness of our instruments and means of observation have no small tendency to baffle the ambition of man in these curious investigations.

"The true quantity of the moon's parallax," says Bonnycastle, "cannot be accurately determined by the methods ordinarily resorted to, on account of the varying declination of the moon, and the inconstancy of the horizontal refractions, which are perpetually changing according to the state the atmosphere is in at the time. For the moon continues but for a short time in the equinoctial, and the refraction at a mean rate elevates her apparent place near the horizon, half as much as her parallax depresses it(54)."

(54) *Astronomy, p. 265.*

"It is well known that the parallax of the sun can never exceed nine seconds, or the four-hundredth part of a degree(55)." "Observations," says Halley, "made upon the vibrations of a pendulum, to determine these exceedingly small angles, are not sufficiently accurate to be depended upon; for by this method of ascertaining the parallax, it will sometimes come out to be nothing, or even negative; that is, the distance will either be infinite, or greater than infinite, which is absurd. And, to confess the truth, it is hardly possible for a person to distinguish seconds with certainty by any instruments, however skilfully they may be made; and therefore it is not to be wondered at, that the excessive nicety of this matter should have eluded the many ingenious endeavours of the most able opetators."(56).

(55) Ibid, p. 268.

(56) Phil. Transactions, Vol. XXIX, p. 456.

Such are the difficulties that beset the subject on every side. It is for the impartial and dispassionate observers who have mastered all the subtleties of the science, if such can be found, to determine whether the remedies that have been resorted to to obviate the above inaccuracies and their causes, have fulfilled their end, and are not exposed to similar errors. But it would be vain to expect the persons, who have "scorned delights, and lived laborious days" to possess themselves of the mysteries of astronomy, should be impartial and dispassionate, or be disposed to confess, even to their own minds, that their researches were useless, and their labours ended in nothing.

It is further worthy of our attention, that the instruments with which we measure the distance of the earth from the sun and the planets, are the very instruments which have been pronounced upon as incompetent in measuring the heights of mountains(57). In the latter case therefore we have substituted a different mode for arriving at the truth, which is supposed to be attended with greater precision: but we have no substitute to which we can resort, to correct the mistakes into which we may fall respecting the heavenly bodies.

(57) See above, Essay XXI.

The result of the uncertainty which adheres to all astronomical observations is such as might have been expected. Common readers are only informed of the latest adjustment of the question, and are therefore unavoidably led to believe that the distance of the sun from the earth, ever since astronomy became entitled to the name of a science, has by universal consent been recognised as ninety-five millions of miles, or, as near as may be, twenty-four thousand semi-diameters of the earth. But how does the case really stand? Copernicus and Tycho Brahe held the distance to be twelve hundred semi-diameters; Kepler, who is received to have been perhaps the greatest astronomer that any age has produced, puts it down as three thousand five hundred semi-diameters; since his time, Riccioli as seven thousand; Hevelius as five thousand two hundred and fifty(58); some later astronomers, mentioned by Halley, as fourteen thousand; and Halley himself as sixteen thousand five hundred(59).

(58) They were about thirty and forty years younger than Kepler respectively.

(59) Halley, apud Philosophical Transactions, Vol. XXIX, p. 455.

The doctrine of fluxions is likewise called in by the astronomers in their attempts to ascertain the distance and magnitude of the different celestial bodies which compose the solar system; and in this way their conclusions become subject to all the difficulties which Berkeley has alleged against that doctrine.

Kepler has also supplied us with another mode of arriving at the distance and size of the sun and the planets: he has hazarded a conjecture, that the squares of the times of the revolution of the earth and the other planets are in proportion to the cubes of their distances from the sun, their common centre; and, as by observation we can arrive with tolerable certainty at a knowledge of the times of their revolutions, we may from hence proceed to the other matters we are desirous to ascertain. And that which Kepler seemed, as by a divine inspiration, to hazard in the way of conjecture, Newton professes to have demonstratively established. But the demonstration of Newton has not been considered as satisfactory by all men of science since his time.

Thus far however we proceed as we may, respecting our propositions on the subject of the solar system. But, beyond this, all science, real or pretended, deserts us. We have no method for measuring angles, which can be applied to the fixed stars; and we know nothing of any revolutions they perform. All here therefore seems gratuitous: we reason from certain alleged analogies; and we can do no more.

Huygens endeavoured to ascertain something on the subject, by making the aperture of a telescope so small, that the sun should appear through it no larger than Sirius, which he found to be only in the proportion of 1 to 27,664 times his diameter, as seen by the naked eye. Hence, supposing Sirius to be a globe of the same magnitude as the sun, it must be 27,664 times as distant from us as the sun, in other words, at a distance so considerable as to equal 345 million diameters of the earth(60). Every one must feel on how slender a thread this conclusion is suspended.

(60) Encyclopaedia Londinensis, Vol. 11, p. 407.

And yet, from this small postulate, the astronomers proceed to deduce the most astounding conclusions. They tell us, that the distance of the nearest fixed star from the earth is at least 7,600,000,000,000 miles, and of another they name, not less than 38 millions of millions of miles. A cannon-ball therefore, proceeding at the rate of about twenty miles in a minute would be

760,000 years in passing from us to the nearest fixed star, and 3,800,000 in passing to the second star of which we speak. Huygens accordingly concluded, that it was not impossible, that there might be stars at such inconceivable distances from us, that their light has not yet reached the earth since its creation(61).

(61) Ibid, p. 408.

The received system of the universe, founded upon these so called discoveries, is that each of the stars is a sun, having planets and comets revolving round it, as our sun has the earth and other planets revolving round him. It has been found also by the successive observations of astronomers, that a star now and then is totally lost, and that a new star makes its appearance which had never been remarked before: and this they explain into the creation of a new system from time to time by the Almighty author of the universe, and the destruction of an old system worn out with age(62). We must also remember the power of attraction every where diffused through infinite space, by means of which, as Herschel assures us, in great length of time a nebula, or cluster of stars, may be formed, while the projectile force they received in the beginning may prevent them from all coming together, at least for millions of ages. Some of these nebulae, he adds, cannot well be supposed to be at a less distance from us than six or eight thousand times the distance of Sirius(63). Kepler however denies that each star, of those which distinctly present themselves to our sight, can have its system of planets as our sun has, and considers them as all fixed in the same surface or sphere; since, if one of them were twice or thrice as remote as another, it would, supposing their real magnitudes to be equal, appear to be twice or thrice as small, whereas there is not in their apparent magnitudes the slightest difference(64).

(62) Encycl. Lond. Vol. II, p. 411.

(63) Ibid, p. 348.

(64) Ibid, p. 411.

Certainly the astronomers are a very fortunate and privileged race of men, who talk to us in this oracular way of "the unseen things of God from the creation of the world," hanging up their conclusions upon invisible hooks, while the rest of mankind sit listening gravely to their responses, and unreservedly "acknowledging that their science is the most sublime, the most interesting, and the most useful of all the sciences cultivated by man(65)."

(65) Ferguson, Astronomy, Section 1.

We have a sensation, which we call the sensation of distance. It comes to us from our sight and our other senses. It does not come immediately by the organ of sight. It has been proved, that the objects we see, previously to the comparison and correction of the reports of the organ of sight with those of the other senses, do not suggest to us the idea of distance, but that on the contrary whatever we see seems to touch the eye, even as the objects of the sense of feeling touch the skin.

But, in proportion as we compare the impressions made upon our organs of sight with the impressions made on the other senses, we come gradually to connect with the objects we see the idea of distance. I put out my hand, and find at first that an object of my sense of sight is not within the reach of my hand. I put out my hand farther, or by walking advance my body in the direction of the object, and I am enabled to reach it. From smaller experiments I proceed to greater. I walk towards a tree or a building, the figure of which presents itself to my eye, but which I find upon trial to have been far from me. I travel towards a place that I cannot see, but which I am told lies in a certain direction. I arrive at the place. It is thus, that by repeated experiments I acquire the idea of remote distances.

To confine ourselves however to the question of objects, which without change of place I can discover by the sense of sight. I can see a town, a tower, a mountain at a considerable distance. Let us suppose that the limit of my sight, so far as relates to objects on the earth, is one hundred miles. I can travel towards such an object, and thus ascertain by means of my other senses what is its real distance. I can also employ certain instruments, invented by man, to measure heights, suppose of a tower, and, by experiments made in ways independent of these instruments, verify or otherwise the report of these instruments.

The height of the Monument of London is something more than two hundred feet. Other elevations, the produce of human labour, are considerably higher. It is in the nature of the mind, that we conclude from the observation that we have verified, to the accuracy of another, bearing a striking analogy to the former, that we have not verified. But analogy has its limits. Is it of irresistible certainty, or is it in fact to be considered as approaching to certainty, because we have verified an observation extending to several hundred feet, that an observation extending to ninety-five millions of miles, or to the incredible distances of which Herschel so familiarly talks, is to be treated as a fact, or laid down as a principle in science? Is it reasonable to consider two propositions as analogous, when the thing affirmed in the one is in dimension many million times as great as the thing affirmed in the other? The experience we have had as to the truth of the smaller, does it authorise us to consider the larger as unquestionable? That which I see with a bay of the sea or a wide river between, though it may appear very like something with which I am familiar at home, do I immediately affirm it to be of the same species and nature, or do I not regard it with a certain degree of scepticism, especially if, along with the resemblance in some points, it differs essentially, as for example in magnitude, in other points? We have a sensation, and we enquire into its cause. This is always a question of some uncertainty. Is its cause something of absolute and substantive existence without me, or is it not? Is its cause something of the very same nature, as the thing that gave me a similar sensation in a matter of comparatively a pigmy and diminutive extension?

All these questions an untrained and inquisitive mind will ask itself in the propositions of astronomy. We must believe or not, as we think proper or reasonable. We have no way of verifying the propositions by the trial of our senses. There they lie, to be received by us in the construction that first suggests itself to us, or not. They are something like an agreeable imagination or fiction: and a sober observer, in cold blood, will be disposed deliberately to weigh both sides of the question, and to judge whether the probability lies in favour of the actual affirmation of the millions of millions of miles, and the other incredible propositions of the travelling of light, and the rest, which even the most cautious and sceptical of the retainers of modern astronomy, find themselves compelled to receive.

But I shall be told, that the results of our observations of the distances of the heavenly bodies are unvaried. We have measured the distances and other phenomena of the sun, the moon, Mercury, Venus, Mars, Jupiter, Saturn, and their satellites, and they all fall into a grand system, so as to convey to every unprejudiced mind the conviction that this system is the truth itself. If we look at them day after day, and year after year, we see them for ever the same, and performing the same divine harmony. Successive astronomers in different ages and countries have observed the celestial orbs, and swept the heavens, and for ever bring us back the same story of the number, the dimensions, the distances, and the arrangement of the heavenly bodies which form the subject of astronomical science.

This we have seen indeed not to be exactly the case. But, if it were, it would go a very little way towards proving the point it was brought to prove. It would shew that, the sensations and results being similar, the causes of those results must be similar to each other, but it would not shew that the causes were similar to the sensations produced. Thus, in the sensations which belong to taste, smell, sound, colour, and to those of heat and cold, there is all the uniformity which would arise, when the real external causes bore the most exact similitude to the perceptions they generate; and yet it is now universally confessed that tastes, scents, sounds, colours, and heat and cold do not exist out of ourselves. All that we are entitled therefore to conclude as to the magnitudes and distances of the heavenly bodies, is, that the causes of our sensations and perceptions, whatever they are, are not less uniform than the sensations and perceptions themselves.

It is further alleged, that we calculate eclipses, and register the various phenomena of the heavenly bodies. Thales predicted an eclipse of the sun, which took place nearly six hundred years before the Christian era. The Babylonians, the Persians, the Hindoos, and the Chinese early turned their attention to astronomy. Many of their observations were accurately recorded; and their tables extend to a period of three thousand years before the birth of Christ. Does not all this strongly argue the solidity of the science to which they belong? Who, after this, will have the presumption to question, that the men who profess astronomy proceed on real grounds, and have a profound knowledge of these things, which at first sight might appear to be set at a distance so far removed from our ken?

The answer to this is easy. I believe in all the astronomy that was believed by Thales. I do not question the statements relative to the heavenly bodies that were delivered by the wise men of the East. But the supposed discoveries that were made in the eighteenth, and even in the latter part of the seventeenth century, purporting to ascertain the precise distance of the sun, the planets, and even of the fixed stars, are matters entirely distinct from this.

Among the earliest astronomers of Greece were Thales, Anaximander, Anaximenes and Anaxagoras. Thales, we are told, held that the earth is a sphere or globe, Anaximenes that it is like a round, flat table; Anaximander that the sun is like a chariot-wheel, and is twenty-eight times larger than the earth. Anaxagoras was put in prison for affirming that the sun was by many degrees larger than the whole Peloponnesus(66). Kepler is of opinion that all the stars are at an equal distance from us, and are fixed in the same surface or sphere.

(66) Plutarch, De Placitis Philosophorum. Diogenes Laertius.

In reality the observations and the facts of astronomy do not depend either upon the magnitudes or the distances of the heavenly bodies. They proceed in the first place upon what may lie seen with the naked eye. They require an accurate and persevering attention. They may be assisted by telescopes. But they relate only to the sun and the planets. We are bound to ascertain, as nearly as possible, the orbits described by the different bodies in the solar system: but this has still nothing to do, strictly speaking, with their magnitudes or distances. It is required that we should know them in their relations to each other; but it is no preliminary of just, of practical, it might almost be said, of liberal science, that we should know any thing of them absolutely.

The unlimited ambition of the nature of man has discovered itself in nothing more than this, the amazing superstructure which the votaries of contemplation within the last two hundred years have built upon the simple astronomy of the ancients. Having begun to compute the distances of miles by millions, it appears clearly that nothing can arrest the more than eagle-flight of the human mind. The distance of the nearest fixed star from the earth, we are informed, is at least 7,000,000,000,000 miles, and of another which the astronomers name, not less than 38 millions of millions of miles. The particles of light are said to travel 193,940 miles in every second, which is above a million times swifter than the progress of a cannon-ball(67). And Herschel has concluded, that the light issuing from the faintest nebulae he has discovered, must have been at this rate two millions of years in reaching the Barth(68).

(67) Ferguson, Section 216. "Light moves," says Brewster, Optics, p. 2,

"from one pole of the earth to the other in the 24th part of a second: a

velocity which surpasses all comprehension."

(68) Brinkley, Astronomy, p. 130.

SECTION III.

The next process of the modern astronomer is to affirm the innumerable orbs around us, discovered with the naked eye, or with which we are made acquainted by the aid of telescopes, to be all stocked with rational inhabitants. The argument for this is, that an all-wise and omnipotent creator could never have produced such immense bodies, dispersed through infinite space, for any meaner purpose, than that of peopling them with "intelligent beings, formed for endless progression in perfection and felicity(69)."

(69) See above, Essay XXI.

Now it appears to me, that, in these assertions, the modern astronomers are taking upon themselves somewhat too boldly, to expound the counsels of that mysterious power, to which the universe is indebted for its arrangement and order.

We know nothing of God but from his works. Certain speculative men have adventured to reason upon the source of all the system and the wonders that we behold, a priori, and, having found that the creator is all powerful, all wise, and of infinite goodness, according to their ideas of power, wisdom and goodness, have from thence proceeded to draw their inferences, and to shew us in what manner the works of his hands are arranged and conducted by him. This no doubt they have done with the purest intentions in the world; but it is not certain, that their discretion has equalled the boldness of their undertaking.

The world that we inhabit, this little globe of earth, is to us an infinite mystery. Human imagination is unable to conceive any thing more consummate than the great outline of things below. The trees and the skies, the mountains and the seas, the rivers and the springs, appear as if the design had been to realise the idea of paradise. The freshness of the air, the silvery light of day, the magnificence of the clouds, the gorgeous and soothing colouring of the world, the profusion and exquisiteness of the fruits and flowers of the earth, are as if nothing but joy and delicious sensations had been intended for us. When we ascend to the animal creation, the scene is still more admirable and transporting. The birds and the beasts, the insects that skim the air, and the fishes that live in the great deep, are a magazine of wonders, that we may study for ever, without fear of arriving at the end of their excellence. Last of all, comes the crown of the creation, man, formed with looks erect, to commerce with the skies. What a masterpiece of workmanship is his form, while the beauty and intelligence of Gods seems to manifest itself in his countenance! Look at that most consummate of all implements, the human hand; think of his understanding, how composed and penetrating; of the wealth of his imagination; of the resplendent virtues he is qualified to display! "How wonderful are thy works, Oh God; in wisdom hast thou created them all!"

But there are other parts of the system in which we live, which do not seem to correspond with those already enumerated. Before we proceed to people infinite space, it would be as well, if we surveyed the surface of the earth we inhabit. What vast deserts do we find in it; what immense tracks of burning sands! One half of the globe is perhaps irreclaimable to the use of man. Then let us think of earthquakes and tempests, of wasting hurricanes, and the number of vessels, freighted with human beings, that are yearly buried in the caverns of the ocean. Let us call to mind in man, the prime ornament of the creation, all the diseases to which his frame is subject,

Convulsions, epilepsies, fierce catarrhs,

Intestine stone and ulcer, colic pangs,

Demoniac frenzy, moping melancholy,

And moon-struck madness, pining atrophy,

Marasmus, and wide-wasting pestilence,

Dropsies, and asthmas, and joint-racking rheums.

The very idea of our killing, and subsisting upon the flesh of animals, surely somewhat jars with our conceptions of infinite benevolence.

But, when we look at the political history of man, the case is infinitely worse. This too often seems one tissue of misery and vice. War, conquest, oppression, tyranny, slavery, insurrections, massacres, cruel punishments, degrading corporal infliction, and the extinction of life under the forms of law, are to be found in almost every page. It is as if an evil demon were let loose upon us, and whole nations, from one decad of years to another, were struck with the most pernicious madness. Certain reasoners tell us that this is owing to the freedom of will, without which man could not exist. But here we are presented with an alternative, from which it is impossible for human understanding to escape. Either God, according to our ideas of benevolence, would remove evil out of the world, and cannot; or he can, and will not. If he has the will and not the power, this argues weakness; if he has the power and not the will, this seems to be malevolence.

Let us descend from the great stage of the nations, and look into the obscurities of private misery. Which of us is happy? What bitter springs of misery overflow the human heart, and are borne by us in silence! What cruel disappointments beset us! To what struggles are we doomed, while we struggle often in vain! The human heart seems framed, as if to be the capacious receptacle of all imaginable sorrows. The human frame seems constructed, as if all its fibres were prepared to sustain varieties of torment. "In the sweat of thy brow shalt thou eat bread, till thou return to the earth." But how often does that sweat prove ineffective! There are men of whom sorrow seems to be the destiny, from which they can never escape. There are hearts, into which by their constitution it appears as if serenity and content could never enter, but which are given up to all the furious passions, or are for ever the prey of repining and depression.

Ah, little think the gay, licentious proud,

Whom pleasure, power and affluence surround,

How many pine in want! How many shrink

Into the sordid hut, how many drink

The cup of grief, and eat the bitter bread

Of misery!

And, which aggravates the evil, almost all the worst vices, the most unprincipled acts, and the darkest passions of the human mind, are bred out of poverty and distress. Satan, in the Book of Job, says to the Almighty, "Thou hast blessed the work of thy servant, and his substance is increased in the land. But put forth thy hand now, and take away all that he hath; and he will curse thee to thy face." The prayer of Agar runs, "Feed me with food convenient for me; lest I be poor, and steal, and take the name of my God in vain."

It is with a deep knowledge of the scenes of life, that the prophet pronounces, "My thoughts are not your thoughts; neither are your ways my ways, saith the Lord."

All reflecting persons, who have surveyed the state of the world in which we live, have been struck with the contrarieties of sublunary things; and many hypotheses have been invented to solve the enigma. Some have maintained the doctrine of two principles, Oromasdes and Arimanius, the genius of good and of evil, who are perpetually contending with each other which shall have the greatest sway in the fortunes of the world, and each alternately acquiring the upper hand. Others have inculcated the theory of the fall of man, that God at first made all things beautiful and good, but that man has incurred his displeasure, and been turned out of the paradise for which he was destined. Hence, they say, has arisen the corruption of our nature. "There is none that cloth good, no, not one. That every mouth may be stopped, and all the world become guilty before God." But the solution that has been most generally adopted, particularly in later days, is that of a future state of retribution, in which all the inequalities of our present condition shall be removed, the tears of the unfortunate and the sufferer shall be wiped from their eyes, and their agonies and miseries compensated. This, in other words, independently of the light of revelation, is to infer infinite wisdom and benevolence from what we see, and then, finding the actual phenomena not to correspond with our theories, to invent something of which we have no knowledge, to supply the deficiency.

The astronomer however proceeds from what we see of the globe of earth, to fashion other worlds of which we have no direct knowledge. Finding that there is no part of the soil of the earth into which our wanderings can penetrate, that is not turned to the account of rational and happy beings, creatures capable of knowing and adoring their creator, that nature does nothing in vain, and that the world is full of the evidences of his unmingled beneficence, according to our narrow and imperfect ideas of beneficence, (for such ought to be our premises) we proceed to construct millions of worlds upon the plan we have imagined. The earth is a globe, the planets are globes, and several of them larger than our earth: the earth has a moon; several of the planets have satellites: the globe we dwell in moves in an orbit round the sun; so do the planets: upon these premises, and no more, we hold ourselves authorised to affirm that they contain "myriads of intelligent beings, formed for endless progression in perfection and felicity." Having gone thus far, we next find that the fixed stars bear a certain resemblance to the sun; and, as the sun has a number of planets attendant on him, so, we say, has each of the fixed stars, composing all together "ten thousand times ten thousand" habitable worlds.

All this is well, so long as we view it as a bold and ingenious conjecture. On any other subject it would be so regarded; and we should consider it as reserved for the amusement and gratification of a fanciful visionary in the hour, when he gives up the reins to his imagination. But, backed as it is by a complexity of geometrical right lines and curves, and handed forth to us in large quartos, stuffed with calculations, it experiences a very different fortune. We are told that, "by the knowledge we derive from astronomy, our faculties are enlarged, our minds exalted, and our understandings clearly convinced, and affected with the conviction, of the existence, wisdom, power, goodness, immutability and superintendency of the supreme being; so that, without an hyperbole, 'an undevout astronomer is mad(e)(70).'"

(70) Ferguson, Astronomy, Section I.

It is singular, how deeply I was impressed with this representation, while I was a schoolboy, and was so led to propose a difficulty to the wife of the master. I said, "I find that we have millions of worlds round us peopled with rational creatures. I know not that we have any decisive reason for supposing these creatures more exalted, than the wonderful species of which we are individuals. We are imperfect; they are imperfect. We fell; it is reasonable to suppose that they have fallen also. It became necessary for the second person in the trinity to take upon him our nature, and by suffering for our sins to appease the wrath of his father. I am unwilling to believe that he has less commiseration for the inhabitants of other planets. But in that case it may be supposed that since the creation he has been making a circuit of the planets, and dying on the cross for the sins of rational creatures in uninterrupted succession." The lady was wiser than I, admonished me of the danger of being over-inquisitive, and said we should act more discreetly in leaving those questions to the judgment of the Almighty.

But thus far we have reasoned only on one side of the question. Our pious sentiments have led us to magnify the Lord in all his works, and, however imperfect the analogy, and however obscure the conception we can form of the myriads of rational creatures, all of them no doubt infinitely varied in their nature, their structure and faculties, yet to view the whole scheme with an undoubting persuasion of its truth. It is however somewhat in opposition to the ideas of piety formed by our less adventurous ancestors, that we should usurp the throne of God,

Snatch from his hand the balance and the rod,

and, by means of our telescopes and our calculations, penetrate into mysteries not originally intended for us. According to the received Mosaic chronology we are now in the five thousand eight hundred and thirty-fifth year from the creation: the Samaritan version adds to this date. It is therefore scarcely in the spirit of a Christian, that Herschel talks to us of a light, which must have been two millions of years in reaching the earth.

Moses describes the operations of the Almighty, in one of the six days devoted to the work of creation, as being to place "lights in the firmament of heaven, to divide the day from the night, to be for signs and for seasons, and for days and years, and to give light upon the earth; two great lights, the greater to rule the day, and the lesser the night; and the stars also." And Christ, prophesying what is to happen in the latter days, says, "The sun shall be darkened, and the moon shall not give her light, and the stars shall fall from heaven." Whatever therefore be the piety of the persons, who talk to us of "ten thousand times ten thousand worlds, all peopled with rational creatures," it certainly is not a piety in precise accordance with the Christian scriptures.

SECTION IV. It is also no more than just, that we should bear in mind

the apparent fitness or otherwise, of these bodies, so far as we are acquainted with them, for the dwelling-place of rational creatures. Not to mention the probable extreme coldness of Jupiter and Saturn, the heat of the sunbeams in the planet Mercury is understood to be such as that water would unavoidably boil and be carried away(71), and we can scarcely imagine any living substance that would not be dissolved and dispersed in such an atmosphere. The moon, of which, as being so much nearer to us, we may naturally be supposed to know most, we are told by the astronomers has no water and no atmosphere, or, if any, such an atmosphere as would not sustain clouds and ascending vapour. To our eye, as seen through the telescope, it appears like a metallic substance, which has been burned by fire, and so reduced into the ruined and ragged condition in which we seem to behold it. The sun appears to be still less an appropriate habitation for rational, or for living creatures, than any of the planets. The comets, which describe an orbit so exceedingly eccentric, and are subject to all the excessive vicissitudes of heat and cold, are, we are told, admirably adapted for a scene of eternal, or of lengthened punishment for those who have acquitted themselves ill in a previous state of probation. Buffon is of opinion, that all the planets in the solar system were once so many portions of our great luminary, struck off from the sun by the blow of a comet, and so having received a projectile impulse calculated to carry them forward in a right line, at the same time that the power of attraction counteracts this impulse, and gives them that compound principle of motion which retains them in an orbicular course. In this sense it may be said that all the planets were suns; while on the contrary Herschel pronounces, that the sun itself is a planet, an opake body, richly stored with inhabitants(72).

(71) Encyclopaedia Londinensis, Vol. II, p. 355.

(72) Philosophical Transactions for 1795, p. 68.

The modern astronomers go on to account to us for the total disappearance of a star in certain cases, which, they say, may be in reality the destruction of a system, such as that of our sun and its attendant planets, while the appearance of a new star may, in like manner, be the occasional creation of a new system of planets. "We ought perhaps," says Herschel, "to look upon certain clusters of stars, and the destruction of a star now and then in some thousands of ages, as the very means by which the whole is preserved and renewed. These clusters may be the laboratories of the universe, wherein the most salutary remedies for the decay of the whole are prepared(73)."

(73) Philosophical Transactions for 1785, p. 217.

All this must appear to a sober mind, unbitten by the rage which grows out of the heat of these new discoverers, to be nothing less than astronomy run mad. This occasional creation of new systems and worlds, is in little accordance with the Christian scriptures, or, I believe, with any sober speculation upon the attributes of the creator. The astronomer seizes upon some hint so fine as scarcely by any ingenuity to be arrested, immediately launches forth into infinite space, and in an instant returns, and presents us with millions of worlds, each of them peopled with ten thousand times ten thousand inhabitants.

We spoke a while since of the apparent unfitness of many of the heavenly bodies for the reception of living inhabitants. But for all this these discoverers have a remedy. They remind us how unlike these inhabitants may be to ourselves, having other organs than ours, and being able to live in a very different temperature. "The great heat in the planet Mercury is no argument against its being inhabited; since the Almighty could as easily suit the bodies and constitutions of its inhabitants to the heat of their dwelling, as he has done ours to the temperature of our earth. And it is very probable that the people there have such an opinion of us, as we have of the inhabitants of Jupiter and Saturn; namely, that we must be intolerably cold, and have very little light at so great a distance from the sun."

These are the remarks of Ferguson(74). One of our latest astronomers expresses himself to the same purpose.

(74) Astronomy, Section 22.

"We have no argument against the planets being inhabited by rational beings, and consequently by witnesses of the creator's power, magnificence and benevolence, unless it be said that some are much nearer the sun than the earth is, and therefore must be uninhabitable from heat, and those more distant from cold. Whatever objection this may be against their being inhabited by rational beings, of an organisation similar to those on the earth, it can have little force, when urged with respect to rational beings in general.

"But we may examine without indulging too much in conjecture, whether it be not possible that the planets may be possessed by rational beings, and contain animals and vegetables, even little different from those with which we are familiar.

"Is the sun the principal cause of the temperature of the earth? We have reason to suppose that it is not. The mean temperature of the earth, at a small depth from the surface, seems constant in summer and in winter, and is probably coeval with its first formation.

"At the planet Mercury, the direct heat of the sun, or its power of causing heat, is six times greater than with us. If we suppose the mean temperature of Mercury to be the same as of the earth, and the planet to be surrounded with an atmosphere, denser than that of the earth, less capable of transmitting heat, or rather the influence of the sun to extricate heat, and at the same time more readily conducting it to keep up an evenness of temperature, may we not suppose the planet Mercury fit for the habitation of men, and the production of vegetables similar to our own?

"At the Georgium Sidus, the direct influence of the sun is 360 times less than at the earth, and the sun is there seen at an angle not much greater than that under which we behold Venus, when nearest. Yet may not the mean temperature of the Georgium Sidus be nearly the same as that of the earth? May not its atmosphere more easily transmit the influence of the sun, and may not the matter of heat be more copiously combined, and more readily extricated, than with us? Whence changes of season similar to our own may take place. Even in the comets we may suppose no great change of temperature takes place, as we know of no cause which will deprive them of their mean temperature, and particularly if we suppose, that on their approach towards the sun, there is a provision for their atmosphere becoming denser. The tails they exhibit, when in the neighbourhood of the sun, seem in some measure to countenance this idea.

"We can hardly suppose the sun, a body three hundred times larger than all the planets together, was created only to preserve the periodic motions, and give light and heat to the planets. Many astronomers have thought that its atmosphere only is luminous, and its body opake, and probably of the same constitution as the planets. Allowing therefore that its luminous atmosphere only extricates heat, we see no reason why the sun itself should not be inhabited(75)."

(75) Brinkley, Elements of Astronomy, Chap. IX.

There is certainly no end to the suppositions that may be made by an ingenious astronomer. May we not suppose that we might do nearly as well altogether without the sun, which it appears is at present of little use to us as to warmth and heat? As to light, the great creator might, for aught we know, find a substitute; feelers, for example, endued with a certain acuteness of sense: or, at all events, the least imaginable degree of light might answer every purpose to organs adapted to this kind of twilight. In that way the inhabitants of the Georgium Sidus are already sufficiently provided for; they appear to have as little benefit of the light as of the heat of the sun. How the satellites of the distant planets are supplied with light is a mystery, since their principals have scarcely any. Unless indeed, like the sun, they have a luminous atmosphere, competent to enlighten a whole system, themselves being opake. But in truth light in a greater or less degree seems scarcely worthy of a thought, since the inhabitants of the planet Mercury have not their eyes put out by a light, scarcely inferior in radiance to that which is reflected by those plates of burning brass, with which tyrants in some ages were accustomed to extinguish the sense of vision in their unfortunate victims. The comets also must be a delectable residence; that of 1680 completing its orbit in 576 years, and being at its greatest distance about eleven thousand two hundred millions of miles from the sun, and at its least within less than a third part of the sun's semi-diameter from its surface(76). They must therefore have delightful vicissitudes of light and the contrary; for, as to heat, that is already provided for. Archdeacon Brinkley's postulate is, that these bodies are "possessed by rational beings, and contain animals and vegetables, little different from those with which we are familiar."

(76) Ferguson, Section 93.

Now the only reason we have to believe in these extraordinary propositions, is the knowledge we possess of the divine attributes. From the force of this consideration it is argued that God will not leave any sensible area of matter unoccupied, and therefore that it is impossible that such vast orbs as we believe surround us even to the extent of infinite space, should not be "richly stored with rational beings, the capable witnesses of his power, magnificence and benevolence." All difficulties arising from the considerations of light, and heat, and a thousand other obstacles, are to give way to the perfect insight we have as to how the deity will conduct himself in every case that can be proposed. I am not persuaded that this is agreeable to religion; and I am still less convinced that it is compatible with the sobriety and sedateness of common sense.

It is with some degree of satisfaction that I perceive lord Brougham, the reputed author of the Preliminary Discourse to the Library of Useful Knowledge, at the same time that he states the dimensions and distances of the heavenly bodies in the usual way, says not a word of their inhabitants.

It is somewhat remarkable that, since the commencement of the present century, four new planets have been added to those formerly contained in the enumeration of the solar system. They lie between the planets Mars and Jupiter, and have been named Vesta, Juno, Ceres and Pallas. Brinkley speaks of them in this manner. "The very small magnitudes of the new planets Ceres and Pallas, and their nearly equal distances from the sun, induced Dr. Olbers, who discovered Pallas in 1802, nearly in the same place where he had observed Ceres a few months before, to conjecture that they were fragments of a larger planet, which had by some unknown cause been broken to pieces. It follows from the law of gravity, by which the planets are retained in their orbits, that each fragment would again, after every revolution about the sun, pass nearly through the place in which the planet was when the catastrophe happened, and besides the orbit of each fragment would intersect the continuation of the line joining this place and the sun. Thence it was easy to ascertain the two particular regions of the heavens through which all these fragments would pass. Also, by carefully noting the small stars thereabout, and examining them from time to time, it might be expected that more of the fragments would be discovered.—M. Harding discovered the planet Juno in one of these regions; and Dr. Olbers himself also, by carefully examining them (the small stars) from time to time, discovered Vesta."

These additions certainly afford us a new epoch in the annals of the solar system, and of astronomy itself. It is somewhat remarkable, that Herschel, who in the course of his observations traced certain nebulae, the light from which must have been two millions of years in reaching the earth, should never have remarked these planets, which, so to speak, lay at his feet. It reminds one of Esop's astrologer, who, to the amusement of his ignorant countrymen, while he was wholly occupied in surveying the heavens, suddenly found himself plunged in a pit. These new planets also we are told are fragments of a larger planet: how came this larger planet never to have been discovered?

Till Herschel's time we were content with six planets and the sun, making up the cabalistical number seven. He added another. But these four new ones entirely derange the scheme. The astronomers have not yet had opportunity to digest them into their places, and form new worlds of them. This is all unpleasant. They are, it seems, "fragments of a larger planet, which had by some unknown cause been broken to pieces." They therefore are probably not inhabited. How does this correspond with the goodness of God, which will suffer no mass of matter in his creation to remain unoccupied? Herschel talks at his ease of whole systems, suns with all their attendant planets, being consigned to destruction. But here we have a catastrophe happening before our eyes, and cannot avoid being shocked by it. "God does nothing in vain." For which of his lofty purposes has this planet been broken to pieces, and its fragments left to deform the system of which we are inhabitants; at least to humble the pride of man, and laugh to scorn his presumption? Still they perform their revolutions, and obey the projectile and gravitating forces, which have induced us to people ten thousand times ten thousand worlds. It is time, that we should learn modesty, to revere in silence the great cause to which the universe is indebted for its magnificence, its beauty and harmony, and to acknowledge that we do not possess the key that should unlock the mysteries of creation.

One of the most important lessons that can be impressed on the human mind, is that of self-knowledge and a just apprehension of what it is that we are competent to achieve. We can do much. We are capable of much knowledge and much virtue. We have patience, perseverance and subtlety. We can put forth considerable energies, and nerve ourselves to resist great obstacles and much suffering. Our ingenuity is various and considerable. We can form machines, and erect mighty structures. The invention of man for the ease of human life, and for procuring it a multitude of pleasures and accommodations, is truly astonishing. We can dissect the human frame, and anatomise the mind. We can study the scene of our social existence, and make extraordinary improvements in the administration of justice, and in securing to ourselves that germ of all our noblest virtues, civil and political liberty. We can study the earth, its strata, its soil, its animals, and its productions, "from the cedar that is in Lebanon, to the hyssop that springeth out of the wall."

But man is not omnipotent. If he aspires to be worthy of honour, it is necessary that he should compute his powers, and what it is they are competent to achieve. The globe of earth, with "all that is therein," is our estate and our empire. Let us be content with that which we have. It were a pitiful thing to see so noble a creature struggling in a field, where it is impossible for him to distinguish himself, or to effect any thing real. There is no situation in which any one can appear more little and ludicrous, than when he engages in vain essays, and seeks to accomplish that, which a moment's sober thought would teach him was utterly hopeless.

Even astronomy is to a certain degree our own. We can measure the course of the sun, and the orbits of the planets. We can calculate eclipses. We can number the stars, assign to them their places, and form them into what we call constellations. But, when we pretend to measure millions of miles in the heavens, and to make ourselves acquainted with the inhabitants of ten thousand times ten thousand worlds and the accommodations which the creator has provided for their comfort and felicity, we probably engage in something more fruitless and idle, than the pigmy who should undertake to bend the bow of Ulysses, or strut and perform the office of a warrior clad in the armour of Achilles.

How beautiful is the "firmament; this majestical roof fretted with golden fire!" Let us beware how we mar the magnificent scene with our interpolations and commentaries! Simplicity is of the essence of the truly great. Let us look at the operations of that mighty power from which we ourselves derive our existence, with humility and reverential awe! It may well become us. Let us not "presume into the heaven of heavens," unbidden, unauthorised guests! Let us adopt the counsel of the apostle, and allow no man to "spoil us through vain philosophy." The business of human life is serious; the useful investigations in which we may engage are multiplied. It is excellent to see a rational being conscious of his genuine province, and not idly wasting powers adapted for the noblest uses in unmeasured essays and ill-concocted attempts.

ESSAY XXII. OF THE MATERIAL UNIVERSE.

In the preceding Essay I have referred to the theory of Berkeley, whose opinion is that there is no such thing as matter in the sense in which it is understood by the writers on natural philosophy, and that the whole of our experience in that respect is the result of a system of accidents without an intelligible subject, by means of which antecedents and consequents flow on for ever in a train, the past succession of which man is able to record, and the future in many cases he is qualified to predict and to act upon.

An argument more palpable and popular than that of Berkeley in favour of the same hypothesis, might be deduced from the points recapitulated in that Essay as delivered by Locke and Newton. If what are vulgarly denominated the secondary qualities of matter are in reality nothing but sensations existing in the human mind, then at any rate matter is a very different thing from what it is ordinarily apprehended to be. To which I add, in the second place, that, if matter, as is stated by Newton, consists in so much greater a degree of pores than solid parts, that the absolute particles contained in the solar system might, for aught we know, he contained in a nutshell(77), and that no two ever touched each other, or approached so near that they might not be brought nearer, provided a sufficient force could be applied for that purpose,—and if, as Priestley teaches, all that we observe is the result of successive spheres of attraction and repulsion, the centre of which is a mathematical point only, we then certainly come very near to a conclusion, which should banish matter out of the theatre of real existences(78).

(77) See above, Essay XXI.

(78) See above, Essay XXI.

But the extreme subtleties of human intellect are perhaps of little further use, than to afford an amusement to persons of curious speculation, and whose condition in human society procures them leisure for such enquiries. The same thing happens here, as in the subject of my Twelfth Essay, on the Liberty of Human Actions. The speculator in his closet is one man: the same person, when he comes out of his retirement, and mixes in intercourse with his fellow-creatures, is another man. The necessarian, when he reasons on the everlasting concatenation of antecedents and consequents, proves to his own apprehension irrefragably, that he is a passive instrument, acted upon, and acting upon other things, in turn, and that he can never disengage himself from the operation of the omnipotent laws of physical nature, and the impulses of other men with whom he is united in the ties of society. But no sooner does this acute and ingenious reasoner come into active life and the intercourse of his fellowmen, than all these fine-drawn speculations vanish from his recollection. He regards himself and other men as beings endowed with a liberty of action, as possessed of a proper initiative power, and free to do a thing or not to do it, without being subject to the absolute and irresistible constraint of motives. It is from this internal and indefeasible sense of liberty, that we draw all our moral energies and enthusiasm, that we persevere heroically in defiance of obstacles and discouragements, that we praise or blame the actions of others, and admire the elevated virtues of the best of our contemporaries, and of those whose achievements adorn the page of history.

It is in a manner of precisely the same sort as that which prevails in the philosophical doctrines of liberty and necessity, that we find ourselves impelled to feel on the question of the existence of the material universe. Berkeley, and as many persons as are persuaded by his or similar reasonings, feel satisfied in speculation that there is no such thing as matter in the sense in which it is understood by the writers on natural philosophy, and that all our notions of the external and actual existence of the table, the chair, and the other material substances with which we conceive ourselves to be surrounded, of woods, and mountains, and rivers, and seas, are mere prejudice and misconception. All this is very well in the closet, and as long as we are involved in meditation, and remain abstracted from action, business, and the exertion of our limbs and corporal faculties. But it is too fine for the realities of life. Berkeley, and the most strenuous and spiritualised of his followers, no sooner descend from the high tower of their speculations, submit to the necessities of their nature, and mix in the business of the world, than they become impelled, as strongly as the necessarian in the question of the liberty of human actions, not only to act like other men, but even to feel just in the same manner as if they had never been acquainted with these abstractions. A table then becomes absolutely a table, and a chair a chair: they are "fed with the same food, hurt by the same weapons, and warmed and cooled by the same summer and winter," as other men: and they make use of the refreshments which nature requires, with as true an orthodoxy, and as credulous a temper, as he who was never assailed with such refinements. Nature is too strong, to be prevailed on to retire, and give way to the authority of definitions and syllogistical deduction.

But, when we have granted all this, it is however a mistake to say, that these "subtleties of human intellect are of little further use, than to afford an amusement to persons of curious speculation(79)." We have seen, in the case of the doctrine of philosophical necessity(80), that, though it can never form a rule for the intercourse between man and man, it may nevertheless be turned to no mean advantage. It is calculated to inspire us with temperance and toleration. It tends impressively to evince to us, that this scene of things is but like the shadows which pass before us in a magic lanthorn, and that, after all, men are but the tools, not the masters, of their fate. It corrects the illusions of life, much after the same manner as the spectator of a puppet-shew is enlightened, who should be taken within the curtain, and shewn how the wires are pulled by the master, which produce all the turmoil and strife that before riveted our attention. It is good for him who would arrive at all the improvement of which our nature is capable, at one time to take his place among the literal beholders of the drama, and at another to go behind the scenes, and remark the deceptions in their original elements, and the actors in their proper and natural costume.

(79) See above, Essay XXII.

(80) See above, Essay XII.

And, as in the question of the liberty of human actions, so in that of the reality of the material universe, it is a privilege not to be despised, that we are so formed as to be able to dissect the subject that is submitted to our examination, and to strip the elements of which this sublunary scene is composed, of the disguise in which they present themselves to the vulgar spectator. It is little, after all, that we are capable to know; and the man of heroic mind and generous enterprise, will not refuse the discoveries that are placed within his reach. The subtleties of grammar are as the porch, which leads from the knowledge of words to the knowledge of things. The subtleties of mathematics defecate the grossness of our apprehension, and supply the elements of a sounder and severer logic. And in the same manner the faculty which removes the illusions of external appearance, and enables us to "look into the seeds of time," is one which we are bound to estimate at its genuine value. The more we refine our faculties, other things equal, the wiser we grow: we are the more raised above the thickness of the atmosphere that envelops our fellow-mortals, and are made partakers of a nature superhuman and divine.

There is a curious question that has risen out of this proposition of Berkeley, of the supposed illusion we suffer in our conceptions of the material universe. It has been said, "Well then, I am satisfied that the chairs, the tables, and the other material substances with which I conceive myself to be surrounded, are not what they appear to be, but are merely an eternal chain of antecedents and consequents, going on according to what Leibnitz calls a 'preestablished harmony,' and thus furnishing the ground of the speculations which mortals cherish, and the motives of their proceeding. But, if thus, in the ordinary process of human affairs, we believe in matter, when in reality there is no such thing as matter, how shall we pronounce of mind, and the things which happen to us in our seeming intercourse with our fellow-men, and in the complexities of love and hatred, of kindred and friendship, of benevolence and misanthropy, of robbery and murder, and of the wholesale massacre of thousands of human beings which are recorded in the page of history? We absolutely know nothing of the lives and actions of others but through the medium of material impulse. And, if you take away matter, the bodies of our fellow-men, does it not follow by irresistible consequence that all knowledge of their minds is taken away also? Am not I therefore (the person engaged in reading the present Essay) the only being in existence, an entire universe to myself?"

Certainly this is a very different conclusion from any that Berkeley ever contemplated. In the very title of the Treatise in which his notions on this subject are unfolded, he professes his purpose to be to remove "the grounds of scepticism, atheism and irreligion." Berkeley was a sincere Christian, and a man of the most ingenuous dispositions. Pope, in the Epilogue to his Satires, does not hesitate to ascribe to him "every virtue under heaven." He was for twenty years a prelate of the Protestant church. And, though his personal sentiments were in the highest degree philanthropical and amiable, yet, in his most diffusive production, entitled The Minute Philosopher, he treats "those who are called Free Thinkers" with a scorn and disdain, scarcely to be reconciled with the spirit of Christian meekness.

There are examples however, especially in the fields of controversy, where an adventurous speculatist has been known to lay down premises and principles, from which inferences might be fairly deduced, incompatible with the opinions entertained by him who delivered them. It may therefore be no unprofitable research to enquire how far the creed of the non-existence of matter is to be regarded as in truth and reality countenancing the inference which has just been recited.

The persons then, who refine with Berkeley upon the system of things so far, as to deny that there is any such thing as matter in the sense in which it is understood by the writers on natural philosophy, proceed on the ground of affirming that we have no reason to believe that the causes of our sensations have an express resemblance to the sensations themselves(81). That which gives us a sensation of colour is not itself coloured: and the same may be affirmed of the sensations of hot and cold, of sweet and bitter, and of odours offensive or otherwise. The immaterialist proceeds to say, that what we call matter has been strewn to be so exceedingly porous, that, for any thing we know, all the solid particles in the universe might be contained in a nutshell, that there is no such thing in the external world as actual contact, and that no two particles of matter were ever so near to each other, but that they might be brought nearer, if a sufficient force could be applied for that purpose. From these premises it seems to follow with sufficient evidence, that the causes of our sensations, so far as the material universe is concerned, bear no express resemblance to the sensations themselves.

(81) See above, Essay XXI.

How then does the question stand with relation to mind? Are those persons who deny the existence of matter, reduced, if they would be consistent in their reasonings, to deny, each man for himself, that he has any proper evidence of the existence of other minds than his own?

He denies, while he has the sensation of colour, that there exists colour out of himself, unless in thinking and percipient beings constituted in a manner similar to that in which he is constituted. And the same of the sensations of hot and cold, sweet and bitter, and odours offensive or otherwise. He affirms, while he has the sensation of length, breadth and thickness, that there is no continuous substance out of himself, possessing the attributes of length, breadth and thickness in any way similar to the sensation of which he is conscious. He professes therefore that he has no evidence, arising from his observation of what we call matter, of the actual existence of a material world. He looks into himself, and all he finds is sensation; but sensation cannot be a property of inert matter. There is therefore no assignable analogy between the causes of his sensations, whatever they may be, and the sensations themselves; and the material world, such as we apprehend it, is the mere creature of his own mind.

Let us next consider how this question stands as to the conceptions he entertains respecting the minds of other men. That which gives him the sensation of colour, is not any thing coloured out of himself; and that which gives him the sensation of length, breadth and thickness, is not any thing long, broad and thick in a manner corresponding with the impression he receives. There is nothing in the nature of a parallel, a type and its archetype, between that which is without him and that which is within, the impresser and the impression. This is the point supposed to be established by Locke and Newton, and by those who have followed the reasonings of these philosophers into their remotest consequences.

But the case is far otherwise in the impressions we receive respecting the minds of other men. In colour it has been proved by these authors that there is no express correspondence and analogy between the cause of the sensation and the sensation. They are not part and counterpart. But in mind there is a precise resemblance and analogy between the conceptions we are led to entertain respecting other men, and what we know of ourselves. I and my associate, or fellow-man, are like two instruments of music constructed upon the same model. We have each of us, so to speak, the three great divisions of sound, base, tenor and treble. We have each the same number of keys, capable of being struck, consecutively or with alternations, at the will of the master. We can utter the same sound or series of sounds, or sounds of a different character, but which respond to each other. My neighbour therefore being of the same nature as myself, what passes within me may be regarded as amounting to a commanding evidence that he is a real being, having a proper and independent existence.

There is further something still more impressive and irresistible in the notices I receive respecting the minds of other men. The sceptics whose reasonings I am here taking into consideration, admit, each man for himself, the reality of his own existence. There is such a thing therefore as human nature; for he is a specimen of it. Now the idea of human nature, or of man, is a very complex thing. He is in the first place the subject of sensible impressions, however these impressions are communicated to him. He has the faculties of thinking and feeling. He is subject to the law of the association of ideas, or, in other words, any one idea existing in his mind has a tendency to call up the ideas of other things which have been connected with it in his first experience. He has, be it delusive or otherwise, the sense of liberty of action.

But we will go still further into detail as to the nature of man.

Our lives are carried forward by the intervention of what we call meat, drink and sleep. We are liable to the accidents of health and sickness. We are alternately the recipients of joy and sorrow, of cheerfulness and melancholy. Our passions are excited by similar means, whether of love or hatred, complacency or indignation, sympathy or resentment. I could fill many pages with a description of the properties or accidents, which belong to man as such, or to which he is liable.

Now with all these each man is acquainted in the sphere of his inward experience, whether he is a single being standing by himself, or is an individual belonging to a numerous species.

Observe then the difference between my acquaintance with the phenomena of the material universe, and with the individuals of my own species. The former say nothing to me; they are a series of events and no more; I cannot penetrate into their causes; that which gives rise to my sensations, may or may not be similar to the sensations themselves. The follower of Berkeley or Newton has satisfied himself in the negative.

But the case is very different in my intercourse with my fellow-men. Agreeably to the statement already made I know the reality of human nature; for I feel the particulars that constitute it within myself. The impressions I receive from that intercourse say something to me; for they talk to me of beings like myself. My own existence becomes multiplied in infinitum. Of the possibility of matter I know nothing; but with the possibility of mind I am acquainted; for I am myself an example. I am amazed at the consistency and systematic succession of the phenomena of the material universe; though I cannot penetrate the veil which presents itself to my grosser sense, nor see effects in their causes. But I can see, in other words, I have the most cogent reasons to believe in, the causes of the phenomena that occur in my apparent intercourse with my fellow-men. What solution so natural, as that they are produced by beings like myself, the duplicates, with certain variations, of what I feel within me?

The belief in the reality of matter explains nothing. Supposing it to exist, if Newton is right, no particle of extraneous matter ever touched the matter of my body; and therefore it is not just to regard it as the cause of my sensations. It would amount to no more than two systems going on at the same time by a preestablished harmony, but totally independent of and disjointed from each other.

But the belief in the existence of our fellow-men explains much. It makes level before us the wonder of the method of their proceedings, and affords an obvious reason why they should be in so many respects like our own. If I dismiss from my creed the existence of inert matter, I lose nothing. The phenomena, the train of antecedents and consequents, remain as before; and this is all that I am truly concerned with. But take away the existence of my fellow-men; and you reduce all that is, and all that I experience, to a senseless mummery. "You take my life, taking the thing whereon I live."

Human nature, and the nature of mind, are to us a theme of endless investigation. "The proper study of mankind is man." All the subtlety of metaphysics, or (if there be men captious and prejudiced enough to dislike that term) the science of ourselves, depends upon it. The science of morals hangs upon the actions of men, and the effects they produce upon our brother-men, in a narrower or a wider circle. The endless, and inexpressibly interesting, roll of history relies for its meaning and its spirit upon the reality and substance of the subjects of which it treats. Poetry, and all the wonders and endless varieties that imagination creates, have this for their solution and their soul.

Sympathy is the only reality of which we are susceptible; it is our heart of hearts: and, if the world had been "one entire and perfect chrysolite," without this it would have been no more than one heap of rubbish.

Observe the difference between what we know of the material world, and what of the intellectual. The material goes on for ever according to certain laws that admit of no discrimination. They proceed upon a first principle, an impulse given them from the beginning of things. Their effects are regulated by something that we call their nature: fire burns; water suffocates; the substances around us that we call solid, depend for their effects, when put in motion, upon momentum and gravity.

The principle that regulates the dead universe, "acts by general, not by partial laws."

When the loose mountain trembles from on high,

Shall gravitation cease, if you go by?

No: the chain of antecedents and consequents proceeds in this respect for ever the same. The laws of what we call the material world continue unvaried. And, when the vast system of things was first set in motion, every thing, so far as depends on inert matter, was determined to the minutest particle, even to the end of time.

The material world, or that train of antecedents and consequents which we understand by that term, goes on for ever in a train agreeably to the impulse previously given. It is deaf and inexorable. It is unmoved by the consideration of any accidents and miseries that may result, and unalterable. But man is a source of events of a very different nature. He looks to results, and is governed by views growing out of the contemplation of them. He acts in a way diametrically opposite to the action of inert matter, and "turns, and turns, and turns again," at the impulse of the thought that strikes him, the appetite that prompts, the passions that move, and the effects that he anticipates. It is therefore in a high degree unreasonable, to make that train of inferences which may satisfy us on the subject of material phenomena, a standard of what we ought to think respecting the phenomena of mind.

It is further worthy of our notice to recollect, that the same reasonings which apply to our brethren of mankind, apply also to the brute creation. They, like ourselves, act from motives; that is, the elections they form are adopted by them for the sake of certain consequences they expect to see result from them. Whatever becomes therefore of the phenomena of what we call dead matter, we are here presented with tribes of being, susceptible of pleasure and pain, of hope and fear, of regard and resentment.

How beautifully does this conviction vary the scene of things! What a source to us is the animal creation, of amusement, of curious observations upon the impulses of inferior intellect, of the exhaustless varieties of what we call instinct, of the care we can exercise for their accommodation and welfare, and of the attachment and affection we win from them in return! If I travel alone through pathless deserts, if I journey from the rising to the setting sun, with no object around me but nature's desolation, or the sublime, the magnificent and the exuberant scenery she occasionally presents, still I have that noble animal, the horse, and my faithful dog, the companions of my toil, and with whom, when my solitude would otherwise become insufferable, I can hold communion, and engage in dumb dialogues of sentiment and affection.

I have heard of a man, who, talking to his friend on the subject of these speculations, said, "What then, are you so poor and pusillanimous a creature, that you could not preserve your serenity, be perfectly composed and content, and hold on your way unvaried, though you were convinced that you were the only real being in existence, and all the rest were mere phantasies and shadows?"

If I had been the person to whom this speech was addressed, I should have frankly acknowledged, "I am the poor and pusillanimous creature you are disposed to regard with so much scorn."

To adopt the sententious language of the Bible, "It is not good for man to be alone." All our faculties and attributes bear relation to, and talk to us of, other beings like ourselves. We might indeed eat, drink and sleep, that is, submit to those necessities which we so denominate, without thinking of any thing beyond ourselves; for these are the demands of our nature, and we know that we cannot subsist without them. We might make use of the alternate conditions of exercise and repose.

But the life of our lives would be gone. As far as we bore in mind the creed we had adopted, of our single existence, we could neither love nor hate. Sympathy would be a solemn mockery. We could not communicate; for the being to whom our communication was addressed we were satisfied was a non-entity. We could not anticipate the pleasure or pain, the joy or sorrow, of another; for that other had no existence. We should be in a worse condition than Robinson Crusoe in the desolate island; for he believed in the existence of other men, and hoped and trusted that he should one day again enter into human society. We should be in a worse condition than Robinson Crusoe; for he at least was unannoyed in his solitude; while we are perpetually and per force intruded on, like a delirious man, by visions which we know to be unreal, but which we are denied the power to deliver ourselves from. We have no motive to any of the great and cardinal functions of human life; for there is no one in being, that we can benefit, or that we can affect. Study is nothing to us; for we have no use for it. Even science is unsatisfactory; unless we can communicate it by word or writing, can converse upon it, and compare notes with our neighbour. History is nothing; for there were no Greeks and no Romans; no freemen and no slaves; no kings and no subjects; no despots, nor victims of their tyranny; no republics, nor states immerged in brutal and ignominious servitude. Life must be inevitably a burthen to us, a dreary, unvaried, motiveless existence; and death must be welcomed, as the most desirable blessing that can visit us. It is impossible indeed that we should always recollect this our, by supposition, real situation; but, as often as we did, it would come over us like a blight, withering all the prospects of our industry, or like a scirocco, unbracing the nerves of our frame, and consigning us to the most pitiable depression.

Thus far I have allowed myself to follow the refinements of those who profess to deny the existence of the material universe. But it is satisfactory to come back to that persuasion, which, from whatever cause it is derived, is incorporated with our very existence, and can never be shaken off by us. Our senses are too powerful in their operation, for it to be possible for us to discard them, and to take as their substitute, in active life, and in the earnestness of pursuit, the deductions of our logical faculty, however well knit and irresistible we may apprehend them to be. Speculation and common sense are at war on this point; and however we may "think with the learned," and follow the abstrusenesses of the philosopher, in the sequestered hour of our meditation, we must always act, and even feel, "with the vulgar," when we come abroad into the world.

It is however no small gratification to the man of sober mind, that, from what has here been alleged, it seems to follow, that untutored mind, and the severest deductions of philosophy, agree in that most interesting of our concerns, our intercourse with our fellow-creatures. The inexorable reasoner, refining on the reports of sense, may dispose, as he pleases, of the chair, the table, and the so called material substances around him. He may include the whole solid matter of the universe in a nutshell, or less than a nutshell. But he cannot deprive me of that greatest of all consolations, the sustaining pillar of my existence, "the cordial drop Heaven in our cup has thrown,"—the intercourse of my fellow-creatures. When we read history, the subjects of which we read are realities; they do not "come like shadows, so depart;" they loved and acted in sober earnest; they sometimes perpetrated crimes; but they sometimes also achieved illustrious deeds, which angels might look down from their exalted abodes and admire. We are not deluded with mockeries. The woman I love, and the man to whom I swear eternal friendship, are as much realities as myself. If I relieve the poor, and assist the progress of genius and virtuous designs struggling with fearful discouragements, I do something upon the success of which I may safely congratulate myself. If I devote my energies to enlighten my fellow-creatures, to detect the weak places in our social institutions, to plead the cause of liberty, and to invite others to engage in noble actions and unite in effecting the most solid and unquestionable improvements, I erect to my name an eternal monument; or I do something better than this,—secure inestimable advantage to the latest posterity, the benefit of which they shall enjoy, long after the very name of the author shall, with a thousand other things great and small, have been swallowed up in the gulph of insatiable oblivion.

ESSAY XXIII. OF HUMAN VIRTUE. THE EPILOGUE.

The life of man is divided into many stages; and we shall not form a just estimate of our common nature, if we do not to a certain degree pass its successive periods in review, and observe it in its commencement, its progress, and its maturity.

It has been attempted to be established in an early part of the present volume(82), that all men, idiots and extraordinary cases being put out of the question, are endowed with talents, which, if rightly directed, would shew them to be apt, adroit, intelligent and acute, in the walk for which their organisation especially fitted them. We are bound therefore, particularly in the morning of life, to consider every thing that presents itself to us in the human form, with deference and attention.

(82) See above, Essay III.

"God," saith the Preacher, "made man upright; but he hath sought out many inventions." There is something loose and difficult of exposition in this statement; but we shall find an important truth hid beneath its obscurity.

Junius Brutus, in the play, says to his son,

I like thy frame: the fingers of the Gods

I see have left their mastery upon thee;

And the majestic prints distinct appear.

Such is the true description of every well-formed and healthful infant that is born into the world.

He is placed on the threshold of existence; and an eventful journey is open before him. For the first four or five years of life indeed he has little apprehension of the scenes that await him. But a child of quick apprehension early begins to have day-dreams, and to form imaginations of the various chances that may occur to him, and the things he shall have to do, when, according to the language of the story-books, he "goes out to seek his fortune."

"God made man upright." Every child that is born, has within him a concealed magazine of excellence. His heart beats for every thing that is lovely and good; and whatever is set before him of that sort in honest colours, rouses his emulation. By how many tokens does he prove himself worthy of our approbation and love—the unaffected and ingenuous sobriety with which he listens to what addresses itself to his attention, the sweetness of his smile, his hearty laugh, the clear, bell tones of his voice, his sudden and assured impulses, and his bounding step!

To his own heart he promises well of himself. Like Lear in the play, he says, "I will do such things!—What they are, yet I know not." But he is assured, frank and light-spirited. He thinks of no disguise. He "wears his heart upon his sleeve." He looks in the face of his seniors with the glistening eye of confidence, and expects to encounter sympathy and encouragement in return. Such is man, as he comes from the hands of his maker.

Thus prepared, he is turned into the great field of society. Here he meets with much that he had not anticipated, and with many rebuffs. He is taught that he must accommodate his temper and proceedings to the expectations and prejudices of those around him. He must be careful to give no offence. With how many lessons, not always the most salutary and ingenuous, is this maxim pregnant! It calls on the neophyte to bear a wary eye, and to watch the first indications of disapprobation and displeasure in those among whom his lot is cast. It teaches him to suppress the genuine emotions of his soul. It informs him that he is not always to yield to his own impulses, but that he must "stretch forth his hands to another, and be carried whither he would not."

It recommends to him falseness, and to be the thing in outward appearance that he is not in his heart.

Still however he goes on. He shuts up his thoughts in his bosom; but they are not exterminated. On the contrary he broods over them with genial warmth; and the less they are exposed to the eye of day, the more perseveringly are they cherished. Perhaps he chooses some youthful confident of his imaginings: and the effect of this is, that he pours out his soul with uncontrolable copiousness, and with the fervour of a new and unchecked conceiving. It is received with answering warmth; or, if there is any deficiency in the sympathy of his companion, his mind is so earnest and full, that he does not perceive it. By and by, it may be, he finds that the discovery he had made of a friend, a brother of his soul, is, like so many of the visions of this world, hollow and fallacious. He grasped, as he thought, a jewel of the first water; and it turns out to be a vulgar pebble. No matter: he has gained something by the communication. He has heard from his own lips the imaginings of his mind shaped into articulate air; they grew more definite and distinct as he uttered them; they came by the very act to have more of reality, to be more tangible. He shakes off the ill-assorted companion that only encumbered him, and springs away in his race, more light of heart, and with a step more assured, than ever.

By and by he becomes a young man. And, whatever checks he may have received before, it usually happens that all his hopes and projects return to him now with recruited strength. He has no longer a master. He no longer crouches to the yoke of subjection, and is directed this way and that at the judgment of another. Liberty is at all times dear to the free-soured and ingenuous; but never so much so, as when we wear it in its full gloss and newness. He never felt before, that he was sui juris, that he might go whithersoever he would, without asking leave, without consulting any other director than the law of his own mind. It is nearly at the same season that he arrives at the period of puberty, at the stature, and in a certain degree at the strength, which he is destined to attain. He is by general consent admitted to be at years of discretion.

Though I have put all these things together, they do not, in the course of nature, all come at the same time. It is a memorable period, when the ingenuous youth is transferred from the trammels of the schoolmaster to the residence of a college. It was at the age of seventeen that, according to the custom of Rome, the youthful citizen put on the manly gown, and was introduced into the forum. Even in college-life, there is a difference in the privileges of the mere freshman, and of the youth who has already completed the first half of his period in the university.

The season of what may be denominated the independence of the individual, is certainly in no small degree critical. A human being, suddenly emancipated from a state of subjection, if we may not call it slavery, and transported into a state of freedom, must be expected to be guilty of some extravagancies and follies.

But upon the whole, with a small number of exceptions, it is creditable to human nature, that we take this period of our new powers and immunities with so much sobriety as we do.

The young man then, calls to mind all that he imagined at an earlier season, and that he promised himself. He adds to this the new lights that he has since obtained, and the nearer and more distinct view that he has reached, of the realities of life.

He recollects the long noviciate that he served to reach this period, the twenty years that he passed in ardent and palpitating expectation; and he resolves to do something worthy of all he had vowed and had imagined. He takes a full survey of his stores and endowments; and to the latter, from his enthusiasm and his self-love, he is morally sure to do justice. He says to himself, "What I purpose to do will not be achieved to-day. No; it shall be copious, and worthy of men's suffrage and approbation. But I will meditate it; I will sketch a grand outline; I will essay my powers in secret, and ascertain what I may be able to effect." The youth, whose morning of life is not utterly abortive, palpitates with the desire to promote the happiness of others, and with the desire of glory.

We have an apt specimen of this in the first period of the reign of Nero. The historians, Tacitus in particular, have treated this with too much incredulity. It was the passion of that eminent man to indulge in subtleties, and to find hidden meanings in cases where in reality every thing is plain. We must not regard the panegyric of Seneca, and the devotion of Lucan to the imperial stripling, as unworthy of our attention. He was declared emperor before he had completed the eighteenth year of his age. No occasion for the exhibition of liberality, clemency, courtesy or kindness escaped him. He called every one by his name, and saluted all orders of men. When the senate shewed a disposition to confer on him peculiar honours, he interposed, he said, "Let them be bestowed when I have deserved them(83)." Seneca affirms, that in the first part of his reign, and to the time in which the philosopher dedicated to him his treatise of Clemency, he had "shed no drop of blood(84)." He adds, "If the Gods were this day to call thee to a hearing, thou couldst account to them for every man that had been intrusted to thy rule. Not an individual has been lost from the number, either by secret practices, or by open violence. This could scarcely have been, if thy good dispositions had not been natural, but assumed. No one can long personate a character. A pretended goodness will speedily give place to the real temper; while a sincere mind, and acts prompted by the heart, will not fail to go on from one stage of excellence to another(85)."

(83) Suetonius, Nero, cap. 10.

(84) De Clementia, Lib. I, cap. II.

(85) De Clementia, cap. I.

The philosopher expresses himself in raptures on that celebrated phrase of Nero, WOULD I HAD NEVER LEARNED TO WRITE! "An exclamation," he says, "not studied, not uttered for the purpose of courting popularity, but bursting insuppressibly from thy lips, and indicating the vehemence of the struggle between the kindness of thy disposition and the duties of thy office(86)."

(86) Ibid., Lib. II, cap. I.

How many generous purposes, what bright and heart-thrilling visions of beneficence and honour, does the young man, just starting in the race of life, conceive! There is no one in that period of existence, who has received a reasonable education, and has not in his very nonage been trod down in the mire of poverty and oppression, that does not say to himself, "Now is the time; and I will do something worthy to be remembered by myself and by others." Youth is the season of generosity. He calls over the catalogue of his endowments, his attainments, and his powers, and exclaims, "To that which

I am, my contemporaries are welcome; it shall all be expended for their service and advantage."

With what disdain he looks at the temptations of selfishness, effeminate indulgence, and sordid gain! He feels within himself that he was born for better things. His elders, and those who have already been tamed down and emasculated by the corrupt commerce of the world, tell him, "All this is the rhapsody of youth, fostered by inexperience; you will soon learn to know better; in no long time you will see these things in the same light in which we see them." But he despises the sinister prognostic that is held out to him, and feels proudly conscious that the sentiments that now live in his bosom, will continue to animate him to his latest breath.

Youth is necessarily ingenuous in its thoughts, and sanguine in its anticipations of the future. But the predictions of the seniors I have quoted, are unfortunately in too many cases fulfilled. The outline of the scheme of civil society is in a high degree hostile to the growth and maturity of human virtue. Its unavoidable operation, except in those rare cases where positive institutions have arrested its tendency, has been to divide a great portion of its members, especially in large and powerful states, into those who are plentifully supplied with the means of luxury and indulgence, and those who are condemned to suffer the rigours of indigence.

The young man who is born to the prospect of hereditary wealth, will not unfrequently feel as generous emotions, and as much of the spirit of self-denial, as the bosom of man is capable of conceiving. He will say, What am I, that I should have a monopoly of those things, which, if "well dispensed, in unsuperfluous, even proportion," would supply the wants of all? He is ready, agreeably to the advice of Christ to the young man in the Gospel, to "sell all that he has, and give to the poor," if he could be shewn how so generous a resolution on his part could be encountered with an extensive conspiracy of the well-disposed, and rendered available to the real melioration of the state of man in society. Who is there so ignorant, or that has lived in so barren and unconceiving a tract of the soil of earth, that has not his tale to tell of the sublime emotions and the generous purposes he has witnessed, which so often mark this beautiful era of our sublunary existence?

But this is in the dawn of life, and the first innocence of the human heart. When once the young man of "great possessions" has entered the gardens of Alcina, when he has drunk of the cup of her enchantments, and seen all the delusive honour and consideration that, in the corruptness of modern times, are the lot of him who is the owner of considerable wealth, the dreams of sublime virtue are too apt to fade away. He was willing before, to be nourished with the simplest diet, and clad with the plainest attire. He knew that he was but a man like the rest of his species, and was in equity entitled to no more than they. But he presently learns a very different lesson. He believes that he cannot live without splendour and luxury; he regards a noble mansion, elegant vesture, horses, equipage, and an ample establishment, as things without which he must be hopelessly miserable. That income, which he once thought, if divided, would have secured the happiness and independence of many, he now finds scarcely sufficient to supply his increased and artificial cravings.

But, if the rich are seduced and led away from the inspirations of virtue, it may easily be conceived how much more injurious, and beyond the power of control, are the effects on the poor. The mysterious source from which the talents of men are derived, cannot be supposed in their distribution to be regulated by the artificial laws of society, and to have one measure for those which are bestowed upon the opulent, and another for the destitute. It will therefore not seldom happen that powers susceptible of the noblest uses may be cast, like "seed sown upon stony places," where they have scarcely any chance to be unfolded and matured. In a few instances they may attract the attention of persons both able and willing to contribute to their being brought to perfection. In a few instances the principle may be so vigorous, and the tendency to excel so decisive, as to bid defiance to and to conquer every obstacle. But in a vast majority the promise will be made vain, and the hopes that might have been entertained will prove frustrate. What can be expected from the buds of the most auspicious infancy, if encountered in their earliest stage with the rigorous blasts of a polar climate?

And not only will the germs of excellence be likely to be extinguished in the members of the lower class of the community, but the temptations to irregular acts and incroachments upon the laws for the security of property will often be so great, as to be in a manner irresistible. The man who perceives that, with all his industry, he cannot provide for the bare subsistence of himself and those dependent upon him, while his neighbour revels in boundless profusion, cannot but sometimes feel himself goaded to an attempt to correct this crying evil. What must be expected to become of that general good-will which is the natural inheritance of a well-constituted mind, when urged by so bitter oppression and such unendurable sufferings? The whole temper of the human heart must be spoiled, and the wine of life acquire a quality acrimonious and malignant.

But it is not only in the extreme classes of society that the glaring inequality with which property is shared produces its injurious effects. All those who are born in the intermediate ranks are urged with a distempered ambition, unfavourable to independence of temper, and to true philanthropy. Each man aspires to the improvement of his circumstances, and the mounting, by one step and another, higher in the scale of the community. The contemplations of the mind are turned towards selfishness. In opulent communities we are presented with the genuine theatre for courts and kings. And, wherever there are courts, duplicity, lying, hypocrisy and cringing dwell as in their proper field. Next come trades and professions, with all the ignoble contemplations, the resolved smoothness, servility and falshood, by which they are enabled to gain a prosperous and triumphant career.

It is by such means, that man, whom "God made upright," is led away into a thousand devious paths, and, long before the closing scene of his life, is rendered something the very reverse of what in the dawning of existence he promised to be. He is like Hazael in the Jewish history, who, when the prophet set before him the crying enormities he should hereafter perpetrate, exclaimed, "Is thy servant a dog," that he should degrade himself so vilely? He feels the purity of his purposes; but is goaded by one excitement and exasperation after another, till he becomes debased, worthless and criminal. This is strikingly illustrated in the story of Dr. Johnson and the celebrated Windham, who, when he was setting out as secretary to the lord lieutenant of Ireland, expressed to his aged monitor, some doubts whether he could ever reconcile himself to certain indirect proceedings which he was afraid would be expected of him: to which the veteran replied, "Oh, sir, be under no alarm; in a short time, depend upon it, you will make a very pretty rascal(87)."

(87) The phrase here used by Johnson is marked with the licentiousness

we sometimes indulge in familiar conversation. Translate it into a

general maxim; and it contains much melancholy truth. It is true also,

that there are few individuals, who, in the urgent realities of

life, have not occasionally descended from the heights of theoretical

excellence. It is but just however to observe in the case of Windham,

that, though he was a man of many errors, he was not the less

characterised by high honour and eminent virtue.

Such are the "inventions of man," or rather such is the operation of those institutions which ordinarily prevail in society. Still, however, much honour ought to be rendered to our common nature, since all of us are not led away by the potent spells of the enchantress. If the vulgar crew of the vessel of Ulysses were by Circe changed into brutes, so was not their commander. The human species is divided into two classes, the successfully tempted, and the tempted in vain. And, though the latter must be admitted to be a small minority, yet they ought to be regarded as the "salt of the earth," which preserves the entire mass from putridity and dishonour. They are like the remnant, which, if they had been to be found in the cities of the Asphaltic lake, the God of Abraham pronounced as worthy to redeem the whole community. They are like the two witnesses amidst the general apostasy, spoken of in the book of Revelations, who were the harbingers and forerunners of the millenium, the reign of universal virtue and peace. Their excellence only appears with the greater lustre amidst the general defection.

Nothing can be more unjust than the spirit of general levelling and satire, which so customarily prevails. History records, if you will, the vices and follies of mankind. But does it record nothing else? Are the virtues of the best men, the noblest philosophers, and the most disinterested patriots of antiquity, nothing? It is impossible for two things to be more unlike than the general profligacy of the reigns of Charles the Second and Louis the Fifteenth on the one hand, and the austere virtues and the extinction of all private considerations in the general happiness and honour, which constitute the spirit of the best pages of ancient history, and which exalt and transfix the spirit of every ingenuous and high-souled reader, on the other.

Let us then pay to human virtue the honour that is so justly its due! Imagination is indeed a marvellous power; but imagination never equalled history, the achievements which man has actually performed. It is in vain that the man of contemplation sits down in his closet; it is in vain that the poet yields the reins to enthusiasm and fancy: there is something in the realities of life, that excites the mind infinitely more, than is in the power of the most exalted reverie. The true hero cannot, like the poet, or the delineator of fictitious adventures, put off what he has to do till to-morrow. The occasion calls, and he must obey. He sees the obstacles, and the adversary he has to encounter, before him. He sees the individuals, for whose dear sake he resolves to expose himself to every hazard and every evil. The very circumstance, that he is called on to act in the face of the public, animates him. It is thus that resolution is produced, that martyrdom is voluntarily encountered, and that the deeds of genuine, pure and undeniable heroism are performed.

Let then no man, in the supercilious spirit of a fancied disdain, allow himself to detract from our common nature. We are ourselves the models of all the excellence that the human mind can conceive. There have been men, whose virtues may well redeem all the contempt with which satire and detraction have sought to overwhelm our species. There have been memorable periods in the history of man, when the best, the most generous and exalted sentiments have swallowed up and obliterated all that was of an opposite character. And it is but just, that those by whom these things are fairly considered, should anticipate the progress of our nature, and believe that human understanding and human virtue will hereafter accomplish such things as the heart of man has never yet been daring enough to conceive.